MW00999740

Christian Prayer

FOR

DUMMIES®

THIS BOOK BELONGS TO

LISA T. LUPTON

Christian Prayer
FOR
DUMMIES®

by Richard Wagner

WILEY

Wiley Publishing, Inc.

Christian Prayer For Dummies®

Published by
Wiley Publishing, Inc.
909 Third Avenue
New York, NY 10022
www.wiley.com

Copyright © 2003 by Wiley Publishing, Inc., Indianapolis, Indiana

Published simultaneously in Canada

No part of this publication may be reproduced, stored in a retrieval system, or transmitted in any form or by any means, electronic, mechanical, photocopying, recording, scanning, or otherwise, except as permitted under Sections 107 or 108 of the 1976 United States Copyright Act, without either the prior written permission of the Publisher, or authorization through payment of the appropriate per-copy fee to the Copyright Clearance Center, 222 Rosewood Drive, Danvers, MA 01923, 978-750-8400, fax 978-750-4744. Requests to the Publisher for permission should be addressed to the Legal Department, Wiley Publishing, Inc., 10475 Crosspoint Blvd., Indianapolis, IN 46256, 317-572-3447, fax 317-572-4447, or e-mail permcoordinator@wiley.com

The following quotes are used by permission of Discovery House Publishers, Box 3566, Grand Rapids, MI 49501. All rights reserved.

From *He Shall Glorify Me.* Copyright © 1946 by the Oswald Chambers Publications Assn. Ltd.:

"We have a God who engineers circumstances." (Chapter 1)

"If you ever prayed in the dawn, you will ask yourself why you were so foolish has to not do it always: it is difficult to get into communion with God in the midst of the hurly-burly of the day." (Chapter 4)

"Specific times and places and communion with God go together. It is by no haphazard chance that in every age men have risen early to pray. The first thing that marks decline in spiritual life is our relationship to the early morning." (Chapter 4)

"Watch the difference between confession and admitting; the majority of us are quite ready to admit, it is the rarest thing to get to the place where we will confess. . . . It is much more difficult to confess to God than we are apt to think. It is not confessing in order to be forgiven; confession is the evidence that I am forgiven." (Chapter 6)

From *The Love of God.* Copyright © 1938 by the Oswald Chambers Publications Assn. Ltd.:

"Fasting means concentration in order that the purpose of God may be developed in our lives." (Chapter 10)

From *So Send I You.* Copyright © 1930 by the Oswald Chambers Publications Assn. Ltd.:

"Whether our work is a success or a failure has nothing to do with us. Our call is not to successful service, but to faithfulness." (Chapter 12)

"When we hear a thing is not necessarily when it is spoken, but when we are in a state to listen to it and to understand. Our Lord's statements seem to be so simple and gentle, and they slip unobserved into the subconscious mind. Then something happens in our circumstances; up comes one of these words into our consciousness and we hear it for the first time and it makes us reel with amazement." (Chapter 19)

From *God's Workmanship.* Copyright © 1953 by the Oswald Chambers Publications Assn. Ltd.:

"Don't say thy will be done, but see it is done." (Chapter 16)

From *If You Shall Ask.* Copyright © 1937 by the Oswald Chambers Publications Assn. Ltd.:

"Some prayers are followed by silence because they are wrong, others because they are bigger than we can understand." (Chapter 18)

From *Our Brilliant Heritage*. Copyright © 1929 by the Oswald Chambers Publications Assn. Ltd.:

> "Before we can hear, we must be trained." (Chapter 19)

From *The Philosophy of Sin*. Copyright © 1937 by the Oswald Chambers Publications Assn. Ltd.:

> "These are cases recorded in the Bible, and in our own day, of people who have been marvelously healed, for what purpose? For us to imitate them? Never, but in order that we might discern what lies behind, namely, the individual relationship to a personal God." (Chapter 20)

From *Not Knowing Where*. Copyright © 1934 by the Oswald Chambers Publications Assn. Ltd.:

> "If it was God's will to bruise his own Son, why should it not be his will to bruise you?" (Chapter 20)

From *The Shade of His Hand*. Copyright © 1924, 1936 by the Oswald Chambers Publications Assn. Ltd.:

> "Prayer is not a preparation for work, it is work. Prayer is not a preparation for the battle, it is the battle. Prayer is twofold: definite asking and definite waiting to receive." (Chapter 4)

> "There will come one day a personal and direct touch from God when every tear and perplexity, every oppression and distress, every suffering and pain, and wrong and injustice will have a complete and ample and overwhelming explanation." (Chapter 18)

Trademarks: Wiley, the Wiley Publishing logo, For Dummies, the Dummies Man logo, A Reference for the Rest of Us!, The Dummies Way, Dummies Daily, The Fun and Easy Way, Dummies.com and related trade dress are trademarks or registered trademarks of Wiley Publishing, Inc. in the United States and other countries, and may not be used without written permission. All other trademarks are the property of their respective owners. Wiley Publishing, Inc., is not associated with any product or vendor mentioned in this book.

LIMIT OF LIABILITY/DISCLAIMER OF WARRANTY: WHILE THE PUBLISHER AND AUTHOR HAVE USED THEIR BEST EFFORTS IN PREPARING THIS BOOK, THEY MAKE NO REPRESENTATIONS OR WARRANTIES WITH RESPECT TO THE ACCURACY OR COMPLETENESS OF THE CONTENTS OF THIS BOOK AND SPECIFICALLY DISCLAIM ANY IMPLIED WARRANTIES OF MERCHANTABILITY OR FITNESS FOR A PARTICULAR PURPOSE. NO WARRANTY MAY BE CREATED OR EXTENDED BY SALES REPRESENTATIVES OR WRITTEN SALES MATERIALS. THE ADVICE AND STRATEGIES CONTAINED HEREIN MAY NOT BE SUITABLE FOR YOUR SITUATION. YOU SHOULD CONSULT WITH A PROFESSIONAL WHERE APPROPRIATE. NEITHER THE PUBLISHER NOR AUTHOR SHALL BE LIABLE FOR ANY LOSS OF PROFIT OR ANY OTHER COMMERCIAL DAMAGES, INCLUDING BUT NOT LIMITED TO SPECIAL, INCIDENTAL, CONSEQUENTIAL, OR OTHER DAMAGES.

For general information on our other products and services or to obtain technical support, please contact our Customer Care Department within the U.S. at 800-762-2974, outside the U.S. at 317-572-3993, or fax 317-572-4002.

Wiley also publishes its books in a variety of electronic formats. Some content that appears in print may not be available in electronic books.

Library of Congress Control Number: 2002114786

ISBN: 0-7645-5500-6

1B/SX/RR/QS/IN

Manufactured in the United States of America

10 9 8 7 6 5

Wiley Publishing, Inc. is a trademark of Wiley Publishing, Inc.

About the Author

Richard Wagner is founder and writer of Digitalwalk.net (www.digitalwalk.net), a Web-based commentary with the purpose of challenging and encouraging Christians to earnestly live out their faith in a digital, postmodern world. Richard has served in church leadership and teaching roles for more than a dozen years. He lives in Princeton, Massachusetts, with his wife and three boys. You can e-mail Richard at rich@digitalwalk.net.

For a study guide and discussion questions for *Christian Prayer For Dummies*, visit www.digitalwalk.net/prayerdummy.

Dedication

To Lori and Aaron: The present mystery of lost prayers will someday be
answered by your smiles.

Author's Acknowledgments

When John Donne penned "No man is an island," I am convinced that he had to be speaking of an author. There are so many people I'd like to acknowledge who helped shape and guide this book and make it possible.

First and foremost, I want to thank my wife, Kim, for her sacrifice, boundless enthusiasm, and unique insights that helped inspire the book, particularly the family prayer and journaling chapters. My sons, Jordan, Jared, and Justus, deserve special thanks for their support, especially during a particularly important crunch time when they fasted from the TV and movies as a way of showing support for the book.

Several people provided marvelous feedback and ideas to help form and shape the book. Joe Wagner, my father, reviewed each chapter and provided his opinions to help make sure the book stood up to the real world. Clint Frank, a go-to person in my life when I need wise counsel, also provided tremendous encouragement and perspective from the very start. I also appreciated the theological perspectives of Eric Hartlen and Randall Matthews to help clarify some tough issues. Bruce Marchiano deserves a warm and special thanks for sharing his unique insights into the prayer life of Jesus. Finally, I'd like to thank those people who were willing to share their personal stories of prayer to me, some of which I chronicle in the book.

The editorial team for this book was a blessing. Heartfelt thanks to Tonya Cupp for her flawless project management, encouragement, and flexibility; Tina Sims for her keen editing prowess and her knack for always spotting the parts of a chapter that needed further explanation; and Dr. Bill Young for his wise theological insights that helped refine the book and keep its overall message consistent. Special thanks also goes to Kathy Cox for her belief in the book's vision from the outset.

Finally, so many people around me were prayer warriors throughout the book writing process. I have a deep sense of gratitude to the people in my home group, e-accountability group, and Heritage Bible Chapel for their prayers

Publisher's Acknowledgments

We're proud of this book; please send us your comments through our Dummies online registration form located at www.dummies.com/register/.

Some of the people who helped bring this book to market include the following:

Acquisitions, Editorial, and Media Development

Project Editor: Tonya Maddox Cupp

Acquisitions Editor: Kathleen M. Cox

Senior Copy Editor: Tina Sims

Acquisitions Coordinator: Holly Grimes

Technical Editor: Dr. William Young

Senior Permissions Editor: Carmen Krikorian

Editorial Manager: Jennifer Ehrlich

Editorial Assistant: Brian Herrmann

Cartoons: Rich Tennant, www.the5thwave.com

Production

Project Coordinator: Maridee Ennis

Layout and Graphics: Amanda Carter, Carrie Foster, Jackie Nicholas, Shelley Norris, Heather Pope, Jacque Schneider, Rashell Smith, Julie Trippetti, TECHBOOKS Production Services

Proofreaders: Laura Albert, Tyler Connoley, Andy Hollandbeck, Angel Perez, TECHBOOKS Production Services

Indexer: TECHBOOKS Production Services

Publishing and Editorial for Consumer Dummies

Diane Graves Steele, Vice President and Publisher, Consumer Dummies

Joyce Pepple, Acquisitions Director, Consumer Dummies

Kristin A. Cocks, Product Development Director, Consumer Dummies

Michael Spring, Vice President and Publisher, Travel

Brice Gosnell, Publishing Director, Travel

Suzanne Jannetta, Editorial Director, Travel

Publishing for Technology Dummies

Andy Cummings, Vice President and Publisher, Dummies Technology/General User

Composition Services

Gerry Fahey, Vice President of Production Services

Debbie Stailey, Director of Composition Services

Contents at a Glance

Table of Contents

Introduction

*I'*ll pray for you."

Have you ever said those words to a friend or loved one after hearing of a tragedy, sickness, or job loss? I often say that phrase as I talk with others about what's going on their lives. Indeed, this expression is a common, second-nature response to a need that is shared. Yet, do you always follow up on your promise to pray? I confess that too many times I've said those words and failed to do so.

"I'll pray for you" is a phrase packed solid with good intentions. However, sorry to say, prayer requests can often go in one ear and out the other, given the frantic, fast-paced lifestyles of today's world. Following through on that pledge to pray has become too much like that to-do list of handyman jobs I keep promising my wife I'll do.

However, I think a reason other than busyness keeps people from praying diligently. People tend to exchange lip service for genuine prayer when they forget the true power that prayer holds. Prayer becomes a nice thing to do rather than something you feel compelled to do for a friend.

In reading this book, you discover that "I'll pray for you" is one of the most significant expressions you can utter. Contained inside this deceivingly simple phrase is a direct line to an all-knowing, all-powerful God, who invites Christians to participate in his work in the world through prayer. Therefore, by following through on that promise to your friend, God can use your earnest and diligent prayers to effect real and lasting change. However, you also discover while reading this book that prayer is more than a one-sided conversation of endless prayer requests. Instead, as a natural part of the relationship you have with a personal God, prayer involves actively listening to him and letting him move freely in your life.

Christian Prayer For Dummies equips you with the know-how you need to deepen and enrich your prayer life. It also helps you know why you're praying, whom you're praying to, what prayer can do, and how to pray effectively. I avoid the two extremes — "touchy-feely" spiritualism and heavy theological prose — that you can so often encounter when reading books on prayer. My aim is to touch a middle ground that is highly practical yet life changing.

How This Book Is Organized

Christian Prayer For Dummies is your practical guide to prayer that helps you wrap your arms around this often misunderstood topic. I divide the book into five parts, each of which builds upon the previous ones.

Part I: Signing Up for Basic Training

As you kick off your journey of prayer, Part I helps you discover the essential aspects of prayer, what prayer is not, and why prayer is central to how God works in the world. You then explore when and how to pray, whether you're at home, on the road, at work, or at play. Before leaving, you study the Lord's Prayer, the most famous prayer of all time, and find out how you can use it as a model for your own prayers.

Part II: Turbocharging Your Prayers

In Part II, it's time to get practical. You begin by exploring how to pray on your own and how to best organize your prayers. From there, you start looking at how to use written prayers and Scripture to keep your prayers on track and prevent them from becoming stale. You also discover several proven prayer techniques and aids, including journaling, meditating, fasting, and singing. Furthermore, because wandering thoughts and emotional blocks can kill your prayer life before it ever gets off the ground, you explore how to overcome these and other common hindrances to prayer.

Part III: Praying Well with Others

In Part III, you find out to pray more effectively with others, starting with the most important place of all — your home. You see how prayer can transform your family relationships and how you can create a legacy of prayer for your children. You also discover how to pray in small, informal groups and get an insight into the hodgepodge of issues to think about when praying in formal occasions, such as church services and graduation ceremonies.

Part IV: Tackling Some Tough Issues

Part IV tackles the most difficult and thorny issues associated with prayer. You find out why God sometimes wants you to wait for answers despite your objections, how you can pray according to God's will and not your own, how to listen to God speak, how God heals in today's world, and what praying in tongues means. Chapters 16, 17, and 18 are the heart of the book.

Part V: The Part of Tens

In Part V, I provide a variety of resources designed to boost your prayer walk. I begin by listing prayers for ten occasions when you really need them. I continue by providing ten prayers well worth teaching your children or grandchildren. Next, I detail ten retreat and pilgrimage locations that you can visit on special occasions when you want to get away to pray. Finally, I close the part by chronicling what I consider the ten best prayer Web sites.

Assumptions Made in the Book

Christian Prayer For Dummies is a book on Christian prayer, not a general guide to prayer spanning all religious faiths. The primary assumption made in this book is that prayer is directed to the God of the Bible and is in synch with historical Christian beliefs.

The great Christian writer C.S. Lewis used the term "mere Christianity" to describe the core essentials of the Christian faith that any believer, regardless of his or her background, can agree to. In the same way, I focus my discussion on "mere Christian prayer," or teachings of prayer and practices that Protestants (including both the evangelical and mainline communities), Roman Catholics, and Orthodox Christians all affirm.

Although all Christians can agree on the essentials of prayer, let me be very frank and say that Christians among the different branches of Christianity disagree and sometimes disagree very loudly. When I encounter these debatable issues, I point them out and distinguish among the various traditions.

Christianity is a faith based on real space and time history. The central event is the life, death, and resurrection of Jesus Christ, some 2,000 years ago. All Christian teaching depends on this historical, literal event. The Apostle Paul, who wrote much of the New Testament, concurred when he said that if this fact weren't true, then everything he and other Christians were doing was a huge waste of time. So, although this book doesn't address issues concerning the historical reliability of the Christian faith, it does assume that what you read in the Bible is trustworthy and reliable.

Finally, although I certainly don't expect anyone to be a Bible scholar, I am assuming some very basic knowledge of the Bible, such as knowing what the

Old Testament is, who the Israelites and Moses were, and the like. If you'd like a primer on the Bible, I recommend checking out *The Bible For Dummies* by Jeffrey Geoghegan and Michael Homan (published by Wiley, Inc.).

Conventions Used in This Book

As you read through the book, keep in mind the following conventions:

✔ Each Bible passage cited in the book is from the *World English Bible* translation (which you can see at www.worldenglishbible.com). On occasion, I paraphrase the text to make it more readable.

✔ Although the Bible uses many terms to describe God, I generally use *God* and *Lord.* Also, in accordance with traditional Christian beliefs, I make use of the traditional masculine pronoun *he* to refer to God.

✔ You find quotes from the some of the top Christian thinkers on prayer scattered throughout the pages of the book. Each quote is relevant to the text of the chapter and helps round out your understanding of the information being discussed.

Icons Used in This Book

Tip draws attention to a key point that can enrich your prayer life.

Pay close attention to the Remember text; it highlights something that is important if you want to deepen your understanding of prayer.

Heed the cautionary tales whenever you see the Warning icon. It saves you from falling into the pitfalls of prayer mistakes and errors.

The Technical Stuff icon identifies cool, hip, and interesting material to read, but it's more theological or advanced than the rest of the stuff in the book. Technical Stuff information is helpful but not essential.

Where to Go from Here

If you decide to read *Christian Prayer For Dummies* from start to finish, you will find the topics logically ordered, with each successive chapter rounding out what you discovered in previous chapters. However, because it is a reference book, you don't have to read the book cover to cover.

What's more, if you have a specific issue that you'd like to jump to, consider the following jumping-off points:

- ✔ For the basics of what prayer is and isn't, see Chapters 1, 2, and 3.

- ✔ For how, when, and what to pray, see Chapters 4, 5, and 6.

- ✔ For the two key concepts of Christian prayer — "Thy will be done" and "Ask and you shall receive" — see Chapters 16, 17, and 18.

- ✔ For knowing how to hear God, see Chapter 19.

- ✔ For what to do when God doesn't seem to answer your prayer, see Chapter 18.

- ✔ For discovering how prayer is related to your relationship with God, see Chapter 3.

- ✔ For prayer techniques, see Chapters 7, 8, 9, 10, and 11.

- ✔ For very practical information about praying with others, see Chapters 13, 14, and 15.

- ✔ For ready-made prayers that kick-start your and your child's prayer life, see Chapters 22 and 23.

Part I
Signing Up for Basic Training

The 5th Wave
By Rich Tennant

"I'm thinking of taking a spiritual journey, but I want to make sure I look right for the trip."

In this part . . .

Prayer is like a greased pig at a county fair — often pursued but rarely grasped. In this part, you discover the basics of prayer and how to get that lasso going in full motion. You find out what prayer is, how it works, and why it is such a pivotal part of how God works in the world.

Chapter 1

Discovering the Real X-Factor

Can you go anywhere these days without seeing someone talking on a cell phone? Take a look around, and you'll see happy "cellulites" walking down the street, driving a car, or watching a movie. Even the church is not immune — on more than one occasion I've heard a cell phone ring in the middle of a service!

In this age of wireless communication, there are virtually no barriers to chatting with a friend on the phone, no matter where you are or what you're doing. In fact, during a recent car trip across the United States, I was amazed to find my cell phone fully usable in the most remote and barren spots of the Nevada desert.

Prayer has many similarities to this wireless revolution; you can dial up God and talk as long as you like anytime, anywhere. At some point, nearly everyone turns to prayer in such a way — from the most devoted believers to the wildest prodigals. Some do so at the top of each morning, while others wait until they're at the top of a cliff, perilously close to the edge.

Prayer is the most universal practice in all of religion. A Christian, a Hindu, a Muslim, and a Buddhist may not agree on the purpose of prayer or to whom one should pray, but they do all agree on the need for prayer. The reason for this instinctive drive to pray must be that, in creating humans, God embedded something like a cellular phone in you and me that is equipped with an unlimited calling plan to him (weekends and nights free, of course). Just as I naturally turn to my wireless device to call my wife in times of need and joy on the road, so do I intuitively turn to God during key times in my life.

The vast majority of both adults and teens in the United States pray during a typical week and believe that their prayers have an impact on what happens in their lives (Barna Research). However, although most Americans practice prayer, they're not necessarily confident about how to pray or how prayer works. What's more, don't go asking one of them to pray in public, because you're likely to get an evasive answer or see them sprinting frantically in the other direction. (See Chapter 15 for more on praying in public.)

If you're in their camp and prayer remains somewhat elusive to you, be assured that you're in good company. Even the most saintly of people, be it evangelist Billy Graham, the pope, or my mother, never have it fully mastered. In fact, prayer is something akin to a greased pig at a county fair — often pursued, but rarely grasped.

As you read *Christian Prayer For Dummies*, think of this book as your lasso for that hard-to-catch concept. In these pages, you discover how to throw the rope and harness prayer: You find out what prayer is and isn't and how prayer can benefit, challenge, equip, and, above all, transform your life. However, a word of caution: After you lasso it, I can't promise that prayer won't still pull you along for a ride as you hold on for dear life. But such is the nature of this wonderfully mysterious thing called prayer.

Having a Chat with God

Prayer is simply communicating with God. There's nothing magical at all about Christian prayer; it's matter of fact. This book covers dozens of prayer methods and techniques, but don't confuse these with the basic truth that prayer is simply an open invitation to talk to God.

However, Christian prayer is more than just telling God your list of requests and expecting him to answer your prayers like he's some kind of cosmic vending machine. Yes, prayer is a way to share with God what's on your mind. But even more important, it's a way to get to know God and what he wants to do in your life and in the world. (Chapters 16, 17, and 18, which together form the heart of this book, focus on these critical issues.)

When you study the Bible, you find people praying left and right, but the subject of prayer itself is actually rarely addressed. I suppose that's not too surprising when you consider that *Basketball For Dummies* probably doesn't spend too much time talking about pumping up the ball with air. A filled ball is essential to playing basketball, but it's also so obvious that nothing need be said about it. In the same way, prayer, or talking with God, is so natural that it's a given in the Bible.

Statistically speaking

Surveys of U.S. adults and teenagers by Barna Research Ltd. from 1991–2001 revealed the following statistics about people's prayer habits:

Who prays?

✔ 82 percent of adults and 89 percent of teenagers pray in a normal week.

✔ 88 percent of women and 75 percent of men pray in a typical week.

✔ People living in the South and Midwest pray more than those living in the West and Northeast (around 86 percent to 76 percent, respectively).

✔ 96 percent of born-again Christians pray weekly, while 72 percent of people not describing themselves as born again pray on a weekly basis.

What do people pray about?

✔ 95 percent of adults thank God for what he has done in their lives.

✔ 76 percent ask for forgiveness for specific sins.

✔ 67 percent spend time in prayer worshiping God by praising his superior attributes.

✔ 61 percent ask for help for specific needs.

✔ 47 percent are silent during prayer to listen for God.

What do people believe?

✔ 89 percent of adults believe "there is a god who watches over you and answers your prayers."

✔ 82 percent of people believe that prayer can change what happens in a person's life.

When and how much do people pray?

✔ An average prayer lasts just under five minutes.

✔ 52 percent of people who pray do so several times a day.

✔ 37 percent of people say they pray once a day.

✔ 21 percent have extended prayer time with other family members (25 percent among Protestants and 13 percent among Catholics).

✔ 33 percent of adults regularly participate in a prayer group or other meeting that has a focus on prayer.

Although the Bible doesn't talk specifically about prayer methods, you do notice that the manner in which people prayed changed through the ages. In the earliest of times, people like Adam, Noah, and Abraham prayed in a very familiar and direct manner to God and tended to focus on the practicalities of life. But from the time of Moses through the rest of the Old Testament period, prayers tended to be more formal and focus less on personal needs and more on national issues related to the Israelites.

Christian prayer has its origins in the prayers of Jesus, particularly the Lord's Prayer (which I cover in detail in Chapter 5). Christian prayer in the New Testament becomes more focused on the spiritual needs of individuals, such as the cleansing of sins, physical healing, and equipping of individuals with spiritual qualities to live like Christ. Prayer in the New Testament is also quite intimate and even goes so far as to tell you to call God your Daddy. (See Chapter 3 for details on this topic.)

Nowhere does the Bible list any specific rules on how to pray. Protestant, Catholic, and Orthodox Christians each have their own distinct traditions of prayer. The refreshing and liberating fact is that God is not much concerned with how you pray; he's more interested in what you pray about and what your attitude is while you pray (see Chapter 6).

Realizing What's So Good about Prayer Anyway

Our society is a no-nonsense one — just give me the facts. So before diving into how to pray, I want to discuss why prayer is advantageous and how it can benefit you.

Having prayer in your life offers five distinct advantages:

- ✔ **Prayer changes your circumstances.** Certainly the most obvious benefit to prayer is that prayer changes things. After all, if prayer never made any difference, why do it? The Bible make it clear that when you pray, things change: "Everyone who asks receives," said Jesus in Matthew 7:8, while James 4:2 adds the contrary message as well: "You don't have, because you don't ask."

    The more I discover about God, the more I agree with Scottish pastor and author Oswald Chambers, who said, "We have a God who engineers circumstances." God is engaged and involved in the world, even when you and I relegate his interventions to being mere "coincidences."

    Sadly, one of the biggest hindrances to believing that prayer changes circumstances is your short-term memory. Even after people see God answer a prayer definitively, they tend to forget about his work the next time they have a pressing need. One way to combat this attention deficit is to write down your prayer requests and answers, a topic I talk about further in Chapter 9.

✔ **Prayer mends relationships.** You can look at prayer as the following:

- **A healing salve that you can apply to the wounds of torn and broken relationships:** When you pray, you open yourself up to God and allow him to work in the situation you're praying about. (See Chapter 13 to find out how prayer can strengthen family and marriage relationships.)

- **A pride buster:** You humble yourself to God when you pray, saying in effect, "I need your help because I can't solve the situation by myself." This attitude of humility can then spill over and make it easier to deal with the other party and be open to a resolution.

- **Something that pulls people together as they mutually submit to a higher authority:** So if you and the other party are willing to pray together about the situation, the two of you can take a big step toward breaking down a major barrier to resolving the problem.

Finally, even when the other party has hardened his heart about coming to a resolution, prayer gives you a listener who knows all about your situation and your frustration and can empathize with you.

✔ **Prayer helps you physically.** Prayer can make a tangible difference in your physical health. The Bible offers many examples of God's healing of people's physical ailments when people prayed, and I often hear of present-day stories of healing. Over the past 20 years, these accounts are being backed up with medical research studies on the effectiveness of prayer on physical healing, suggesting that prayer can indeed have a positive impact on those people who are being prayed for. (See Chapter 20 for more on physical healing prayer.)

What if?

Don't you wonder why God doesn't answer 100 percent of the prayers in the manner you and I expect? After all, wouldn't that take all the "ifs" away about God, causing everyone to believe? Ironically, even if the Lord answered everyone's prayers in spectacular and miraculous ways, it probably wouldn't change most people's minds about God. In Jesus' day, for example, when he performed miracles, those supernatural events tended to make his followers more committed to him and those against him angrier at him. Check out Chapter 18 for more about prayers that aren't answered like you expect.

Show me the data

Once viewed skeptically by doctors, prayer is becoming more valued by many in the medical community. Several scientific studies over the past two decades give credence to what Christians have been saying for 2,000 years: God heals people. Here are a few noteworthy examples:

✔ Two studies on heart patients showed impressive results. In the first, patients who received an angioplasty procedure and were prayed for suffered much fewer complications than those who were not. In the second, prayed-for heart patients had fewer problems and shorter hospital stays. (For more information about these studies, see the November 2001 issue of *American Heart Journal* and the May 1999 issue of *Internal Medicine*.)

✔ A fertilization study found a doubling of in vitro pregnancies among women who were prayed for by others. The women involved didn't know that they were being prayed for, so the results can't be attributed to psychological factors. (The September 2001 issue of *The Journal of Reproductive Medicine* has more on this study.)

✔ Perhaps the best-known study was one conducted in the late 1980s by Dr. Randolph Byrd, who looked at the impact of Judeo-Christian prayer on nearly 400 heart attack patients. Half of those patients were prayed for by groups around the country, resulting in fewer deaths, faster recovery, and fewer complications. However, other aspects of

the study were far less clear, because not all factors were statistically different, allowing critics to question the true effectiveness of the study. (You can read about this in the July 1988 issue of *Southern Medical Journal*.)

However, when you hear about scientific studies on the effectiveness of prayer, take them with a grain of salt, for two reasons:

✔ Prayer isn't a simple cause-and-effect equation. Because God does answer prayers, healing may take place as a result of the prayers in these studies, but it will not be the case 100 percent of the time. Your own experiences bear that out — sometimes God heals, but sometimes he chooses not to answer your prayers in that way. As you discover in Chapter 18 and 20, God has reasons that go beyond that particular person's well-being when it comes to healing or choosing not to heal someone.

✔ God is not a pawn to be manipulated. I'm sure that he must laugh at some of the attempts humans make in measuring his involvement in the world. God can do what he pleases and so can influence the results of the research as much or as little as he pleases.

However, in spite of these caveats, the studies being conducted by researchers today continue to indicate that prayer makes a difference in the physical recovery of the patients being prayed for.

✔ **Prayer helps you emotionally.** When you think of healing, physical healing may be the first thing that comes to mind. But the Gospels give many examples of Jesus' emotional and spiritual healing of people.

Many people today live with painful memories from the past that can enslave and rule their lives, even in ways that they don't consciously realize. Through prayer, God can free you from the bondage of memories and past sin and provide a release in such a way that they no longer become a dominating force in your life. (See Chapter 12 for ways around emotional and spiritual barriers to prayer.)

✔ **Prayer changes you.** Perhaps the greatest irony of prayer is that when you're truly open to God's answer, you — not the circumstance — are often what changes. Just as I'm discovering that God does engineer circumstances, he also uses circumstances to change me. Although this discovery may be a surprise, it really shouldn't be that unexpected. The God of the Bible makes it clear that he is most interested in how people are being transformed on the inside, because those changes are eternal.

Seeing How Prayer Works: Past, Present, and Future

Although "X-factor" is technically a term that describes an arcane economic principle, it has become a popular way to describe the hidden key or mysterious ingredient that, when added to the mix, makes a difference. A quick search on the Web shows you that so many people use the term X-factor these days to describe what they're doing, whether it's a golf swing, a diet plan, a software product, or a comic book character. Indeed, the expression is a great marketing device: People yearn for a missing piece that will help solve their problems.

In contrast to these imitators, prayer has been the *real* X-factor throughout history, from Adam's first breath down through this digital, high-tech age. Because of prayer, God has gotten many a person out of a fix or saved them from certain danger. For reasons I explain in Chapter 16, God does not *always* choose to answer prayers in the way you or I may want or expect. However, you can find countless examples of times when God's explicit response to a specific prayer proved to be the critical agent of change used to turn circumstances on a dime. Consider a handful of remarkable examples from Biblical, historical, and modern times. (See Chapter 20 for more real-life examples of physical healing and turn to Chapter 18 for stories of when God chooses not to answer prayers in the manner that you or I expect.)

A vintage Hollywood story: How Esther saved the Israelites

The Book of Esther in the Old Testament tells the gripping story of how a young Jewish girl named Esther came to marry King Xerxes and then served as queen of Persia. Like something out of a Hollywood movie, Esther's charmed life as a queen turned sour when Haman, a power-hungry advisor to the king, felt that Esther's father, Mordecai, had slighted him. Turning a personal vendetta into an ethnic-cleansing scheme, Haman decided to trick Xerxes into doing away with all the Jewish people in the kingdom. But before Haman could carry out this evil plan, Mordecai learned of it and promptly appealed to Esther to stop the impending massacre.

Esther's ability to change the situation, however, was easier said than done. You see, Persia wasn't exactly a politically correct society at that time, as evidenced by the fact that the queen wasn't permitted to approach the king without his sending for her first. Esther found herself in a catch-22 situation: If she appealed to the king, he would likely take offense at her initiative and kill her on the spot, but if she didn't, the Jews (and she too if the king finds out that she is Jewish) would meet a certain doom.

In the midst of this quandary, Esther intuitively turned to the Lord in prayer and asked for his intervention in the situation. She commanded all Jewish people to *fast* (pray and go without food, a topic you can read more about in Chapter 10) for three days; after that time, she went and saw the king.

Esther's X-factor proved to be that prayer. Not only did the king not get angry at her, but Haman was eventually exposed for his true sinister self. In the end, Esther, Mordecai, and all the Jewish people were saved because God answered their earnest prayers.

The absent-minded doctor

Even from his teenage years, Hudson Taylor had a lifelong passion to become a Christian missionary to inland China, and not just because he liked Kung Pao chicken. Although you can find many stories of answered prayer in his decades of work in 19th century China, one of the most fascinating occurred before he ever left the shores of his native England.

Resolved that he needed medical training before leaving for the mission field, Hudson started working as a doctor's apprentice when he was 20 years old. While working in that job, however, Hudson began wondering whether he had the kind of rock-solid faith that he needed to make it as a missionary: Was he trusting in the Lord to supply his needs or relying on himself? (See Chapters 16 and 17.)

Hudson decided to find out. After much prayer, he concluded that he'd start relying on God for his paycheck rather than on himself. You see, he was paid a salary and boarding allowance every four months, but in those days before direct deposit, he didn't always get paid when he was supposed to. Without a daily planner or personal digital assistant, the kindly but forgetful doctor for whom Hudson worked needed regular reminding about payday. In the past, Hudson had prompted him, but he resolved from that point on to let God do the prompting instead. When the next payday rolled around, Hudson found himself without a paycheck.

He watched his wallet growing ever thinner as day after day went by. After three weeks had passed, Hudson was in dire straits: He'd just given his last coin to a needy family and eaten the last of his food, and his rent was due the next morning. Hudson began questioning why God hadn't answered his prayer yet, and he wondered whether his whole scheme was a mark of obedience or just plain foolishness.

As he awoke the next morning, he knew it was time to face the music. Yet as he prayed, the postman came and delivered an unsigned letter containing a single pair of gloves and a sovereign coin — worth four times as much as the half crown he'd given away the day before!

This gift kept him solvent for another two weeks, but eventually he found himself in the same situation as before — without any money or food and the rent due the following day. On a Saturday evening, the doctor and Hudson were talking after the last patient had gone, when, lo and behold, the absent-minded doctor finally remembered to pay Hudson. However, because it was a Saturday night, the doctor couldn't do anything about paying Hudson until Monday when the banks opened. Taylor was torn up inside: He was relieved that the doctor finally remembered but desperate that no solution seemed possible until Monday.

The doctor went home and left Hudson to close the office. After uttering a final prayer for help, Hudson was preparing to leave the office at 10 p.m. when the doctor burst through the door laughing. After catching his breath, the doctor told Hudson the strange story of what had just transpired. As the doctor was preparing to go to bed around 9 p.m., one of his wealthy patients came to his house to pay his bill. And instead of paying with a check as he usually did, he paid in cash. With a smile, the doctor handed over the cash to Hudson — enabling him to pay the rent on time and to buy breakfast the next day.

Hudson's story is a reminder that even though his prayers proved to be the X-factor, God's timing (see Chapter 16) is not exactly our own. God didn't make it easy for Hudson for those many weeks, but look at the result: Hudson was changed in a way that he wouldn't have been had God answered on that first payday. And that trust proved critical to his missionary success in China years later.

Elijah Jones and the altars of Carmel

Elijah was an Old Testament *prophet,* a special messenger representing God to the people of the day. I think of Elijah as something like the Indiana Jones of the Bible. He was bold, energetic, and zealous and always seemed to find himself in the midst of the action.

Prayer to Elijah was like Indiana Jones's whip, making him one not to be messed with. His prayers caused a multiyear drought in Israel to start and end and brought back a young boy from death. However, Elijah's defining moment came at a big showdown with the evil King Ahab concerning which god — Elijah's or King Ahab's — was real.

To determine who was the real god, Elijah challenged King Ahab and his 450 prophets to the first ever battle of the gods between the God of Israel and their god of Baal. The challenge: Whose god could light an *altar* (a table that serves as the centerpiece for a religious ceremony) on Mount Carmel?

The Baal prophets went first. With Elijah smiling all the while, they worked all day, dancing and prancing, crying out to Baal but having no luck. And when that didn't work, they pulled a trick you'd expect to see in *The Temple of Doom*, getting so desperate that they started cutting themselves with swords and knives to get their god to listen. Unsuccessful, they finally gave up and gave Elijah his turn.

But in true Indiana Jones fashion, Elijah wasn't simply content to pray for God to light a dry altar. Instead, he made it more interesting by having his altar doused with water several times beforehand. He then thundered out a prayer (from 1 Kings 18:36–37):

> *[Lord], the God of Abraham, of Isaac, and of Israel, let it be known this day that you are God in Israel, and that I am your servant, and that I have done all these things at your word. Hear me, [Lord], hear me, that this people may know that you are God, and that you have turned their heart back again."*

You can guess what happens next: God answered his prayer in a big and mighty way — sending fire to burn up the sacrifice and everything around it. Indiana Jones would have been proud!

Elijah discovered on that day that God does indeed answer prayers in visible and tangible ways (see Chapter 17).

Elijah's experience on Mount Carmel could have given him the impression that God's way of working in the world was always through lightning and thunder, but if you read on later in 1 Kings, you find out that God also responds to Elijah in more subtle ways with a "still small voice." See Chapter 19 for more details on how God communicates.

Putting your faith where your mouth is

Prayer warrior is a term often used to describe someone who is especially diligent in prayer. George Müller, who established a series of orphanages in 19th century England, is perhaps my favorite prayer warrior of all time. He started out with a single house to care for a handful of orphans, but by the time he died, George had fed, clothed, and taught over 10,000 orphans.

Although the philanthropic work he performed over his lifetime is remarkable, what is truly extraordinary is *how* George did it. He let prayer be the centerpiece of his life's work. In reading Psalms 81:10 ("Open your mouth wide, and I will fill it."), he believed that this passage meant that God would do as he promised and provide for the needs of the orphans and his family. So, instead of doing the expected fundraising gigs in churches and Rotary Clubs and appearing on late-night TV commercials, he simply prayed for God to prompt people to give money to them. In all his years of caring for thousands of orphans, he never once asked a person for a dime!

And, over the span of decades, God never failed to provide materially for George — not that he never had any hard times, because he had more than his share. On countless occasions, the orphanage ran completely out of money immediately before a breakfast or dinner. But, each time, the Lord miraculously intervened before anyone missed a meal. Müller was a fanatic at writing down his prayers and their answers and said later that some 5,000 of his prayers had been answered on the day he asked for them. (You can read more about writing down your prayers in Chapter 9.)

Human-sized fishing bait

Why is it that some people become permanently associated with a single event in their lives and, like it or not, they just can't shake it off? Lindberg and Paris, Nixon and Watergate, Bill Buckner and the 1986 World Series, and Gilligan and his three-hour tour. But when it comes to big fish, only one name springs to the mind of most anyone who ever attended Sunday School as a child: Jonah.

Jonah, another Old Testament prophet, was called by God to go to the bustling city of Nineveh and warn the people there of God's impending judgment if they refused to turn from their wicked ways. God may have chosen Jonah for this assignment, but to put it mildly, he wasn't exactly thrilled with the mission. Did Jonah like Nineveh? Well, let me put it this way: He probably would never have volunteered to be a spokesman for the Nineveh Office of Tourism.

Determined not to obey this command, Jonah makes one of the silliest moves in history when he decides to run away from God. Evidently, he played hooky on the day in Prophet School when they learned about God being everywhere!

Jonah set out on a fishing boat in the opposite direction of Nineveh, and sure enough, God caused a great storm to disrupt his plans. Jonah eventually told the boat's crew what he did and begged them to throw him into the sea to save themselves. Though reluctant, they agreed and threw him overboard. Once in the water, Jonah splashed around in the sea, fully expecting a watery grave any moment. To his surprise, however, he was swallowed by a big fish (or whale) and ended up staying inside of it for three smelly days.

Jonah used those 72 hours not only to freshen up on his "God is everywhere" knowledge but also to have a change of heart. After a long prayer thanking God for saving him from drowning, Jonah vowed that he would do whatever the Lord asked of him.

His prayer of thanksgiving proved the X-factor, for the Lord promptly caused the fish to throw up Jonah, letting him wash onto dry land. Then, after taking a nice, long, hot shower and swearing never to eat seafood again, Jonah went to Nineveh and began carrying out God's plan.

Peter's great escape

The Great Escape, the 1962 Steve McQueen classic film about British and American officers escaping from a Nazi prison camp during World War II, has always been one of my favorite movies. The prisoners formulate a grand scheme to tunnel their way out of the camp and then dig for months on end to carry it out.

The Apostle Peter had a great escape of his own, but unlike Steve McQueen, he didn't have to dig a tunnel to get away. He was imprisoned by King Herod after the ruler began cracking down on the early Christian church leaders. Herod killed the Apostle James and intended to have Peter be the next leader put on trial.

Peter's outlook looked bleak. The night before the trial was to begin, Peter was tied up in chains and forced to sleep between two jailers, and sentries stood guard outside the entrance to his cell. Not even Steve McQueen could have gotten out of this tight spot. But unknown to Herod, the church had an X-factor all its own when members prayed diligently for Peter's safety. In the nick of time, God answered their prayers when an angel appeared that night and freed Peter from his prison cell, enabling him to continue his ministry unencumbered.

Don't forget the postage

Les Nimigan was the director of a modern-day, Canadian-based evangelistic ministry reaching out to people in the transportation industry. Several years ago, when he was traveling in Alberta, Canada, the old car he was driving broke down and was beyond repair, leaving Les in dire need of a car to continue his working trip. There was just one problem: The ministry had no money to pay for the expense. So, in true Müller fashion (see the section "Putting your faith where your mouth is," earlier in this chapter), Les prayed earnestly that God would provide a car.

Les walked into an auto dealership the next day to see what his options were. Les found out that the owner was a Christian, so Les shared some information about his ministry. When the owner learned of his need for a car, the dealer sold him a Chevrolet Nova at dealer cost of $9,740.20 on the condition that Lee would send him a check for payment when the Lord provided the money. So Les took the car and drove to Toronto.

Once back at the ministry headquarters, Les and his staff had a prayer meeting to ask God to send additional funds to pay for their new purchase. The moment they finished praying, the secretary opened the mail and discovered a check from an elderly donor in the amount of $9,740.42. His secretary was dumbfounded that the check was so close to the price of the car, but she wondered why the amount would be off 22 cents. Les responded, "Why, of course, that's the amount to cover the postage."

Transforming Your ABC's into the X

Other than "Which came first: the chicken or the egg?" no issue on the planet is more perplexing than the question of why God intervenes in the world at some times but not others. After all, if he is all powerful, he controls everything. And if he is all-knowing, then he knows everything — including what your prayers will be before you speak them! Given this power and knowledge monopoly, the prayers of mere mortals almost seem like a waste of breath.

The obvious question then is, why bother praying? The answer to this is simple but also profoundly complex: For reasons you and I will never fully comprehend, the Lord *wants* you to pray to him, and by and large, he releases his power in the world and in your life through prayer. Don't make the mistake, however, of thinking that the power is in the prayer itself. The prayers are only messages to the one who holds the power. God's the one who chooses how to act upon them.

Given this, what transforms a simple prayer into an X-factor that can save a nation, free a prisoner, feed thousands of orphans, and pay for a new car? After all, Elijah and the Baal prophets both prayed sincerely, but only Elijah's prayer was effective. Therefore, what was so special about the prayers of Elijah, Esther, George Müller, and the others whom I discuss earlier in this chapter?

One response may be that these groups of people were God's favorites, ones whom he actually listened to. But, if you take the Bible at its word, then this is certainly not true. Scripture makes it abundantly clear that God treats everyone equally. Given that reality, then the way in which they prayed must have proved to be the difference.

Notice that I didn't say X-factor means praying in a certain way, praying the rosary (see Chapter 11), praying in tongues (see Chapter 21), or praying on your knees (see Chapter 6). These are simply techniques people use. God looks past all that and into the heart of the prayer.

Indeed, I see five attitudes that I call the "Five Be's" (which I discuss further in Chapter 18) that you need for an effective prayer life:

- ✔ **Be aware.** The first and foremost quality of effective prayers is a keen awareness of whom you're praying to. Trying to pray without acknowledging God is similar to trying to hold an intelligent conversation with someone who doesn't know who you are or even care to get to know you.

- ✔ **Be real.** Prayer becomes an X-factor when you're earnest. When you pray, God wants nothing more than for you to be genuine. *Real* refers not only to the words you use (not Shakespearean English) but also to what you're praying about. (See Chapters 4 and 15 for more discussion on being real in your prayers.)

  We must lay before Him what is in us, not what ought to be in us.

  C.S. Lewis

- ✔ **Be repentant.** Sin in your life can be a serious obstacle to your prayers, so you should always approach prayer with a spirit of repentance or willingness to seek forgiveness and abandon sin in the future. (See Chapter 3 for more discussion on sin and repentance.)

- ✔ **Be dogged.** Prayer becomes an X-factor when you're diligent. On occasion, God answers your prayer on the first and only request, such as Elijah's prayer to light the altar. However, more often than not, his timing is longer term than yours and mine, and he wants us to be patient and wait on his timing. Hudson Taylor's paycheck trial (see the section "The absent-minded doctor," earlier in this chapter) serves as a great example of the need to be tenacious in your prayer life. God answered him, but only after Taylor spent a lot of time in fervent prayer.

The insistent prayer of a righteous person is powerfully effective.

James 5:16

✔ **Be expectant.** Prayer becomes an X-factor when you trust God to answer it. George Müller (see the section "Putting your faith where your mouth is," earlier in this chapter) is a great example of a person who had faith that anticipated God to answer. He had so much confidence in the Lord that he considered his prayer requests as good as answered after he uttered them.

The people of great faith whose stories I tell earlier in this chapter all knew to whom they were praying and were diligent, earnest, and trustful in their prayers. When you combine these factors, you have the X-factor. Therefore, the lynchpin in transforming the ABC's of prayer into the X-factor is not God at all, but you and me. God is always ready and willing to intervene. It's up to you and me to come alongside God and allow him to do his work.

Chapter 2

Prayers: We Don't Need No Stinkin' Prayers

• •

• •

My parents love to tell the story of the time when I was a bright-eyed, spunky 8-year-old who, after reading the Dr. Seuss classic, *Green Eggs and Ham,* tried to order this special meal in a restaurant: "I'd like green eggs and ham, please." But after being sternly rebuffed by an overworked wait-ress, I had to settle for eggs and bacon instead. No, I've not tried to order them since, although I occasionally try to prod my own kids into doing the same thing.

Green Eggs and Ham tells the story of Sam-I-Am, a persistent, weird-looking creature who tries to get his friend to eat green eggs and ham, hounding him wherever he goes. Convinced that he won't like the dish, his friend refuses a whopping 70 times until he finally agrees to try them if Sam-I-Am will stop bugging him. But when the friend finally tastes the first bite, he discovers that he loves them after all.

Prayer is something like green eggs and ham. Misconceptions abound about what it really is, and they can be hard to shake. Mistaken beliefs influence not only people who avoid prayer but also those who pray religiously. Therefore, before you go further into finding out how to improve your prayer life, allow me to first clear up any misconceptions about what prayer is *not*. Read this chapter closely; I don't want to be forced to chase you to pray in a boat or with a goat or in the rain or on a train.

Debunking the Top Excuses

If you avoid prayer, you probably have a single reason or a combination of reasons for not praying. Perhaps you dismiss the concept of prayer altogether, or maybe you believe that something about you prevents prayer from working for you personally. Overall, I've found six major reasons people give for not praying:

- ✔ Prayer is a crutch.
- ✔ Prayer is only for good people.
- ✔ Prayer is too good to be true.
- ✔ Prayer is just a self-help technique.
- ✔ God is a "big-picture guy."
- ✔ I'd like to, but I can't speak in King James.

Prayer is a crutch

A common excuse for not praying is that prayer is simply a crutch for those who are weak, needy, or faint of heart. The thinking is that those who are strong and able pick themselves up by their own bootstraps and persevere through hard times. This attitude isn't surprising in societies (such as the United States) that glorify the concept of rugged individualism.

Even those who believe in prayer can fall into this trap. When circumstances are going good, I sometimes find myself starting to think and act as a self-reliant, independent creature who doesn't need anyone or anything. I don't consciously accept this, but my actions sure speak that way. Yet as most everyone discovers, this attitude can last for a while, but not forever. Sooner or later, all people need help beyond themselves.

Rock climbing offers a good illustration of this fact. There are two ways of rock climbing on steep cliffs: using equipment (such as ropes, harnesses, and spikes) or going freehand.

Expert freehand climbers may scoff at the idea of using equipment, relegating its use to the inexperienced or faint of heart. They take pride in never getting into a position in which they need the safety net of ropes. But freehand climbers with such an attitude forget one thing: Although many rock formations allow a climber with know-how to climb using no equipment, some sheer, smooth cliffs are utterly impossible to climb freehand. Climbing equipment, therefore, serves a dual purpose. It does provide a safety plan in case you slip during a climb. But, just as important, this equipment also provides the tools needed to travel upward on those otherwise impossible vertical ascents.

In the same way, prayer provides a safety net through hard times when you slip and fall as the Lord picks you up. But prayer also supplies the tools to equip you to "climb higher" when you put your life into the hands of God through prayer.

A freehand climber can be pleased with his self-sufficiency, but any gloating by this climber must be done at the bottom of the toughest cliffs, not at their top. In the same way, rugged individualists ironically limit themselves rather than free themselves when they stubbornly go it alone. Like the equipped climber, the praying person is able to reach the "impossible peaks," in this case by asking for God's help.

> *It is vain, O men, that you seek within yourselves the cure for your miseries. All your insight only leads you to the knowledge that it is not in yourselves that you will discover the true and the good.*

Blaise Pascal

Prayer is only for good people

Some people would like to pray but don't think they're good enough to do so; they think that they have too many skeletons in their closet. Or, in the words of Dana Carvey's Garth, "I'm not worthy! I'm not worthy!" On first take, this attitude is totally understandable because you and I both have done plenty of things that have gone against what we know is right.

Natural though this attitude may be, however, Jesus makes it clear that it is a faulty one, because he died for the sins of every saint and scoundrel, not for a select few good people. For example, Luke 23 says that when Jesus was dying on the cross, a thief who was being crucified beside him defended Jesus from the curses of the other crucified thief. He then proclaimed Jesus as Messiah and asked Jesus to remember him in heaven. The response Jesus gave to that thief should give encouragement to you and me, no matter the plight faced: "Today, you will be with me in paradise."

Jesus didn't utter this to a holy man; he said it to a convicted habitual felon. If a thief who was plain evil 99.9 percent of his life can still be redeemed in his last .1 percent of life, when death was but moments away, then I suggest there's hope for you and me.

Prayer can't be only for good people, because no one can be called "good" by God's standard. On many occasions in the gospels, Jesus says that he came into the world for people who need him, not for those who didn't need any help. When Jesus said this, he must have had a sense of humor because, of course, there aren't any people who don't need his help. The Bible says that everyone has sinned, so if God applied his standard that only the perfect could pray, then no one would be able to, not even Billy Graham or Mother Teresa.

It's too good to be true

A third excuse for not praying is that prayer sounds great but is too good to be true. God's got the universe to take care of. He doesn't have time to be concerned about my itty-bitty life. Answered prayers, then, are mere coincidences, events that would have happened anyway, even without prayer. The God of the Bible makes it abundantly clear that he does answer prayer, however. So if you believe in him, then prayer is a freebie. (See Chapter 3 and Chapter 17 for more on how God answers your prayers.)

The deeper issue for this excuse is more of a belief issue rather than a prayer issue. I'm not sure whether anyone can ever fully prove that an answered prayer wasn't luck or a twist of fate, but when you see enough so-called coincidences in your prayer life, you begin to realize that God engineers those happenstances.

Prayer is just a self-help technique

A fourth reason that some people don't pray is that they relegate prayer to being yet another self-help method. According to this view, prayer is a technique that allows you to channel your physical and spiritual energies to achieve inner peace and tranquility. Many try to explain the effectiveness of prayer that heals people physically as self-help (see Chapter 1), saying that such prayers elicit a "mind over body" response in the patient that enables the prayers to come true.

Self-help may be the definition of prayer for some other world views, but not Christian prayer. In fact, Christian prayer is a "God-help" technique. Christianity maintains that God is in control of everything, and prayer is asking God to use his overwhelming power to alter your circumstances.

Let there be curtains

My pastor, Eric Hartlen, tells the story of a time early in his married life when he and his wife, Joan, were strapped financially. Unable to afford new drapes for their house, Joan prayed privately that God would provide them. Meanwhile, at work, Eric went to the home of a man he knew who was moving out of his apartment and into a boarding house to receive more personal care. While there, the man was packing boxes and asked Eric if he would like some new, unopened drapes that he was getting rid of.

Eric went ahead and took them, but he had no idea of his wife's prayer request. As he arrived

home, Eric brought in the drapes and asked Joan whether she had any use for them. Joan was floored: what a perfect answer to her prayer —the sizes were exactly what she needed, and the colors were precisely what she would have chosen had she selected them herself! This simple but powerful story illustrates that God is concerned not only about major life-and-death issues of your life but also about something as small as curtains in your house.

God is a big-picture guy

Have you ever met a chief executive officer, governor, or similar executive of a company or political body? Nearly all these corporate or political leaders are what may be called "big-picture guys." In other words, they focus on the strategic directions of a company or state and let their staffs deal with the implementation details of a decision. This leadership mind-set looks at reality from a 10,000-foot level and doesn't deal with the ground-level details.

Many people look at God similarly, as CEO of the Universe, and use this perception as an excuse not to pray. The thinking is that, because God has 5 billion people to deal with, a universe to run, and an age-old battle with Satan and his underlings to press, he's simply got too much on his plate to be concerned with the minute details of each person's life. After all, when was the last time the head of a company, state, or nation made a house call to your home to ask how things were going? My guess is that's it been quite a while (unless a TV camera is nearby, and then all bets are off).

But God doesn't fit into any kind of human personality type. He's able to deal not only with the big picture but also with the minutiae of your life and my life as well. In Matthew 6:26, Jesus says that God himself is concerned with such details as feeding the birds, not forming a committee of angels to do it for him. Then, in John 14:14, Jesus says, "If you will ask anything in my name, I will do it." Notice he said "anything," not "big, important things." (See Chapter 17 for more on this topic.)

But I can't speak King James

Growing up, I had a cool walkie-talkie set that had a Morse code beeper on each device and a chart on its back that gave the codes for each letter of the alphabet. Determined to speak from that day forth in just Morse code, my best friend and I each took a walkie-talkie and set out a distance a football field apart to learn our new lingua franca.

Our enthusiasm for this new code language lasted all of five minutes, because I kept mistaking my friend's letters. As I translated his message, I was in a panic when I thought that a wild tiger was attacking him, when instead he reported that he had to go home and feed his cat. In the end, we gave up and just sent S-O-S (three short, three long, three short) messages back and forth because that was the only message we could figure out how to communicate.

Many people look at prayer as something akin to speaking in Morse code. The idea is that, before you can communicate with God, you have to learn an arcane language first. And so people often stumble along in "Godspeak," speaking in Shakespearean English rather than from the heart. (See Chapters 5 and 6 for more on this subject.)

Unfortunately, many in the clergy help promote "Godspeak" each Sunday, as they move from normal speech in their sermon into Shakespearean English the moment they begin to pray.

Now, I'm not sure what God's native language is, but it surely isn't Morse code or Shakespearean English. God doesn't want you to talk to him in some artificial language. If your name isn't Hamlet, don't use words like "thou" and "thee." Instead, the Lord wants straight talk and doesn't care whether you talk with a drawl, jive, or Cockney accent. Simply be real in prayer.

Correcting Eight Really Bad Ideas about Prayer

The people who avoid prayer aren't the only ones with misconceptions of what prayer is *not*. Many people who pray also have skewed ideas on what prayer is. The problem is that some of these ideas, such as those in the following list, aren't only wrong but can also derail your prayer life altogether.

- No patience is required.
- Prayer comes naturally.
- Prayer is like a wish list for Santa.
- Prayer is a one-way conversation.
- Prayer is a silver bullet.
- Prayer is like lobbying in front of Congress.
- My way is the right way to pray.
- I'll live my life the way I want to (also known as the Frank Sinatra syndrome).

No patience required

Modern civilization has so abandoned the virtue of patience that it risks being placed on the endangered virtues list. Call this devaluation of patience an unintended side effect of the "instant society." Who can have patience when you're used to instant photos, instant coffee, and instant divorces; overnight and same-day shipping; and downloadable music on demand via the Internet?

The drive to speed up the delivery of goods and services isn't inherently bad, as society can use it for humanitarian as well as monetary purposes. However, this progressive force, whether motivated by good or ill, incessantly speeds up the pace of life. Life today moves at an exponentially faster rate than in centuries past.

So when you enter prayer with an instant-society mind-set, there's just one catch: God's timetable is the same today as it has been since the beginning of time. He doesn't bend to innovative new delivery models or preprocessed foods. The Lord will answer prayer in the time he knows to be best, even though delays irritate you and me to no end.

Compared to people who lived in earlier times in history, when the pace of life was slower, you and I are at a spiritual disadvantage. All the world is telling you to speed up, while God is asking you to slow down and wait on him. The Scriptures say, "Be still and know that I am God," not "Sprint and catch me." Therefore, when you pray, focus on God and his timing, not your timetable or the timetable of the world around you.

Prayer comes naturally

The second bad idea on prayer is that prayer is easy, something that comes naturally. So, this line of thinking goes, when you pray, just do what comes to mind. I quite agree that prayer is natural in times of distress and agony and when you have no one to turn to for help (as I explain in Chapter 22).

Yet the Apostle Paul instructs Christians in his first letter to the Thessalonians to pray 24/7 (as I talk about in Chapter 4). This day-in, day-out prayer is anything but natural, at least for me, and I suspect that I'm not alone in this struggle. In fact, prayer is hard work, a discipline that takes energy and focus to be effective.

I think of prayer as being similar to running or singing. At first, both of these practices seem perfectly natural. What can be more second nature than running across the yard or singing a tune you heard on the radio? These activities may indeed be quite natural for the easy jogs or radio tunes, but consider running a marathon or singing an opera. When you get serious about either task, you start to realize how complex these disciplines become, requiring years to master in order to be truly proficient. You need training, instruction, and discipline to be effective in singing and running, as well as in prayer.

Prayer is like a wish list for Santa

An easy trap to fall into is to begin to look at God as the Great Santa Claus In The Sky. You know the words to the song: "He's making a list and checking it twice, gonna find out who's naughty and nice." You start approaching God like the Santa in your local shopping mall, coming to him with your wish list.

Petition, or asking God to answer your prayers, is a perfectly legitimate part of prayer, but that's only a part of what prayer should be. God does love you, but don't mistake him for Santa Claus. Jesus says, "Ask and you shall receive," but that doesn't mean that you can ask for a Porsche, as some people mistakenly believe. Petition is a component of prayer, but just one component. Prayer has other equally important parts. See Chapter 6 for a discussion on the ingredients of a complete prayer.

Prayer is a one-way conversation

Do you know any "talkers"? You know the kind — the friend who absolutely loves to hear himself talk and hardly lets you get a word in edgewise. I've known or worked with my share of talkers over the years, and as much as I still like them as people, I'm quite frustrated at times by those one-sided conversations.

God must look on prayer the same way. Although he's not going to talk to you verbally, when you're properly focused on God, he does speak to you in other ways, as you find out in Chapter 19. Schedule your prayer so that you have the quiet and solitude you need to receive this guidance and instruction.

Prayer is a silver bullet

Prayer is not the silver bullet you take out of your gun belt when all else is lost. It's not a panacea or a cure-all. One of the most natural things that human beings do is to rely on themselves until all goes bad and then pull out prayer as a solution to getting out of a tight spot. As you discover in Chapter 4, you and I should be praying 24/7, making it constantly the *current* thing to do rather than saving prayer as the *last resort*.

Prayer is like lobbying Congress

Some people have the tendency to view prayer as the spiritual equivalent to lobbying Congress. When they're convinced of the rightness, validity, and justification of a specific prayer request, they go about formulating a strategy for getting their bill (prayer) passed into law. God's answering of prayer then becomes something like a legislative process, as people lobby him for the answer they want.

This approach, however, is not prayer. God isn't going to be swayed by any lobbying efforts. In addition, prayer is meant to change you, not just to change God's mind. But if you approach God like a lobbyist does, you won't be open to change.

My way is the right way

One of the most frequent temptations in the Christian church is believing that the manner in which *you* worship and pray is the only right way. However, within the framework of historical Christianity, the different religions pray in vastly different ways: Catholics pray the rosary and say the Hail Mary, Pentecostals regularly pray by speaking in tongues, Orthodox believers focus on ceremonial prayer, and evangelicals focus on the simplicity of free-form prayer as part of their tradition. (See Chapters 7, 11, and 21 for more information on different prayer traditions.)

However, as I say in Chapter 1, the Bible gives no rules about prayer, other than your attitude. Therefore, each religion's traditions are the right ways to pray if the praying is done in humility, earnestness, and diligence.

 Major on the majors, and minor on the minors. In other words, a Christian needs to stand firm on a half dozen core issues (see Chapter 3), but prayer styles and techniques or traditions are not among them. God is open to flexibility, and his people should be, too.

The selfish syndrome

One of Frank Sinatra's most memorable songs was *My Way*. Many people today have that same attitude concerning their prayer lives. They live their life the way they want, without regard for the need to obey God's will, and then expect God to bless their life. They then are perplexed why their prayers aren't answered in the manner they expect.

 But, as you may recall if you read Chapter 1, what makes prayer effective is an earnest, humble spirit. So when you approach God in humility, you have to submit to his will. Therefore, if you're going to have an effective prayer life, you need to change your tune to "I did it his way."

> *Heaven is too busy to listen to half-hearted prayers or to respond to pop-calls.*
>
> E. M. Bounds

Chapter 3

Relating to God: More than the Sum of All Prayers

● ●

In This Chapter

▶ Repenting of your sin before you pray

▶ Understanding how your view of God dictates the quality of your prayer life

▶ Deciding to whom you should pray

▶ Calling God your "daddy"

▶ Taking a behind-the-scenes look at prayer after it leaves your lips

● ●

Christian prayer may sound like a noun, but it's really an action verb. Prayer is something you *do*, not a thing you make the object of your attention. When the Bible mentions prayer, it almost always refers to the act of prayer and isn't much interested in dwelling on prayer as an art form or spiritual discipline to get a black belt in. Yet, prayer itself is often treated by people as the primary subject, the life of the party, an end in itself, rather than for what it really is: simply the means by which you can talk with God.

Prayer is a natural outflow of your relationship with God, much like the communication that exists between a married couple is an extension of their marital bond. A healthy marriage has growing, lively interaction, whereas a stale marriage has an ever decreasing amount of contact between the two spouses.

In this chapter, you discover how your prayer life is fundamentally impacted by the relationship you have with the Lord. You explore how issues that surface in any friend or family relationship also come up when you're dealing with your father in heaven:

✔ What gets in the way of effective communication?

✔ Does God ever stop listening?

> ✔ How does your perception of God impact the way you relate to him in prayer?
>
> ✔ How do you address God in prayer?
>
> ✔ Does God treat my prayers seriously?

The key to an effective prayer life is a healthy bond between God and yourself. The quality of your relationship, not the quantity of your prayers, is what counts. Looked at in this light, the sum of all prayers matters only so much as the intimacy of your relationship with him.

Naming the Elephant in the Room: Sin

Whenever you consider the relationship between God and humans, there's one issue that no one much likes to discuss: that nasty stuff called sin. It's a topic that people avoid and ignore, and sometimes they deny its very existence, even in a fair share of Christian churches. But you can see the evidence of sin simply by taking a drive in rush hour traffic or spending an evening with your 8-year-old terror of a nephew. You don't have to go far to see that sin is often the elephant in the room, the thing that people can see so clearly but tend to walk and talk around instead of acknowledging.

> *For all have sinned, and fall short of the glory of God.*
>
> Romans 3:23

From a Christian perspective, *sin* is any deliberate action, attitude, motivation, or thought that goes against God, whether it be done by one person or a group of people. Sin is often an obvious act, such as murder, stealing, or adultery, but it's just as often a subtle, perhaps imperceptible, transgression, such as pride, envy, and even worry. Sin involves *trespassing,* or going beyond a boundary set by God. But sin can also occur when you "miss the mark," falling short of what God expects due to fear, laziness, or some other reason.

> *Take this rule: whatever weakens your reason, impairs the tenderness of your conscience, obscures your sense of God, or takes off the relish of spiritual things; in short, whatever increases the strength and authority of your body over your mind, that thing is sin to you, however innocent it may be in itself.*
>
> Susanna Wesley, mother of John Wesley

Ignore sin? Not on your ice

Sometimes people wonder why God doesn't just overlook sin by looking the other way. The simple but definitive answer is that doing so is impossible for him, because sin is against his perfect, holy nature. Therefore, by the very act of ignoring it, he'd cease to be who he is. In the same way, an ice cube can't simply overlook a pot of boiling water. For if the cube ignores reality and jumps into the steaming fluid, it ceases to be an ice cube anymore.

Managing sin

A once-popular belief that still has advocates today is the idea that humans are basically good, not sinful. However, the tendency of people to rebel against their Creator is one of the central messages of the Bible, both in the Old and New Testaments. I don't need to rely on the Bible alone as proof or point to extreme examples like Hitler, Stalin, or Idi Amin. Instead, I can stay closer to home (actually, my office) and make the same point.

Anyone who doesn't believe in the reality of sin has surely never been a manager. In a former job, I managed an organization of 70 employees. My group was composed of highly talented, friendly, and energetic people with whom I enjoyed working. But in spite of their good qualities, I still had to deal with endless headaches: incessant bickering and squabbling among individuals, the pride and self-aggrandizement produced by competing job offers, the sometimes questionable ethical decisions from above, and my own sinful tendencies.

I came away from that experience realizing how sin creeps into every aspect of people's lives, although they typically don't see it as sin at all. Ironically, my primary role in the company was not managing people, but managing sin, trying to minimize sin's harmful effects within the division I was responsible for.

Sin may be an unpleasant topic to dwell on, but a recognition of sin is essential when you think about Christian prayer. After all, Christianity (and, it follows, Christian prayer) doesn't really make sense until you understand this elephant in the room and how God responded to it before everyone in the room was stomped on. (See the sidebar "Buzzword-free Christianity," later in this chapter.)

Christ without cleansing

The people of Jesus' day were in eager expectation of a Messiah, but many expected a political leader, like King David of old, to rise up and defeat the Roman occupiers. They weren't expecting a sacrificial savior. Therefore, when it became clear that Jesus had no interest in a political or military victory, many turned on him, ultimately sending him to his execution.

Sadly, some people today make the same mistake by focusing exclusively on the promises of Jesus Christ ("peace on earth") while overlooking the very reason for his coming in the first place ("the elephant in the room"). Beware of wanting a "Christ without cleansing," seeking a savior while ignoring his forgiveness of sins. However, as shown through his life and teaching, Jesus made it very clear that he came to be the savior on *his* terms: cleansing first and promises after that.

Does God wear earplugs?

In your prayer life, sin can end up becoming an elephant-sized barrier that can block effective communication with God. In fact, if you have sins that you cling to and don't want to give up, then this sin actually puts up a brick wall between God and you that prevents him from hearing your prayers. Not a fun prospect to consider, but two sobering verses back that idea up:

> *If I cherished sin in my heart, The Lord wouldn't have listened.*

Psalm 66:18

> *But your iniquities have separated between you and your God, and your sins have hidden his face from you, so that he will not hear.*

Isaiah 59:2

On first take, this reality may sound harsh, but this response is a fundamental part of any relationship, whether on earth or in heaven. Suppose that a wife has an affair and brazenly brings her lover home. With the man hanging all over her neck, she can't possibly carry on a normal conversation with her husband, expecting him to ignore the man she brought through the door. The husband may still deeply love her and want the marriage to survive, but the wife has baggage she has to shed first before he can talk to her. Moreover, the block isn't just on his side — she needs to get rid of the other guy before she's in a position to productively communicate with her husband.

No one would blame someone with a cheating spouse for backing off on communicating with the partner until the guilty party sorted things out. In the same way, you and I should never blame God for not listening to prayers of people who have sin draped around their necks. They're the ones supplying the earplugs to God, preventing their prayers from being heard.

Removing the earplugs

Perhaps no prospects are scarier in life than the idea that God might refuse to hear your prayers. Fortunately, God provides a way out of this mess. According to 1 John 1:9:

> *If we confess our sins, he is faithful and righteous to forgive us the sins, and to cleanse us from all unrighteousness.*

This passage gets to the heart of what Christianity is all about: Because Jesus Christ took on the punishment for all the sins of the world by dying on the cross, you can confess your sins to God, and he'll consider them road kill, dead and forgotten, and wipe the slate clean. He'll then take off those earplugs and look forward to a deeper relationship with you.

Although God isn't one to be trifled with, he is extremely patient, so don't lose heart if you find yourself struggling with a particular sin. Because of Jesus Christ's covering for sin, God doesn't require Christians to be perfect in order to pray. Rather, God refuses to listen only if your life is characterized by chronic, unremorseful, and unrepentant sin. (However, keep in mind that God always hears any prayer crying out for repentance.)

Sin does become a barrier to your prayer life *unless* you explicitly do something about it. However, if you have confessed your sins yet remain worried that God isn't hearing your prayers, take heart. Such concern is a good indication that you're indeed remorseful and repentant about sin in your life.

Buzzword-free Christianity

Christians love buzzwords. When it comes to explaining what Christianity is to people who aren't quite sure what it is, Christians can easily fall into the trap of explaining the Christian faith by using words such as "gospel," "salvation," "born again," and "saved." However, this lingo can be confusing if you aren't sure what it means. Therefore, if you need a refresher on the basics of Christianity, here's one that is guaranteed to be 100 percent buzzword free.

(Obviously, in trying to summarize the Christian faith in this manner, I leave out a lot of the nuances and honest differences of opinion that people inside the church have on its various particulars. Nonetheless, many Christians today accept the perspective expressed here.)

God's bold decision

A long time ago, in a land far away, God was alone and yearned for children to love and be with, perhaps in the same way that people today desire kids at some point in their lives. So he decided to create the world and populate it with living creatures. But before he created children, he had a big decision to make: Do I make robots who will follow me dutifully? Or do I create humans who will have the freedom to choose whether they want to obey me or not?

(continued)

(continued)

A robot world would have been perfectly controlled — no problems or pain — but it also would have been sterile, monotone, and without any true love. This scenario wasn't something God wanted to be a party to, so he decided on human freedom. Because of this self-determination, a human world is now the best of all possible worlds or the worst of all, depending solely on the combined decisions that people make over the millennia.

A cancer festers

God gave humans a great start and a perfect world, but people quickly chose to disobey the Lord, thinking that they knew better. Little did they know that this fateful decision set the wheels in motion to slowly turn their perfect world into an ever-deteriorating one. A cancerous gene known as sin was introduced and passed down to the rest of the human race.

As the population grew, this cancer of sin festered inside each person and the human race as a whole, putting God's perfect love, holiness, and justice at odds: God loved humans intensely, but their sin prevented him from accepting them as his children because of the uncompromising nature of his holiness. What's more, his justice demanded that a penalty be paid for each person's sin.

A line in the sand

A line in the sand was then formed. On one side, God couldn't accept any humans as his children anymore due to their impurity; on the other side, humans wallowed in their sin, occasionally remorseful but often thriving in it. As the Old Testament spells out in great detail, a group of folks known as the Israelites were given the opportunity to bridge the gap on a day-to-day basis by following rules and making sacrifices, but the solution was temporary and the cancer was just too strong. Ultimately, humans proved incapable of conquering sin on their own.

The miracle cure

Because God equipped people with souls that live forever, either with him or not, he had a decision to make: Do I send all sin-infested creatures away to hell forever? Or do I develop a "miracle cure" for their cancer, so that those people who really want to be "cancer survivors" can do so with my help?

Because of his enduring love for his children, he chose the second option, sending himself to earth in the form of Jesus Christ to live a sin-free, perfect life. As a substitute for the "terminally ill," Jesus voluntarily took on all the cancer of sin himself, receiving all its damaging effects and sparing the rest of the human race. The cancer killed him, but only for a short time. Miraculously, God brought Jesus back from the dead after three days, and in so doing, he conquered the deadly consequences of sin once and for all.

Humanity's bold decision

The heart of Christianity boils down to a decision: Either you believe that God gave people this gift of grace as the only true cure for the cancer of sin inside you or you don't. If you don't, then God is unable to treat you and leaves you to look elsewhere for a magic potion you'll never find. But if you earnestly do believe, then God can make you "cancer free" permanently.

Ultimately, in spite of the centuries-old detour brought on by the cancer of sin, God's solution, Jesus Christ, reunites his children with his perfect love, holiness, and justice. Because some of the self-determining humans choose to follow him, God will eventually be able to bring about that elusive best of all worlds after all. And then God will finally be able to enjoy his true children for eternity.

Viewing God: Taskmaster or Loving Father?

How do you view God? Do you see him as a stern taskmaster waiting to pounce on lowly humans the moment you make a mistake? Or do you see him as a devoted father who loves you?

Your perception of who God is and how he views you makes a significant impact on your prayer life. This perception dictates what you pray about and your attitude toward prayer itself. Your lips may be saying one thing, but your heart is uttering something else. For example, consider the prayers in Table 3-1 and how these prayers might be translated based on your perception of God.

Table 3-1	How Perceptions of God Impact Your Prayers	
Prayer	*View God as Loving Father*	*View God as Taskmaster*
"Forgive me."	"I'm so sorry I hurt you. Please forgive me."	"I know, I'm a jerk. Please somehow overlook that misdeed, although I know I won't be able forgive myself for what I have done."
"Thanks, God."	"Wow, what an example of your love! Thanks!"	"Thanks for the handout. I'll take anything I can."
"Lord, heal me."	"I'm hurting, Father. Please heal me and take this pain away."	"I beg your pardon, sir. I know I don't deserve it, but could you please heal me just this one time?"

Daddy dearest

Studies show that your perception of God usually mirrors the way you look at your earthly father. If you have a kind, affectionate dad, you're able to think of God in a like manner. But if you have a grumbling, overly strict father, you tend to think of God behaving in the same unforgiving way toward you.

What's different about Christianity?

Religion is often the attempt by people to attain approval by God by earning their way; they strive to become better persons, not do bad things, and help their neighbor. But Christianity claims that people can't earn their rescue by themselves and instead need God to do the hard work for them.

The parable of the prodigal son that Jesus told in Luke 15 gives a strong insight into how the father views his wayward son. In this most famous of parables, Jesus tells of a punky son who demands his inheritance before his father is dead and of an amazing father who actually grants the insulting request.

A loose description of what happens next is that after the son collects his money, he leaves home and goes off to a distant land, gambling away money by playing blackjack, making bad investments on the DSE (Damascus Stock Exchange), and squandering the rest of his cash by buying lousy products from those late-night infomercials. In the end, he finds himself bankrupt and starving, so, as a last resort, he decides to return home with his tail between his legs.

In the Middle Eastern culture of the day, his father would have been relentlessly harsh in his treatment of his returning son. He wouldn't even have permitted the son back into his house until he was severely punished. And for years after, the son would be expected to work off his debt like a slave and would never be fully accepted again within the household as a son. But the father in the story responds exactly the opposite of what would be expected, in a manner unheard of in the culture of Jesus' time.

Luke 15:20 says:

> *While the younger son was still far off, his father saw him, and was moved with compassion, and ran, and fell on his neck, and kissed him.*

The father's response includes three stunning aspects:

- ✔ **The father makes the first move.** Instead of letting the son sleep outside his gate for a couple days and then grudgingly letting him back inside, the father makes the first move by going to the son.

- ✔ **The father takes on the humiliation that was due his son.** The father sprints to the son. Because people of all ages jog and exercise today, you could easily gloss over this detail, but during Jesus' day, that was an important element in the story. The father running in such a public manner would have been humiliating, because no older person ever ran, regardless of the situation. But instead of allowing the son to be publicly humiliated, which would be the expected response in those days (oh, can't you just see those tabloid headlines?), the father took on that shame for himself.

✔ **The father is passionate about his love for his son.** Even after all this, when the father gets to his child, he again surpasses all expectations of the younger son. He didn't just walk over and shake his son's hand or give him a pat on the back and say that all is well. That would have been surprising enough to the listeners of the parable, but Jesus paints a far more vivid portrait of what the father does, a picture that is unmistakable in the affection expressed. The great 19th century evangelical preacher Charles Spurgeon spoke memorably about this love:

God on the neck of a sinner! What a wonderful picture! Can you conceive it? I do not think you can; but if you cannot imagine it, I hope that you will realize it. When God's arm is about our neck, and His lips are on our cheek, kissing us much, then we understand more than preachers or books can ever tell us of His . . . love.

In the parable, the father realizes the instant he sees his son that he is returning home ready to seek forgiveness. In the same way, God is delighted when people are earnestly sorry for what they've done. Repentance (see the sidebar "Repent! The end is near!" later in this chapter) may be thought of as a harsh demand from God before he begrudgingly forgives someone. But looking at this story, you can see that repentance is, as C.S. Lewis once said, "simply a description of what going back is like." Once again, Spurgeon paints an unforgettable picture of the encounter with the father and son:

Everyone is a prince or a princess

Most people go through times when they get down on themselves, thinking that they amount to nothing. But the New Testament is clear that God loves everyone in the world (John 3:16) and that everyone who truly believes in Jesus Christ is considered a son or daughter of God (Romans 8:17). Therefore, if you're a Christian but feeling like a loser, remember that you're the son or daughter of a king. You're a prince or a princess. British author George MacDonald expresses it well in his classic tale *The Princess and the Goblin*:

"There was once a little princess who . . ."

"But, Mr. Author, why do you always write about princesses?"

"Because every little girl is a princess."

"You will make them vain if you tell them that."

"Not if they understand what I mean."

"Then what do you mean?"

"What do you mean by a princess?"

"The daughter of a king."

"Very well, then every little girl is a princess. . . ."

Repent! The end is near!

"Repent" is a word that is often associated today with a shaggy-bearded man carrying a placard that says "Repent! The end is near!" While that word may conjure images of the lunatic fringe, it actually is a very useful word that properly expresses the attitude you and I should have when approaching God about sin. Repentance is more than just saying, "I'm sorry." It is saying three things: I'm sorry. I'm seeking God's forgiveness. And I want nothing more to do with that sin in the future.

Let me try to describe the scene. The father has kissed the son, and he [asks] him to sit down; then he comes in front of him, and looks at him, and feels so happy that he says, "I must give you another kiss," then he walks away a minute; but he is back again before long, saying to himself, "Oh, I must give him another kiss!" He gives him another, for he is so happy. His heart beats fast; he feels very joyful; the old man would like the music to strike up; he wants to be at the dancing; but meanwhile he satisfies himself by a repeated look at his long-lost child. Oh, I believe that God looks at the sinner, and looks at him again, and keeps on looking at him, all the while delighting in the very sight of him, when he is truly repentant, and comes back to his Father's house.

Seeing the father's love for his really bad but now repentant child in this parable renders words like "ruthless" and "harsh" obsolete when talking about God. According to Jesus, God is passionate about his love for his children. That's the attitude God has when you pray in a repentant spirit, regardless of what you've done in the past.

Talking to God: Dear (fill-in-the-blank)

Tough questions abound when talking about prayer, but how exactly you address your prayers doesn't seem like it would be one of them. After all, isn't "Dear God" sufficient? On one hand, this simple address is indeed perfectly acceptable. On the other hand, the issue can become murkier when you think about how prayer relates to one of the central teachings of Christianity: the belief that there is one God but that he consists of the Father, Son, and Holy Spirit. This concept is known as the *Trinity*. (See the sidebar "Uno, dos, tres," later in this chapter, for more on the Trinity.)

If you're praying to the Christian God, doesn't it then follow that you're in a sense praying to all three? If so, does it matter whom you address your prayers to? Or can you interchangeably pray to God, Father, Jesus, and even the Holy Spirit?

When you look to the Bible for answers, by far the clearest example is to pray to God the Father. For starters, in the Lord's Prayer that Jesus gives as a blueprint for prayer, he begins with "Our Father." The Scriptures include many other examples of praying *to* the Father, but *in* Jesus' name. (See Chapter 17 for more information on praying "in the name of Jesus.")

However, many Christians also regularly direct their prayers to Jesus and support their position by pointing to Acts 7:59, a passage that talks about the early church leader Stephen crying out specifically to Jesus in prayer moments before he dies. No one can cite any clear Biblical precedent for praying directly to the Holy Spirit, although some Christians do address their prayers to him as well.

Given that the Bible points to praying to the Father, some argue passionately that praying to Jesus and the Holy Spirit is invalid and should never be done. However, I think that argument treads on becoming overly legalistic, giving the words you utter priority over the state of your heart. If your heart is earnestly seeking God, I don't believe that God the Father is going to feel slighted if you pray to Jesus or the Holy Spirit, even with the weight of Biblical precedent pointing to God the Father.

Moreover, Romans 8:26 talks about how the Holy Spirit can take your skewed, confused, and disjointed prayers and transform them so they make sense to the Father. Even if prayer to Jesus or the Holy Spirit weren't valid, this passage indicates that the Holy Spirit corrects the mistake and redirects the prayer, much like the post office forwards a letter to you when you move across town to a new address.

Because prayers in the Bible are nearly always directed to God the Father, I recommend following this example to avoid any potential confusion you may experience during your prayer life.

Uno, dos, tres

One concept that will fry your brain if you think about it too much is Christianity's belief that God is a Trinity. The basic idea of the Trinity is that God is one, but he has three distinct identities: God the Father, Jesus the Son, and the Holy Spirit. British theologian and author C.S. Lewis used a cube as a way to describe the Trinity: A cube consists of six squares, but the cube itself is distinct from each of these individual squares. Therefore, each member of the Trinity has a unique personality and role, but they're all unified.

I certainly don't understand this mystery completely (I'm waiting to read *Trinity For Dummies*), nor do I think any human can really grasp what it all means. Therefore, don't dwell too much on the mystery of the Trinity or feel that you need to fully understand it. Rather, simply recognize that each "person" of the Trinity has a unique role in prayer, as I discuss later in this chapter.

Praying to Mary and the saints

Undoubtedly, when it comes to prayer, the greatest area of disagreement within the Christian church is whether it is permissible to pray to Mary and the other saints who are now in heaven. Catholics believe that such a practice is permissible, whereas Protestants do not.

Catholics maintain that when they pray to Mary, they're asking her to pray *with* them and *for* them. They don't see her as the actual mediator between man and God (because Jesus is the one and only Mediator). They believe that she is a special intercessor, maintaining a special, unique role with respect to Jesus Christ.

When Catholics pray to a patron saint, they're asking the saint to join with them in prayer for a particular request. Catholics assert that their teachings are rooted in the Bible and that any attempt to throw them out needlessly removes part of the essence of Christianity.

Protestants counter by saying that the Catholic Church's addition of these teachings blurs or waters down the Christian faith. Their main argument is that praying to anyone but God has no Biblical basis. Moreover, believing that these prayers are a distraction, they hold that when you pray to Mary or a patron saint, you're focusing on the middleman rather than going directly to the only one who can actually answer the prayer.

Ultimately, given that this centuries-old argument continues today, Catholics and Protestants must learn to agree to disagree on this issue. Despite this disagreement, however, all Christians, be they Catholic, Protestant, or Orthodox, agree that the *most* important aspect of prayer is the relationship that each individual has with Jesus Christ.

Deciding Between "Heavenly Father" or "Daddy"

If you walk into any church on any given Sunday morning and listen to a spoken prayer, chances are that it starts off in a very formal tone:

> *O most honorable and worthy heavenly Father, creator of the heavens and earth and our blessed redeemer, we tellurians most humbly beseech your presence amid the mitterlschmerz of this peccant and flagitious world that we live in.*

Such a prayer may be theologically accurate and display the kind of reverence that you and I are to show to God. However, it sure doesn't sound like an intimate conversation with your spouse or best friend on a warm summer night!

The New Testament has a much different, more radical take on how to address God in your prayers. Paul suggests that you don't use the same titles you would use to introduce a baccalaureate speaker on graduation day. Instead, Paul tells you to call God not just "father" but, amazingly enough, "daddy." He writes in Romans 8:15–16:

> *You received the Spirit . . . by whom we cry, "Abba! Father!" The Spirit himself testifies with our spirit that we are children of God.*

Paul is saying here that Christians can call out to God, "Abba, Father." No, Paul isn't referring to that 1970s pop band that sang that annoying *Momma Mia* song. Instead, "Abba" is an Aramaic term (Aramaic was the dominant language in 1st century Palestine) that suggests deep affection and intimacy and is a word that a child would use to refer to her father, much like "daddy" or "papa" is used today.

Jesus used this same word in Mark 14:36 when he prayed to his Father the night before he died on the cross:

> *Jesus said, "Abba, Father, all things are possible to you. Please remove this cup from me. However, not what I desire, but what you desire."*

In the same way, Christians are encouraged to call God their "Abba, Father," just like Jesus did. If you grew up in a formal church, the idea of referring to God as "daddy" may sound strange or even irreverent. Yet Jesus and Paul make it very clear in their teachings that that is exactly the kind of intimate relationship God wants with Christians; he doesn't want a distant relationship characterized by formality and four-syllable adjectives.

At the same time, don't let intimacy turn into casualness or even outright disrespect. If you go overboard and forget about the reverence that you should have for God, "Dear Abba, Father" can become "Howdy, Pops." Balance deep reverence with intimacy, just like Jesus demonstrated throughout his time on earth. (See Chapter 15 for details on how to balance intimacy and reverence in public prayer settings.)

After Your Prayer Leaves Your Lips: A Behind-The-Scenes Guide

When I watch a film I really like, I want to know more about how the movie was made: How did the director put the movie together? How were particular actors chosen? For true stories, what are the real people depicted in the film actually like? Until recently, such information was hard to come by if you weren't in the Hollywood crowd, but DVDs today regularly provide these juicy tidbits of information to interested folks like me. Many DVDs contain more than just the movie itself; you can view deleted scenes, watch alternate endings, and listen to director's commentaries, getting a scene-by-scene account of the movie from the filmmaker's perspective.

Like films, prayers too can seem like a mystery. You're left guessing about what happens behind the scenes after you pray. Fortunately, the Bible provides something similar to a director's commentary that helps explain what God does with your prayers after you pray them.

In a broad sense, a prayer is a conversation with a friend: God hears it and responds, and you respond back. You can think of prayer at that level and be perfectly satisfied and accurate. At the same time, the Bible gives a further insight into what happens behind the scenes. I think God provided these nuggets of information so that you can take comfort in the fact that each prayer is treated as a precious, valuable item; it's not something that God relegates to the bottom of his in box until he gets around to it.

The Bible shows that all three members of the Trinity are involved in your prayers, each with a very distinct role: The Holy Spirit serves as a translator, Jesus Christ is the mediator, and God the Father is the listener. Figure 3-1 depicts how the three members of the Trinity are involved in the prayer process.

Because of the inherent mysteries surrounding prayer and the Trinity, this behind-the-scenes tour is an issue that can seem very confusing and even make your head spin. So use the information on this topic only as much as you find it helpful. Don't ever let the complexities of the Trinity get in the way of thinking of prayer simply as an intimate talk between you and your Father in heaven, because it is just that. At the same time, you may find it encouraging to study the topic further to better understand how much promised assistance you have in your prayers from each member of the Trinity.

Translating your prayers: The Holy Spirit

I'm a lousy linguist. Although I had two years of French in both high school and college, the only sentences I retained from those years of study are "Let's go to the beach" (*On va à la plage*) and "The janitor lives alone" (*La concierge est seule*), neither of which would prove too useful if I decide to tour France.

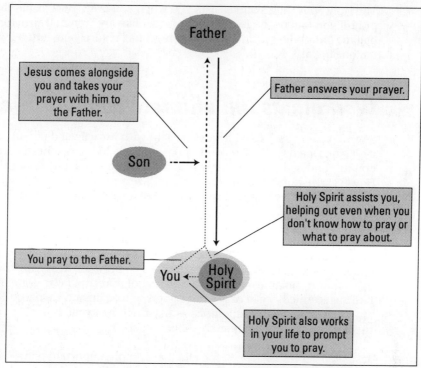

Father

Jesus comes alongside you and takes your prayer with him to the Father.

Father answers your prayer.

Son

Holy Spirit assists you, helping out even when you don't know how to pray or what to pray about.

You pray to the Father.

You

Holy Spirit

Holy Spirit also works in your life to prompt you to pray.

Figure 3-1: Each member of the Trinity is involved in the prayer process.

Given that I am linguistically challenged, my prospects of having a smooth trip throughout the French countryside don't seem too promising. However, if I could convince a native French speaker to come along with me, he could order my meals, bargain with the hotel clerk, and turn my broken tunes into a fluent melody that French people could immediately understand.

The Holy Spirit serves in a similar capacity to that French speaker. When you pray, the Holy Spirit serves as a translator of sorts for your prayers. After all, you may find that when you pray, you sometimes can't find the right words to speak or don't know exactly how to ask for something. Instead of letting you fend for yourself, the Holy Spirit comes to the rescue, as described in Romans 8:26–27:

> *In the same way, the Spirit also helps our weaknesses, for we don't know how to pray as we ought. But the Spirit himself makes intercession for us with groanings which can't be uttered. He who searches the hearts knows what is on the Spirit's mind, because he makes intercession for the saints according to God.*

The Holy Spirit helps and assists you when you pray, even prompting you to pray. If you foul up, he fixes it for you, just like my French translator would bail me out of the communication screw-ups I'd surely get into if I were going it alone in Paris. Merci!

Working as the ultimate mediator: Jesus

Several years ago, I spent a week in Haiti with my wife and parents on a mission trip. One day, we decided to take a trip up to the northern part of the country and had to make our way along the country's lone national highway. However, we quickly found out that, with several military checkpoints on the route, the journey was far less easy and enjoyable than a trip to the local grocery back home.

During one stop in particular, a solider with an automatic machine gun gave us a hard time, refusing to let us through the checkpoint. To the rescue, our guide stepped up and served as a trusted go-between, resolving the situation in a smooth, amiable manner. For the rest of that trip, I was grateful that we had an intermediary in case things got rough again and we needed help in any potentially hostile situations — like the time I yelled "fire" in a crowded theater, but that's a completely different subject.

Jesus too serves as a mediator, albeit a far more important one — between God the Father and every Christian. He played this role in a grand way when he died on the cross to take on the punishment for human sins. But he also plays this go-between role on a day-in, day-out basis as well. Hebrew 7:25 says:

> *Jesus is able to fully save those who approach God through him, since he lives continually to intercede for them.*

If you examine this verse closely, you can see that it's packed with meaning. Jesus not only fully and completely saves people who come to God through him, but he does so in the present tense. In other words, more than just dying on the cross 2,000 years ago, he continues to intercede and look out for your interests. Christians, therefore, have constant, real-time access to God through Jesus. In effect, Jesus prays for you all the time, picking up your prayer requests and communicating them to God the Father.

Listening with love: God the Father

You pray. The Holy Spirit assists you in your prayers. Then Jesus mediates for you. All this activity is pointing towards a single direction — the Father, the final member of the Trinity. As you discover earlier in the chapter, prayers are best directed to the Father, as described by Jesus in the Lord's Prayer in Matthew 6:9:

> *Our father, who is in heaven . . .*

God serves as the loving listener to your prayers and answers them according to his will.

See Chapters 16, 17, and 18 for more details on how God answers your prayers according to his will.

Chapter 4

Taking a 24/7 Prayer Adventure

· ·

In This Chapter

▶ Praying 24/7

▶ Developing the habit of prayer

▶ Discovering the best times to pray in your day

▶ Exploring how to pray on your way to work and in the office

▶ Making prayer a priority

▶ Persevering when prayer becomes a struggle

· ·

The film *Oh Brother, Where Art Thou?* tells the story of three prison escapees on a futile search for treasure in an adventure much like Homer's *Odyssey.* Throughout the tale, a ruthless sheriff bent on capturing them and tying a noose around each of their necks is continually hunting down the trio. Each time the sheriff comes close to finding them, Ulysses Everett McGill, the ringleader of the bunch, exclaims, "We're in a tight spot!" as they scramble to escape their predicament. They relax afterward and continue on their merry way, but they soon find themselves yet again close to being caught. After this cycle repeats itself a few times, you begin to realize that the trio has a knack for getting into these tight spots.

McGill reminds me of the attitude that I've so often had in my life. I live a carefree, content life when circumstances are good, but the moment events begin to look bad, I start crying to God on my knees, "Help, I'm in a tight spot! Get me outta here!" But then, once the pressure is off, I stop praying and go on my merry way.

Although this feast/famine cycle of prayer may be quite natural to fall into, it's not the kind of prayer life that God wants you to have, nor are these types of prayers the ones that you'll find to be life changing. If you want to make prayer an X-factor in your life (see Chapter 1), you'll want to get into the regular practice of prayer and integrate it into all aspects of your life, not just the tight spots. In this chapter, you discover how to do this through 24/7 (24 hours, 7 days a week) prayer.

Praying Around the Clock

I've had the privilege of spending some time around a couple "celebrities," and one common element with both people was that their assistants carefully guarded their time. Trying to schedule time with celebrities is often a long shot at best, even if you have a legitimate reason for the encounter. And, if you're successful at getting on their calendar, then you're allotted a measly amount of time to get done what you need to do.

With this backdrop, just sit back and think about how utterly amazing it is that God, the Creator and Lord of the Universe, offers you and I unlimited access 24/7. You don't have to fight with Michael the Archangel to get on his appointment calendar or go through a gauntlet of secretaries or assistants to set the agenda. He's available anytime, anywhere. That fact is so astounding given the reality of the world you and I live in, it's sad how one so easily glosses over that priveledge.

God wants you to actually use this open access to him, however, and not just be content with having his ear available when you get into a tight spot. Paul writes in 1 Thessalonians 5:17 to "pray without ceasing." No, I didn't say "pray without sneezing" (that is assumed), but rather that Paul is exhorting Christians to offer continual prayers throughout the day.

God doesn't recommend that you sit at home on your knees in your room all day, neglecting your responsibilities. Instead, Paul's instructing you to think of God as being beside you as you carry on the day's business, talking with him in a constant, real-time conversation. Other verses back up this 24/7 idea, including the following:

> *With all prayer and requests, praying at all times in the Spirit, and being watchful to this end in all perseverance and requests for all the saints.* (Ephesians 6:18)
>
> *Continue persistently in prayer, being watchful and thankful.* (Colossians 4:2)
>
> *He also spoke a parable to them that they must always pray, and not give up.* (Luke 18:1)

The 24/7 type of prayer, therefore, consists of dedicated prayer time (as discussed in the section "Knowing When You're at Your Best," later in the chapter) coupled with prayer *sound bites* (quick one- or two-sentence prayers) throughout the day. In many ways, 24/7 prayer is similar to a marriage relationship: Sometimes a couple spontaneously talks about practical matters that come up, while on other occasions, they have extended discussions about a given topic. A healthy marriage has a balance of the two.

The sound-bite prayers can be about anything that comes up during the day:

- ✔ When you see a beautiful sunrise, offer God praise for his creation.

- ✔ When you shake your fist at a driver who cuts you off, confess your sin immediately to God.

✔ When your boss shortens an already unrealistic project deadline, go to God for help before you leave the conference room.

✔ When your assistant tells you he finished up the project early in his spare time, express gratitude to your assistant and then give God immediate thanks for this blessed news.

You get the idea. Prayer sound bites keep you continually aware that God is right next to you, deepening your relationship with him all the while.

Packing Your Own Prayer Saber

Whether you're a *Star Wars* fan or not, odds are that you've seen at least one of the films in the popular sci-fi series. If you have, you probably remember the Jedi knights, the fighters of good over Darth Vader and his minions. In order to combat the Evil Empire, the Jedi knight is never without his futuristic sword, known as a light saber. The light saber is the Jedi weapon of choice, and whenever a Jedi knight loses his light saber in a battle, bad things always seem to happen to him. A Christian should look on prayer in the same way: as the weapon of choice to have in his possession at all times, keeping him out of danger and heartache.

> *Prayer is not a preparation for work, it is work. Prayer is not a preparation for the battle, it is the battle. Prayer is two-fold: definite asking and definite waiting to receive.*

> Oswald Chambers

But you obviously can't just pick up a "prayer saber" with your hand and carry it with you as you carry on your business. Instead, this tool needs to be developed from within you. Prayer needs to become a habit for you, something as common and ordinary as flossing your teeth. Hmmm, on second thought, flossing comes naturally to very few people, so let me change that example to brushing your hair.

This prayer habit should include these two practices:

✔ **Setting up a daily dedicated prayer time:** You need to develop a regular daily prayer schedule that involves more than uttering a few quick words here and there; you need to carve out a chunk of your day that's specifically devoted to prayer. After you get into this habit, prayer becomes much easier and, over time, can almost seem second nature. Being consistent with a dedicated prayer time is the single most important component to achieving 24/7 prayer.

✔ **Putting prayer on the front burner:** You also need to get into the practice of turning to God at the instant a crisis occurs, instead of waiting until the last possible moment. To do that, prayer needs to be at the forefront of your mind, not on the back burner. Front-burner prayer continually strives for a closer relationship with God so that he is then available when crises do occur.

Knowing When You're at Your Best

The first step toward establishing prayer as a habit is to discover the best time for you to have a period of dedicated prayer. Look for a block of time, spanning from a few minutes to perhaps an hour, in which you are free from other distractions and can be quiet and communicate with God. There is no biblically mandated time of day, no Bible passage that says, "Thou shalt start thouest prayers at 7 a.m. CST." God gives you the flexibility to figure out what works best for you. Therefore, consider the three major options and then settle on what works optimally in your situation.

The early bird gets his word in

The morning has always been considered a special time to pray. Jesus certainly did that regularly, such as in Mark 1:35: "Very early in the morning, he rose up and went out, and departed into a deserted place, and prayed there."

> *If you ever prayed in the dawn, you will ask yourself why you were so foolish as to not do it always: it is difficult to get into communion with God in the midst of the hurly-burly of the day.*
>
> Oswald Chambers

Jesus wasn't the only one to get up early in prayer. If you look back through history, all the great Christians seemed to focus their prayer time at the start of the day. In fact, the thought of a God-fearing man rising early before sunrise to pray is the mental picture that comes to my mind when I think of a saint.

Because Jesus and all these model Christians got up in the morning to pray, I wonder whether something is intrinsically important about the morning or whether these people prayed in the early part of the day simply because they were morning people. Oswald Chambers is pretty outspoken on this issue when he says the following:

> *Specific times and places and communion with God go together. It is by no haphazard chance that in every age men have risen early to pray. The first thing that marks decline in spiritual life is our relationship to the early morning.*

Strong words indeed. However, call me crazy, but I also wonder how much technology factors into this equation. After all, through nearly all of human history, people lived their lives by the rising and setting of the sun. After sundown, people's activities were limited: They could read — but only by candlelight, of course — or spend the time talking. Therefore, people tended to follow the motto "early to bed, early to rise." I'm sure that, with few exceptions, there were far more morning people and fewer night owls back then because fewer options were available for nocturnal activities. Electricity changed all that in a big way, eliminating any natural limits (other than fatigue) to what one does at any given hour of the day.

> *He who runs from God in the morning will scarcely find him the rest of the day.*
>
> John Bunyan

Regardless of how much technology levels the playing field, three big advantages to morning prayer remain:

- ✔ **You can avoid the rush.** The early morning is often the quietest time of the day — no phone calls, no TV shows to catch, and no appointments to meet. As a result, this time can be one of quiet reflection, before the rush of the day sets in.

- ✔ **Prayer sets the tone for the rest of the day.** Morning prayer allows you to pray about the coming day, approaching it purposefully rather than letting the day control you. It also gives you a fresh, godly perspective at the start, setting the tone for the entire morning and afternoon, and allows you to recommit yourself daily to serve God in all you do.

- ✔ **You can give God your "first fruits."** The Old Testament talked about the Israelites giving their "first fruits" of the harvest to God as an offering. In the same way, giving the first part of your day to the Lord is a way of expressing God's lordship in your life, giving him the first helping of the day, rather than its leftovers.

However, the reality is that morning prayer can be terribly difficult for two types of people:

- ✔ **Dozers:** For dozers, getting out of bed at 5 a.m. is something akin to getting their teeth drilled at the dentist. Instead of diving into morning prayer, they'd much rather dive under the covers for another hour of sleep. Morning prayer can become a titanic struggle for dozers, due to a sleepy mind and body. Consequently, the morning prayers of dozers become incoherent, or else sleep wins outright.

- ✔ **Doers:** The rush of the day hits doers the moment the alarm clock rings. And the thought of being still at the beginning of the day is like trying to swim against the tide. When doers try to pray in the morning, they can become distracted by the feeling that they have to get busy and start doing something productive. (In Chapter 12, I talk more about how a doer's racing mind can be a major distraction to one's prayer life.)

Your daily bread at noon

A second option is to use your lunch hour for prayer, whether you're at home or at work. Lunchtime can be ideal for some because of the following reasons:

- It's a welcome break in the midst of the rush of the day.
- It's a time that you can use to temporarily escape and be with God.
- It enables you to reflect on the day so far and still pray about what's coming up in the afternoon and evening.

Noontime prayer, however, does have some big potential snags:

- Your prayers can get squeezed out if you don't fiercely guard your time. Last-minute errands, meetings, and phone calls can hinder your noontime plans if you're not careful.
- Midday is a much more difficult time to find a place where you can get isolated from others and have a moment of quiet focus. Both the morning and evening are far better in that regard.

Just resting your eyes, huh?

One place I'd be wary of using as your primary place to pray is your bed, even if you're a night owl. For a while, my wife and I had been using bedtime as a supplemental time to pray together beyond our individual dedicated prayer times earlier in the day. But as much of a night owl as I consider myself to be, I occasionally found myself slipping into a dreamlike state during prayer when all the lights were out, so what came out of my mouth ended up making no sense at all. Too many times, my wife ended up laughing hysterically at the nonsense that I said. To solve this problem, we recently decided to move up our prayer time to earlier in the evening to prevent fatigue from overtaking our prayers.

Not everyone has this problem. In fact, some people who aren't sleepyheads find that praying in bed as they unwind at night and the first thing when they wake works well for them as favorite times to pray. However, if you're like me, when you pray in bed in a horizontal position, you're often just asking for trouble. Falling asleep while praying isn't a huge deal if your prayers then are a supplement to your other prayers. But it is a problem if you're relying on bedtime to be your primary prayer time. British author and scholar C.S. Lewis puts it well: "No one in his senses, if he has any power of ordering his own day, would reserve his chief prayers for bedtime — obviously the worst possible hour for any action which needs concentration. . . . My own plan, when hard pressed, is to seize any time and place, however unsuitable, in preference to the last waking moment."

Wishing God good night

The final option is to find a chunk of time in the evening or night and dedicate it to prayer. Jesus was a morning prayer, but he occasionally spent time at night as well, such as in Luke 6:12:

> *Jesus went out to the mountain to pray, and he continued all night in prayer to God.*

Night prayer has these advantages:

- ✔ The rush of the day is behind you, so you're free to reflect and spend as much time as you'd like without having the demands of the day at hand.

- ✔ Night can be very peaceful, an environment conducive to quality prayer time. What's more, if you're a night owl like me, the nighttime can be a hoot, an ideal time to have creative energy for your communication with God.

Obviously, the biggest potential distractions for evening prayer are the following:

- ✔ **Fatigue:** At the end of a long day, spending quiet moments with the Lord can be a major struggle to staying awake.

- ✔ **Entertainment:** Because so many people tend to watch TV or a video in the evening, finding quiet time alone with God can be hard. (See Chapter 12 for more details on this distraction.)

Plotting your prayers

Which prayer time works best for your schedule? All things being equal, morning prayer is optimal (see the section "The early bird gets his word in," earlier in this chapter) if you can get it to work with your body clock. But if you have a pillow fight each morning and the pillow invariably wins, instead of giving up and feeling defeated, figure out a better time that works for you. God isn't so concerned about the time of the day that you pray; what he wants is your attention and focus.

Don't try to force a time that is unnatural for you, but remember that prayer isn't going to be a breeze for you to do at any time of the day. Prayer takes discipline, so whatever time of the day you choose, appreciate the fact that prayer takes work and effort to do regularly.

Wanna get away?

Psalms 46:10 tells you and me to "be still and know that I am God." Yet, being still in today's world is far easier said than done. Working, taking care of children, attending school, going to your child's soccer games, and exercising are active tasks that can dominate your schedule. When you have time to relax, you're probably more likely to go out for a dinner or movie or watch TV on the sofa, more activities that don't create an environment conducive to sitting quietly and listening to God.

Yet, if you're going to have a successful prayer life, you have to find a place to get away from the hustle and bustle of the world. This location is often called your *prayer closet,* a term that comes from Matthew 6:6: "When you pray, enter into your closet, and having shut your door, pray to your Father who is in secret, and your Father who sees in secret will reward you openly."

The Bible has countless examples of people going off to a quiet place for prayer. On one occasion, Jesus got up early in the morning, left the house in which he was staying, and went off

to a private place to pray (Mark 1:35). On another occasion, he went out on the mountainside to pray at night (Luke 6:12). In fact, Luke 5:16 says that Jesus regularly went off by himself to lonely places to pray. Peter too shows an example of how to be creative in finding a quiet spot; he went out on a roof to pray in Acts 10:9, presumably because he wanted to get someplace in a city where he could be by himself.

You don't actually have to use a real closet for your prayer closet unless you like tight spaces, but the idea is the same: a location that is away from the others in your house and removed from the telephone, TV, and any other outside distractions. Prayer closets can also differ by personality. Some people want total peace and quiet. If you're one of these people, then look for the quietest place you can find. Others have a hard time concentrating in a perfectly silent space and prefer a location with low-level noise that they can tune out. For these people, activities like driving a car, riding a bike, or jogging in the park can serve as their mobile prayer closet.

As you consider a prayer time, know that the quality of your prayer time is typically impacted by your body clock. A morning person is up and rolling the moment the alarm rings but tends to slow down gradually as the day wears on. The true night owl tends to be half alert for much of the morning but finally kicks in to high gear close to lunch, after the morning Starbucks cappuccino takes effect. After a slight slump in the afternoon, the night owl powers up with energy as night approaches and doesn't start to fade until close to bedtime.

Now it's your turn. Use the empty chart in Figure 4-1 and do the following:

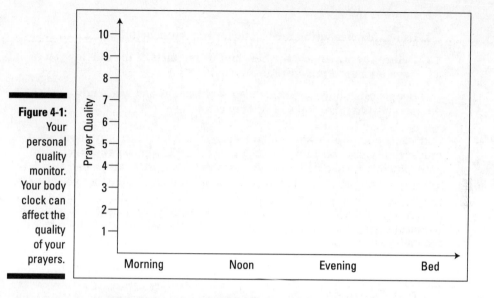

Figure 4-1:
Your
personal
quality
monitor.
Your body
clock can
affect the
quality
of your
prayers.

1. **Place a dot at each of the parts of the day at the place you think you have the most energy.**

   The more energy, the higher the point on the chart. For instance, Figure 4-2 shows a morning and a night person.

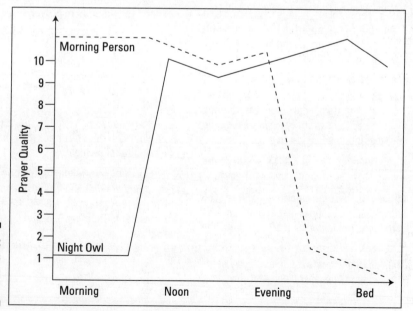

Figure 4-2:
Whoooooo's
a morning
person?

2. **Connect the dots.**

3. **Using this measuring device, factor in your schedule.**

4. **Determine which are the best and worst parts of the day for you to have a focused prayer time.**

   People often have two schedules — weekdays and weekends — so think about what time works best for each of them.

God wants you to pray about all things. So don't forget to pray about what prayer time works best for you. Jesus said that God knows the number of hairs on your head. If he knows you that well, I suspect that he can also provide a good recommendation for you about what time is best for you to pray.

After you select a time for weekdays and weekends, your next step is simply to start praying. Start out with just a few minutes of prayer, and then incrementally expand as you get more used to it and into the habit. Remember that developing the habit of prayer is equivalent to getting into shape. Some people get motivated to get into shape, but they exercise too hard, too soon, before their body is ready for it, and eventually they give up out of soreness and frustration. The same can be the case with prayer. Start slowly and build up your "prayeracity," or capacity to pray.

Three-week prayer adventure

Experts say that it takes 21 days to develop and retain a habit. So if you struggle with prayer, make a commitment to taking a three-week prayer adventure. Simply follow these steps:

1. **Determine your optimal prayer schedule as discussed in the section "Knowing When You're at Your Best," earlier in this chapter, and set morning, noon, or night as the time you're going to set aside to pray.**

   If your weekend schedule differs from the weekday, select specific times for each.

2. **Choose a specific location where you know you can be quiet at that time, such as your room, deck, car, or, if all else fails, the roof.**

   Then go to that same place each day at the specific time you've set aside for prayer.

3. **Spend ten minutes in prayer.**

   Eventually, you'll want to expand your time, but keep to ten minutes for this initial time period.

4. **For those 21 days, stick with it, no matter what.**

   If you happen to miss a day, don't get down on yourself. Just get back into the routine again the following day.

By following this schedule, you'll be surprised at how much prayer has already become part of your life after just three weeks. I present the externals here. Chapters 3, 5, and 6 present the internals.

Pray@Work

Given the reality that so many men and women work full time in the market-place, the act of balancing prayer with work is as important a topic as it's ever been before. What's more, start adding the commute time of people going to and from the office or child care facility, and you see that people spend most of their waking time during the week getting to and from work and doing their job, whether it's in an office, a factory, or their home. If you share this same time commitment, think about how you can better incorporate prayer into your workday.

You don't need exact change to pray

Commute time can be an ideal way to transform what is usually dead time into quality time with the Lord. Whether you travel by car, bus, or subway, consider using your commuting time as a dedicated prayer time. For example, suppose that you drive 40 minutes to work each morning. Instead of listening to a CD or talk radio, you can use this time as a guaranteed 40 minutes of prayer each weekday.

In a perfect world, commute time wouldn't be an ideal time to pray. No matter how you commute, you can't focus your full attention on prayer, or else you'd wind up in a ditch or miss your subway stop. Further, some people simply don't have the personality type that can easily filter out distractions around them, so trying to pray in this situation only causes their minds to stray wildly. However, some people have a knack for being able to focus well in the midst of distractions. If you have this ability, then consider "commuting by prayer."

If you're a praying commuter, turn off your radio and cell phone when you pray so that you can be alone with God and free from external distractions.

If you pray while driving a car, make sure that your first priority is safe driving. God wants to talk with you everywhere, but not when it endangers you or others around you. Besides, if you're not careful, you'll need a special section called "Pray@hospital" added to this book.

Taking a coffee-and-prayer break

Because work isn't just a 9-to-5 gig anymore, many people find themselves in the office from 8 a.m. to 6 p.m. or 9 p.m. to 7 a.m. If you spend a great deal of time in your office, then consider how you can carve out time on your break to pray.

If you do pray at work, be discreet about doing so. I don't recommend, for example, kneeling in the middle of the break room at lunch each day and saying your prayers aloud. Instead, if you have an office, close your office door or, if not, take a walk around the building. You don't need to be outspoken or call attention to yourself, no matter your motives. If you quietly go about your own business and not let it impact your dedication to your work, then praying should be a nonissue to your employer and co-workers.

Wimping on the weekends

When I first established a regular prayer time during the week, I worked hard to get it to fit perfectly with my work routine. Once the habit formed, I was excited to have a consistent pattern developed that actually was working! But once the weekend hit, my schedule was blown to bits, so I ended up wimping out on prayer time every Saturday and Sunday, when I had far more free time but no defined schedule.

The good news about the weekends is that the weekday rush should be a nonissue, but the bad news is that family commitments and a desire to veg out can often get in the way. Therefore, to be successful on the weekends, you need to deliberately set a different routine that suits you and then stick to it.

Penciling in Some Prayer Time

Not having time to pray is an issue that has always dogged me. I get busy with my commitments to projects at work, the books I'm writing, and my wife and children. Therefore, the normal time that I've set aside for prayer gets infiltrated. This intrusion on my prayer time happens most often when I have a tight deadline for a writing project. I tend to write late into the evening and, upon waking, get right back again on the old typewriter. (I confess that it's actually my computer, but doesn't a typewriter sound so much more like something an author should be using?) I justify putting off spending time with the Lord, telling him it is work that I am responsible for and need to do.

> *Work, work, from early until late. I have so much to do that I shall spend the first three hours in prayer.*
>
> Martin Luther

How long do I pray?

When people first start setting a regular prayer schedule, one big question they have is, "How long do I pray?" When I first started praying consistently, I'd read about great Christians from ages past who spent hours in prayer, and I'd panic, thinking, "How could I ever do that? I can't even think of enough to pray about for 10 minutes, let alone an hour or two."

Don't let the amount of time intimidate you. It tends to take care of itself. Start out by committing yourself to five minutes or so. After you develop a habit of prayer, the prayer time tends to naturally extend as you begin to see more

matters to pray about. When it does, just increase the amount of time you commit yourself to prayer.

As I've prayed over the years, I've been astonished at how quickly time goes by when I really start to pray for those around me. Before I know it, an hour has passed, and I'm not even through all the matters I want to pray about.

Finally, don't have the clock rule your prayer time. Pray until you run out of things to pray about and then end it. As Martin Luther said, "The fewer the words, the better the prayer."

Yet, over time, I've begun to understand that I was looking at everything from a skewed perspective. I realized that, in trying to do the busy work in place of spending time with God, I was wrestling control from him in the midst of the rush and trying to do everything myself.

You can do more than pray, after you have prayed, but you cannot do more than pray until you have prayed.

John Bunyan

Therefore, when I have other pressing matters bearing down on me, I see three reasons why I should continue to pray in spite of them:

- **Prayer acknowledges your dependency on God.** Praying before your rush time begins honors God by tangibly giving your time to God. In doing so, you're surrendering your ability to get things done to live in obedience, asking him to bless your efforts.

- **Prayer gets God's help.** Rather than trying to go solo, you're asking God to be an active participant in helping you tackle the issues you need to face. Why hopelessly swim upstream when you have someone who can actually change the flow of the water?

✔ **Prayer gives you perspective.** Prayer gives you a solid foundation, enabling you to reflect on the rush of activities and look on the situation as God does, instead of rushing off like a chicken with its head cut off. When you're truly focused on seeing his will, the decisions you make after prayer will be wiser and more in line with God's will.

Sailing through the Sand

One common misconception of prayer is that after you develop the habit of prayer, it's smooth sailing from there on out. However, as with everything else in life, sometimes prayer is just plain tough. Even the most disciplined of praying Christians have times in which they feel like they're trekking through the desert without food, water, or shelter. Try as they might, prayer becomes a grand struggle, with little energy or enthusiasm left to give God.

Prayers offered in a state of dryness are those which please [God] best.

C.S. Lewis

I see three main causes of these prayer deserts:

✔ **Other priorities encroach upon your prayer life.** Perhaps the biggest factor that can send you packing your backpack for the desert is that other parts of your life inevitably will try to invade your schedule. These other obligations or diversions first eliminate your dedicated prayer time and then distract your mind to rid you of what's left of your 24/7 prayers. To combat this problem, you have to weigh your priorities, decide what's most important, and make sure that prayer remains unimpeded, no matter the pressure from other factors.

In fact, this problem is so big that I set aside Chapter 12 to talk about all these roadblocks to prayer.

✔ **Unrepentant sin can derail your prayer life altogether.** As I say in Chapter 3, unconfessed sin can impede your prayers, kicking sand in your face while you walk through the desert. Sin has a way of not only blocking your relationship with God but, just as significant, hindering your desire to *want* to talk to God.

If you have sin that you haven't confessed or you're being defiant to God about confessing, then you're falling right into the devil's plans, because behaving in this way will wreck your prayer life. However, to stop this ten-car pileup, confess your sins to God and have a genuine desire to remain obedient. Your prayer life will immediately get back on track. Chapter 3 goes into detail about this, as do Chapters 5 and 6.

✔ **Humans live on a roller coaster.** Like all men and women living on this planet, you live on a lifelong roller coaster, periodically climbing a high hill, then descending to a low point, and finally smoothing out and riding the same loop again and again. Many people think something is wrong when they go through this roller coaster experience, but this undulating is simply a normal part of being human in a sin-filled world. Just as you have highs and lows in other aspects of your life, you should expect that you'll naturally have peaks and valleys in your prayer life as well. If your stomach is getting queasy from these roller coaster ups and downs, your best strategy is simply to hang in there, keep your hands and feet in the car at all times, and ride out the coaster, praying all the way.

When you find yourself in a desert with no water or camel, press on and keep focused on the horizon, looking for that oasis of God's presence. Keep with it, and in doing so, 24/7 prayer will gradually become a reality in your life.

Does posture matter?

Praying is traditionally associated with specific postures. Centuries ago, the common practice was standing in public prayer and kneeling in private prayer. Most churches today are less stringent on this issue, but some still contend that specific postures matter.

When I think of prayer posture, kneeling, clasping your hands, and bowing one's head come to mind. But does your posture really matter while you pray? On the one hand, no: God isn't going to decide whether to listen to your prayers based on your posture. Posture is of secondary importance when it comes to your prayer life and far less of a concern than your attitude when you pray.

Yet, at the same time, you can't so easily toss out your posture as meaningless, because what you do with your body is an outward manifestation of what's inside you. Posture shows reverence and facilitates concentration on the task at hand. So when you kneel, bow your head, or clasp your hands, you're showing a visible sign of submission to and respect for God, submitting before him much like you would a king. If you do that action on the outside, chances are likely that same attitude is going to spill over into your spirit when you pray.

At the same time, if praying while you walk is the way in which you feel closest to God, don't let your preference for a nonkneeling posture concern you. Instead, just make sure that your attitude is one of reverence. God won't feel slighted.

Chapter 5

The Original *Christian Prayer For Dummies:* The Lord's Prayer

In This Chapter

▶ Discovering the master blueprint for your prayer life

▶ Looking at the Lord's Prayer from all angles

For Dummies books became a household name because they were uniquely able to make complex issues understandable for normal folks, without treating you and me like we didn't have a brain. And as much as my publishers would like to take credit for their original idea, I'm sorry to tell them that Jesus beat them to the punch some 2,000 years ago.

In Jesus' day, prayer could be a confusing, intimidating subject for the average person on the street. Oh, it was a discipline that the Pharisees, the religious of the day, could master, but the burdensome system of procedures and rules that they placed on prayer made it hard for the rest of the population to undertake. As Jesus started his ministry, he realized that the Pharisees' concept of prayer had become skewed from its original intent, that is, a conversation between God and a person.

Always the innovator, Jesus decided to straighten out this distorted view. He did so by laying out a prototype of prayer and presenting it in a manner that any average Joe could grasp. You and I have come to call this prayer the Lord's Prayer (or the Our Father to some). The Lord's Prayer truly is the original *Christian Prayer For Dummies*: Jesus took a seemingly unreachable concept and put it into the eager arms of his followers.

In this chapter, as you explore the Lord's Prayer, you discover that Jesus intended it to be a model for how you approach your prayer life. You also explore the Lord's Prayer by looking at it from two different angles, both of which shed new light on what Jesus was teaching.

However, before talking about this most famous of Christian prayers, you better check it out first. Read Matthew 6:9–13:

> *Jesus said, pray like this:*
>
> *Our Father in heaven, hallowed be thy name.*
> *Thy Kingdom come.*
> *Thy will be done,*
> *on earth as in heaven.*
> *Give us today our daily bread.*
> *Forgive us our debts, as we also forgive our debtors.*
> *Bring us not into temptation, but deliver us from the evil one.*
> *For thine is the Kingdom, the power, and the glory forever.*
> *Amen.*

The Lord's Prayer is also known as the *Pater noster,* the Latin term for "Our Father."

Viewing the Lord's Prayer as a Model, Not a Carbon Copy

"Nice prayer. I memorized that one in Sunday School." That's the sort of reaction you'll probably get if you ask a man on the street about the Lord's Prayer. (Ever wonder if that street-walking man gets tired of answering everyone's questions?) Indeed, memorizing the Lord's Prayer is a part of the routine for any boy or girl who goes to Sunday School, and the prayer is one of the first prayers a parent teaches a child.

The Lord's Prayer is a great one to memorize and recite often, but the moment you relegate it to a canned prayer for recitation only, then you miss the point that Jesus was trying to make. Ironically, the biggest problem with the Lord's Prayer is that it's a victim of its own popularity. It seems to have a cotton-candy-like texture: You say the words, but they melt in your mouth and seem to disappear before they go anywhere else inside. So too the words can be swallowed up by its sound and cadence, coming out bouncy rather than gracefully and slowly. When I hear my kids say that prayer at night, I occasionally wonder how much of it is sinking in.

The single most important key to understanding the Lord's Prayer is that Jesus taught it to his followers as a *model* of prayer; not necessarily to be repeated as a memorized prayer. Notice that Jesus doesn't start off with "pray these words." Instead, he prefaces the prayer with "pray like this,"

which you can also translate to mean "this is how you should pray" or "pray in this manner." Clearly, Jesus is telling his disciples *how* to pray, not *what* to pray.

Therefore, think of Jesus as giving you a blueprint for your prayers. A *blueprint* is defined in the dictionary as a "guide for making something else" or a "plan of action." A builder uses a blueprint as a model or pattern from which he builds a house, not as something from which he can make a duplicate blueprint; doing so would serve a different purpose than what the architect intended.

The Lord's Prayer remains perhaps the best recitative prayer to pray regularly and to teach kids. But if you stay at the surface level, you simply utter its words in 17 seconds and go on with life pretty much like you did before. It's time to dig deeper.

Getting the Big Picture

Last year, my wife and I built a new home. To be clear, I should qualify that I *personally* didn't construct it, because I have a hard time hitting a screw with a hammer. (Oops, I mean a nail with a hammer. Well, you get the idea.) Before this experience, I never paid much attention to the details of a house, except the essentials: the location of the cappuccino maker, the C.S. Lewis books, the DVD player, and the computer. Everything else was just filler.

But after we started making decisions on paint colors, windows, side molding, and shingles, I found myself driving around town looking at houses in a completely different way. I was amazed at what I'd missed before, completely overlooking details that had been there right in front of me all along. I began noticing the color of houses and then started paying attention to windows, doors, and other features that I'd overlooked before. Each time I drove around, I passed by the same houses that I had seen countless times before, but I looked at them from a different viewpoint. Finally, when I combined the perspectives into one image, I was able to envision a full picture of what the house actually was. What I once described simply as a "nice house" in my mind had become a "cedar-sided, New England red, Deerfield Colonial with 12-x-12 windows and a 4-panel wooden front door."

The Lord's Prayer, which seems like just a nice prayer on the surface, is far more than that. It has lot of texture that you won't notice through a simple recitation. Use this section to analyze the Lord's Prayer from telephoto and wide-angle views. Then, as you combine these perspectives, you'll start to get a fuller picture of what the Lord's Prayer is all about.

Using your telephoto lens for a close-up view of the Lord's Prayer

The most traditional way to dive into the Lord's Prayer is to dissect it and reflect on each line. In this way, you can begin to study the nooks and crannies of the prayer, reflecting on the actual word choices of Jesus to better understand the meaning of the prayer.

✔ **Our Father in heaven, hallowed be thy name.** Jesus begins the prayer with a simple declaration to God as "Our Father." Jesus' word choice was deliberate. He didn't say "My father" or "Father" but went out of his way to use the plural pronoun. In an individual-oriented world where democracy and personal freedoms take priority, the notion of emphasizing group over self is not natural. And yet Paul tells us that the Christian church is a whole body, not a bunch of disassembled parts that live independent lives.

Of course, you and I are still supposed to pray in private. Jesus, for one, often went off alone to pray, as did countless others in the Bible. But in the lone model of prayer that he gave, Jesus gave top billing to praying together rather than going solo. Don't overlook this subtlety.

Jesus' word choice of "Father" is also significant, and he undoubtedly shocked everyone when he began his prayer with the simplicity, intimacy, and succinctness of that statement. You see, in Jesus' day, people didn't refer to God in as intimate a term as "Father." If you read Chapter 3, you discovered that God yearns for you to call him "dad" or "papa." Here in the Lord's Prayer, Jesus underscores this same level of intimacy with his bold use of the word "Father."

Jesus continues by giving praise to the Lord as he emphasizes the holiness of God's name. He underscores that reverence and worship should be at the start of any prayer.

✔ **Thy Kingdom come.** God's kingdom has both present and future aspects to it. It exists today on earth in the Christian church as a whole as well as in individual Christians. But God's kingdom will become complete when Jesus Christ returns to earth (an event known as the Second Coming).

When his kingdom does arrive in full on earth, then the age-old problem of evil will be resolved, ushering in a lasting peace for all eternity. Christians can eagerly look forward to this promised future event. By saying "let your Kingdom come," you affirm your wishes to the Lord, saying in effect, "I can't wait. Bring it on!"

A prayer meeting on Wall Street?

Corporate prayer sounds like a group of business executives clad in three-piece suits who are sitting around a boardroom praying that their quarterly sales numbers will improve. But the term actually refers to the original Latin roots of "corporate," meaning "to make into a body." Therefore, corporate prayer signifies praying together as a group of Christians to become one body of Christ. I like the original meaning, but given the connotations of "corporate" these days, I'm not sure whether I like using the term. It just sounds too impersonal and too sterile.

The Kingdom of God is a frequent topic for Jesus throughout the Gospels and refers not to a particular time or place but to situations in which God's rule is embraced. He uses the word *kingdom* 49 times in Matthew, 16 in Mark, and 38 in Luke.

✔ **Thy will be done.** The first call to submission is to affirm his kingdom plans. Next, you are to forget your own will and submit to God's will, inviting him to have his way with all matters both in the future and present, and in the world as a whole as well as in your personal life.

Praying for God's will is a meaty topic, so I devote Chapter 16 to a full discussion on how to do this.

✔ **On earth as in heaven.** In heaven, God's kingdom is already a "done deal" and his will perfectly accomplished. Jesus then reminds you and me in this phrase to invite him, even plead with him, to do so in this world as well.

✔ **Give us today our daily bread.** Jesus then switches gears, moving into the section of the prayer that makes successive requests to God. Notice that Jesus doesn't start off by praying for spiritual issues but instead gets intensely practical. When he says to ask for bread, he's not talking about some lofty spiritual provision; instead, he's talking about rye bread, yogurt, and SPAM luncheon meat. (Okay, I admit he'd never be referring to SPAM in this passage.) Jesus thus gives his seal of approval to pray for your material needs and makes it clear that God is eager to hear and answer them. (See Chapter 17 for more on this issue.)

Jesus emphasizes in this section that the life of a Christian is to live in daily communion with him as you trust that he'll provide. The emphasis is on *daily* bread, not a storehouse of food for the winter.

Living one day at a time is not a concept that is natural for you and me these days. The modern age dictates the necessity of securing a nest egg through retirement planning, investments, and a 401(k). Society says that you need to live a generation at a time, not one day at a time.

In the Lord's Prayer, Jesus isn't telling you to be reckless and live your life for the moment. (His prodigal son parable in Luke 15 makes it clear that squandering is a dead-end road.) Instead, he teaches that living a life of trust becomes a delicate balance: being wise and generous with today's resources while fully relying on God to provide for tomorrow.

Out of the six words in this phrase, two of them refer to the present moment ("today" and "daily"). Jesus thus emphasizes that the material needs you're supposed to focus on are for today, not the future.

✔ **Forgive us our debts, as we also forgive our debtors.** The second request that Jesus includes is a plea to God for cleansing, a wiping away of debts that you have incurred that you can't possibly pay back. The word "debts" is sometimes translated as "sins," but the idea is the same no matter which word you use: Because of your sins, you're in debt to God.

However, Jesus doesn't just stop there. He adds a phrase that you and I would just as soon he left out: "as we also forgive our debtors." Jesus clearly sees a relationship between God's forgiveness of you with your forgiveness of others. (See the sidebar "You want *me* to forgive *her*" in this chapter.) I know, I know, you're thinking, "That stinks!" But what can you do?

But when you examine the pain that others have caused you and when you accept the notion that what you've done to God is far worse (see Chapter 3 for a discussion on sin), only then can you truly start grasping how much you and I owe God. These sins serve as a reminder of the depth of God's grace, made possible by Jesus Christ.

✔ **Bring us not into temptation, but deliver us from the evil one.** The final request Jesus includes is to ask the Lord to guide you through the narrow road of life without getting detoured into temptations brought on by the "evil one" (the devil) that take you away from him. This passage is more than just a nice wish. God actually promises to back up that prayer with power to resist. Paul confirms this in 1 Corinthians 10:13 when he writes:

No temptation has taken you except what is common to man. God is faithful, who will not allow you to be tempted above what you are able, but will with the temptation also make the way of escape, that you may be able to endure it.

✔ **For yours is the Kingdom, the power, and the glory forever.** This portion of the prayer isn't actually part of the oldest manuscripts of Matthew, and it doesn't appear in the Gospel of Luke's version of the prayer. As a result, many scholars don't believe it was actually something Jesus said, but was added later by the early church. However, even if Jesus didn't say this, this phrase makes a good conclusion to the prayer, as it reaffirms God's kingdom, his power to carry out the kingdom and all the requests in your prayer, and glory in all things that will never diminish.

✔ **Amen.** Amen is used 30 times in the Bible and literally means "so be it." When you speak it to close a prayer, you affirm everything you just said with "let it be so."

You want *me* to forgive *her*?

Forgiveness may be the single hardest act that some people will ever have to do, but Jesus consistently stressed the importance of doing so if you're going to receive God's forgiveness for your even greater debt. Jesus provides a parable speaking of this in Matthew 18:21–35:

Then Peter came and said to him, "Lord, how often shall my brother sin against me, and I forgive him? Until seven times?" Jesus said to him, "I don't tell you until seven times, but, until seventy times seven.

"Therefore the Kingdom of Heaven is like a certain king, who wanted to reconcile accounts with his servants. When he had begun to reconcile, one was brought to him who owed him ten thousand talents. But because he couldn't pay, his lord commanded him to be sold, with his wife, his children, and all that he had, and payment to be made. The servant therefore fell down and kneeled before him, saying, 'Lord, have patience with me, and I will repay you all!' The lord of that servant, being moved with compassion, released him, and forgave him the debt.

"But that servant went out, and found one of his fellow servants, who owed him one hundred denarii, and he grabbed him, and took him by the throat, saying, 'Pay me what you owe!'

"So his fellow servant fell down at his feet and begged him, saying, 'Have patience

with me, and I will repay you!' He would not, but went and cast him into prison, until he should pay back that which was due. So when his fellow servants saw what was done, they were exceedingly sorry, and came and told to their lord all that was done. Then his lord called him in, and said to him, 'You wicked servant! I forgave you all that debt, because you begged me. Shouldn't you also have had mercy on your fellow servant, even as I had mercy on you?' His lord was angry, and delivered him to the tormentors, until he should pay all that was due to him. So my heavenly Father will also do to you, if you don't each forgive your brother from your hearts for his misdeeds."

Does Jesus say then that God won't forgive you if you don't forgive someone who wronged you? Bible teachers argue on both sides of that debate. But one thing is for certain: If you claim God's forgiveness while refusing it to others, at a minimum, your perspective is skewed. Respected theologian and author John Stott sums it up well when he says: "Once our eyes have been opened to see the enormity of our offense against God, the injuries which others have done to us appear by comparison extremely trifling. If, on the other hand, we have an exaggerated view of the offenses of others, it proves that we have minimized our own."

Viewing the Lord's Prayer with your wide-angle lens

A second approach to discovering the Lord's Prayer is to step back from the verses themselves and look at the major building blocks (see Figure 5-1) of the prayer of Jesus and see how they fit together as you apply them to your prayer life. Think of the Lord's Prayer as a house consisting of three parts: foundation, support walls, and living quarters.

- **Foundation:** Worship is the foundation of the Lord's prayer. Jesus begins by acknowledging the holiness of God's name:

  Our Father in heaven, sacred is your name.

  The prayer closes with the traditional ending:

  For yours is the Kingdom, the power, and the glory forever.

  If you use Jesus' model, the root of your prayers should simply reflect on the holiness and glory of God. For if God were not holy, powerful, and in control, why would you and I pray to him in the first place?

- **Support walls:** Once you comprehend the greatness and fullness of God, what other rational response can you make but surrender to him? True worship begets absolute surrender. Therefore, a surrendering spirit is built on top of the worship foundation and provides the framework to support everything else.

- **Living quarters:** The rest of the Lord's Prayer can be summarized in three verbs: provide, forgive, and protect. Jesus is being "practical" in the final part of the prayer, because these verbs deal with the nitty-gritty issues of daily life, not some lofty, esoteric ideas to simply contemplate from a mountaintop. But God's provision, forgiveness, and protection can exist only with the support of a solid foundation and framework.

Just as you'd never live in a house without a foundation and support walls, asking for stuff simply doesn't make sense without a worshipful and surrendering heart.

Figure 5-1:
Building
block
approach to
the Lord's
Prayer.

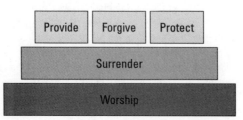

Chapter 6

Revealing Prayer's Secret Recipe

Secret recipes always intrigue people. Kentucky Fried Chicken has its original secret recipe chicken. McDonald's has a special sauce for its Big Mac sandwich. Coca-Cola has its top-secret concoction locked up in a bank vault somewhere in Georgia. All these secrets, however, don't stop interested consumers from trying to crack these codes and coming up with cloned versions on their own. Take a look on the Web, and chances are, you'll find supposed original or cloned recipes of your favorite meal or drink. However, as my wife and I try out some of these copycats, we discover that they're usually flawed wannabes of the real thing.

Prayer too has a secret recipe of ingredients that make up a complete, well-rounded Christian prayer. But that doesn't stop people from taking shortcuts or coming up with cloned versions. However, when it comes to prayer, sticking with the real thing is vital; when you start removing or replacing the active ingredients of prayer, your prayer life begins to lose its effectiveness, much like trying to make bread without the yeast.

In this chapter, you explore the secret ingredients to mix together to make your prayer life complete. These parts include adoration, confession, thanksgiving, intercessory prayer, and petitionary prayer.

Responding in a Most (Un)Natural Way: Adoration

The first ingredient to add to your prayer recipe is adoration. *Adoration* is giving God praise and honor for who he is as Lord over all. As you can discover from reading about the Lord's Prayer in Chapter 5, adoration is not just a section of your prayer; it's the very foundation of all prayer. Everything you say when you pray should be done in a manner that adores God, but you should also take time to specifically worship and give adoration to him, usually at the start of your prayer.

> *God thirsts to be thirsted after.*
>
> St. Augustine

When your head is clear and fully focused on God, adoration can be a natural response to him when you pray. After all, if you stop and think about whom you're actually talking to, you'll find that chills start running down your spine.

Unfortunately, my head at least isn't often as engaged as this, so adoration and worship can become a most unnatural activity for me. Instead of focusing on who God is, I get distracted with my own concerns and activities going on around me. When this happens, I may mutter a few nice-sounding praises to pad the prayer, but my real focus is on the issues I'm concerned about.

A second reason why adoration can be hard is that it's not directly related to my experience, whereas every other part of prayer is. Consider these examples:

- When I sin and feel remorseful, confession comes naturally off my tongue.
- When I find my lost journal, thanksgiving abounds spontaneously.
- When my friend is sick, I get on my knees for him in prayer.
- When I lose my job and have a family to feed, I cry out to God from the bottom of my heart.

Even when I see a beautiful waterfall or a starry sky, I may offer praises to God, but more often than not, thanking him for that creation is easier than adoring him as the one who created it.

So while other parts of prayer come out of your experience, adoration has *nothing* to do with you or me, but solely with God. As a result, if you give adoration and praise, you have to put effort into it because it's the least intuitive part of prayer.

Complete prayer's secret recipe

To pray a complete prayer, follow this recipe.

Cooking time: 5 to 60 minutes

Servings: 1

Ingredients:

1 cup of adoration

1 cup of confession

1 cup of thanksgiving

1 cup of intercessory prayer

1 cup of petitionary prayer

1 teaspoon salt

1. Prepare yourself and then go into your prayer closet (see Chapter 4).

2. Add adoration into a large mixing prayer.

3. Mix equal or near-equal parts of confession, thanksgiving, intercessory prayer, and petitionary prayer into this mixture to form a complete prayer.

4. Add salt. (I'm not sure why, but every recipe always includes salt.)

5. Bake complete prayer at room temperature. Allow 5 minutes for rare, 15 minutes for medium, 40 minutes for well done, and 60 minutes for really well done.

Serving note: Worship can be freely used in place of adoration. However, you can't substitute excuses for confession.

When you first start out with worship prayer, you may find that coming up with words to express yourself is hard. As a result, after a couple lines of worship, you may find yourself mixing in thanksgiving prayer instead of adoration. You can easily confuse these two parts of prayer, but note the difference between the two. Adoration gives glory to God for *who he is,* while thanksgiving praises him for *what he's done.*

Assuring you that God isn't conceited

An issue that plagues some people concerning adoration is that the business sounds too much like God is on a world-class ego trip. I mean, the only people you hear of on earth who ask for adoration and acclaim have heads the size of a watermelon, like some champion athletes and movie stars.

This perspective may ring true when speaking of people, but it misses the point of what true adoration is to God. Consider the following reasons for adoring God:

✔ **Spontaneous joy:** Being a New Englander, I was more than a little excited when the New England Patriots won Super Bowl XXXVI on a last-second field goal. Watching the players celebrate immediately after the game concluded was like seeing kids running loose in a candy store. It was pure, spontaneous joy. Their instant reaction wasn't "look at me"; it was "wow, a Super Bowl victory." In other words, the nature of the event — winning the Super Bowl — demanded a response of spontaneous joy, apart from any egos.

✔ **Awe and respect:** Imagine that the president of the United States is coming to your house for dinner. When you greet him at the door, your natural response is to show awe and respect for his office, even if you don't much agree with his politics. What's more, the honor you show doesn't have anything to do with whether he demands it; instead, your awe is based on the very nature of his position.

Looking to the Bible: Adoration

Psalm 8 vividly captures how you and I can adore God by looking at his glory revealed in his mighty works.

O Lord, our Lord, how majestic is your name in all the earth,

Who has set your glory above the heavens!

From the lips of babes and infants you have established strength,

Because of your adversaries, that you might silence the enemy and the avenger.

When I consider your heavens, the work of your fingers,

The moon and the stars, which you have ordained;

What is man, that you think of him?

The son of man, that you care for him?

For you have made him a little lower than God,

And crowned him with glory and honor

You make him ruler over the works of your hands.

You have put all things under his feet:

All sheep and oxen,

Yes, and the animals of the field,

The birds of the sky, the fish of the sea,

And whatever passes through the paths of the seas.

Lord, our Lord,

How majestic is your name in all the earth!

These two illustrations may not seem related, but when you combine the two, they point to the root of why you and I adore God. The spontaneous joy of the game and the awe of the president were based not on the actions or attitudes of the people involved, but rather on the *nature* of the event or office held. In the same way, the nature of who God is cries out for adoration and worship; you're not adoring him because of some ego-driven demand he places on you and me.

Overcoming the adoration struggle

If you struggle with adoration prayers, apply the following ideas to your prayer life:

✔ **Be quality driven.** When you pray prayers of adoration, one of the biggest challenges is knowing what to praise God for. One can only say "holy, holy, holy" for so long. One of the best ways to better know what to say is to concentrate on the following qualities of God:

- Creativity in the world, as seen by the diversity in nature and the gifts that he gives humankind

- Holiness that makes him without a blemish

- Faithful, selfless love for you and me

- Boundless mercy and grace shown by Jesus' dying on the cross

- Perfect justice so you know you'll never get a raw deal

- Power that can and will conquer all evil

- Sovereignty showing that he's in full control and doesn't have any needs

- Unchangeability so that you don't have to worry about him reversing course or doing something less than perfect

- Wisdom and perfect will so that all things truly work for the good of those who love him

In your prayer, consider how each attribute and capability expresses a part of who God is. Reflect on how they're revealed in the world around you. Plus, when you focus on these qualities, you not only show God adoration but also draw closer to him as a result.

✔ **Get to a Psalm.** If you find yourself suffering from an inability to get beyond "praise you," check out the Psalms. Many chapters in the Psalms are devoted to worship and adoration, making them ideal for discovering how exactly to express adoration to God.

As you read worship-oriented Psalms, note that this book contains two kinds of adoration: *Descriptive praise* adores who God is, and *declarative praise* adores what God does to demonstrate his character.

Recommended worship Psalms include Psalms 8 (see the sidebar "Looking to the Bible: Adoration"), 19, 46, 47, 66, 95, 96, 100, 148, 149, and 150.

✔ **Begin where you are.** When discussing worship and adoration, a friend once taught C.S. Lewis to "begin where you are." This simple advice had a significant impact on how Lewis approached adoration in the future. Rather than try and arrange theological words for prayer, Lewis used what he saw and experienced around him as a starting point for adoration. Take Lewis's advice: Look around you and see God's creative powers and imagination at work in the world.

✔ **Don't stretch it out.** Worship only as long as you're praying from the heart and then wrap up that portion of your prayer. Don't descend into empty accolades to fill a quota. When you first start, you may have only a few seconds of praise and worship, but the more you do it, the more natural adoration will become.

Honesty Required: Improving Your Confession

Confession is prayer's natural response to dealing with sin. *Confession* is an active ingredient to add to prayer because it puts you into a right relationship with God. John emphasizes this in 1 John 1:9:

> *If we confess our sins, he is faithful and righteous to forgive us the sins, and to cleanse us from all unrighteousness.*

Confession also has the effect of transforming your life into an open book, inviting God to work in your life.

> *Watch the difference between confession and admitting; the majority of us are quite ready to admit, it is the rarest thing to get to the place where we will confess. . . . It is much more difficult to confess to God than we are apt to think. It is not confessing in order to be forgiven; confession is the evidence that I am forgiven.*
>
> Oswald Chambers

Looking to the Bible: Confession

Psalm 51 is a heartfelt cry to God for mercy and forgiveness. The writer grieves over the sins he has done and repents over them.

Have mercy on me, God, according to your loving kindness.

   According to the multitude of your tender mercies, blot out my transgressions.

Wash me thoroughly from my iniquity.

   Cleanse me from my sin.

For I know my transgressions.

   My sin is constantly before me.

Against you, and you only, have I sinned,

   And done that which is evil in your sight;

That you may be proved right when you speak,

   And justified when you judge.

Behold, I was brought forth in iniquity.

   In sin my mother conceived me.

Behold, you desire truth in the inward parts.

   You teach me wisdom in the inmost place.

Purify me with hyssop, and I will be clean.

   Wash me, and I will be whiter than snow.

Let me hear joy and gladness,

   That the bones which you have broken may rejoice.

Hide your face from my sins,

   And blot out all of my iniquities.

Create in me a clean heart, O God.

   Renew a right spirit within me.

Don't throw me from your presence,

   And don't take your holy spirit from me.

Restore to me the joy of your salvation.

   Uphold me with a willing spirit.

Then I will teach transgressors your ways.

   Sinners shall be converted to you.

Deliver me from bloodguiltiness, O God, the God of my salvation.

   My tongue shall sing aloud of your righteousness.

(continued)

(continued)

> Lord, open my lips.
>   My mouth shall declare your praise.
> For you don't delight in sacrifice, or else I would give it.
>   You have no pleasure in burnt offering.
> The sacrifices of God are a broken spirit.
>   A broken and contrite heart, O God, you will not despise.

However, Scottish pastor and author Oswald Chambers makes the point that there's a world of difference between confessing and admitting a sin. If, for example, a girl says "sorry" after getting caught with her hand in the cookie jar, that response may have two meanings. She may be sorry that she got caught or sorry that she disobeyed her parents. If she's sorry for being found out, then she did nothing more than admit her mistake. But if she is remorseful for her disobedience, then she understands the true meaning of confession.

When you confess, you first take ownership and responsibility of the sin and recognize the impact that it has on God and other people. Next, you ask for forgiveness and express your intent to avoid the sin thereafter.

Consider the following when you confess your sins to the Lord:

- ✔ **Be specific.** Get into the habit of being as specific as possible in your confession. Lumping all your sins into a quick "please forgive me for everything I did wrong today" isn't true confession or repentance; it's checking confession off your to-do list. Being specific helps you face the reality and frequency of your sins. Doing so also makes you aware of the traps and weaknesses of your life.

- ✔ **Be receptive**. Pray for a deep sensitivity to sin so that you'll recognize sin when it occurs in your life. God will then help you get rid of the sin in your life, much like you peel an onion. He works on one layer of sin, and then after you have success in that area, he'll move on to the next. He never overloads you by trying to fix all the layers of sin at one time.

Making Every Day Turkey Day: Thanksgiving

In the film *Groundhog Day*, Phil Conner is a man who is condemned to repeat the same day (February 2) over and over again in what ultimately turns into a personal odyssey to discover meaning in life. By the end, Phil realizes that helping others is what gives his life purpose, even though that meant he had to simply start all over again the next repeating day. In one scene, Phil comes to the last-minute rescue of a boy who is falling out of a tree, catching him in his arms just before he hit the sidewalk. On each day that Phil repeats this heroic act, the frightened boy always runs home without saying a word, leaving Phil to yell to him, "Someday you're going to thank me. I'll be back tomorrow . . . maybe."

That boy reminds me too much of myself in my prayers to God. So often I get into a difficult situation and pray for God's assistance. But when I actually receive his help, I rush off all excited about the good news but forget to thank the One who made it all possible.

Thanksgiving prayer is, therefore, the next active ingredient to add to your prayer life. It simply verbalizes that you're grateful for what God has done in your life and in the world around you.

Adoration and thanksgiving are easy to confuse. Although you should recognize the distinction and make sure that both of them are part of your prayer life, don't worry if they blur together. I think it's natural for adoration and thanksgiving to do so. Take, for instance, Psalm 103, in the "Looking to the Bible: Thanksgiving" sidebar, which has both thanksgiving and adoration parts to it.

When you give thanks to the Lord, think about the following ways to improve your thanksgiving:

- ✔ **Call the 24/7 thanksgiving hotline.** Keep that 24/7 hotline open so that you can thank God the instant a blessing happens during the day. Don't put it off until later, because you'll often forget. (You can read more on 24/7 prayer in Chapter 4.)

- ✔ **Write it down.** Another way to improve your thanksgiving prayer is to use a journal to write down your blessings as they happen. Journaling helps you to thank God and gives you a spiritual autobiography of your blessings over time, providing a great resource to look at when you need an encouraging word.

Looking to the Bible: Thanksgiving

Psalm 103 praises God for all the wondrous deeds that he does for his people.

Praise the Lord, my soul!

> *All that is within me, praise his holy name!*

Praise The Lord, my soul,

> *And don't forget all his benefits;*

Who forgives all your sins;

> *Who heals all your diseases;*

Who redeems your life from destruction;

> *Who crowns you with loving kindness and tender mercies;*

Who satisfies your desire with good things,

> *So that your youth is renewed like the eagle's.*

The Lord executes righteous acts,

> *And justice for all who are oppressed.*

He made known his ways to Moses,

> *His deeds to the children of Israel.*

The Lord is merciful and gracious,

> *Slow to anger, and abundant in loving kindness.*

He will not always accuse;

> *Neither will he stay angry forever.*

He has not dealt with us according to our sins,

> *Nor repaid us for our iniquities.*

For as the heavens are high above the earth,

> *So great is his loving kindness toward those who fear him.*

As far as the east is from the west,

> *So far has he removed our transgressions from us.*

Like a father has compassion on his children,

> *So the Lord has compassion on those who fear him.*

For he knows how we are made.

> *He remembers that we are dust.*

As for man, his days are like grass.

> *As a flower of the field, so he flourishes.*

For the wind passes over it, and it is gone.

> *Its place remembers it no more.*

> But the Lord's loving kindness is from everlasting to everlasting with those who fear him,
>
> His righteousness to children's children;
>
> To those who keep his covenant,
>
> To those who remember to obey his precepts.
>
> The Lord has established his throne in the heavens.
>
> His kingdom rules over all.
>
> Praise The Lord, you angels of his,
>
> Who are mighty in strength, who fulfill his word,
>
> Obeying the voice of his word.
>
> Praise The Lord, all you armies of his,
>
> You servants of his, who do his pleasure.
>
> Praise The Lord, all you works of his,
>
> In all places of his dominion.
>
> Praise the Lord, my soul.

Going to the Rug for Others: Intercessory

"Ardent defender of the oppressed." That's the nickname I coined for one of my three sons because of his lawyerlike persona when his brothers are being disciplined by my wife or me. He invariably rushes to their defense and tirelessly pleads their case, so much so that, more often than not, he winds up getting into more trouble than they do. Although my son's methods leave a lot to be desired in these situations, I love what's in his heart. His spirit expresses well the sacrificial way in which Christians are called to intercede or plead for others in prayer.

Intercessory prayer, or praying on behalf of others, is another ingredient to mix into a complete prayer. When you begin to understand that God releases his power in the world largely through prayer (see Chapter 1), this idea of intercessory prayer moves from being "nice" to "essential." After all, *your* prayer can be the missing link between a friend's problem or a family member's sickness and God's provision and healing.

> *I sought for a man among them, who should build up the wall, and stand in the gap before me for the land. . . .*
>
> Ezekiel 22:30

Mobsters have the expression "going to the mattress" as a way of denoting starting a war with someone else. Christians should have their own comparable expression: "going to the rug," which means kneeling on your prayer rug (see Chapter 4) as you relentlessly pray for others on their behalf.

Moses gives a vivid illustration of the power of intercession in Exodus 17: 8–13 when the Israelites faced attack from the enemy Amalek:

> *Moses said to Joshua, "Choose men for us, and go out, fight with Amalek. Tomorrow I will stand on the top of the hill with God's rod in my hand." So Joshua did as Moses had told him, and fought with Amalek; and Moses, Aaron, and Hur went up to the top of the hill. It happened, when Moses held up his hand, that Israel prevailed; and when he let down his hand, Amalek prevailed. But Moses' hands were heavy; and they took a stone, and put it under him, and he sat on it. Aaron and Hur held up his hands, the one on the one side, and the other on the other side. His hands were steady until sunset. Joshua defeated Amalek and his people with the edge of the sword.*

In a most amazing demonstration of intercessory prayer, the Israelite army's success or failure depended solely on Moses as an intercessor. You and I most likely won't be called to intercede by raising a rod in front of an army, but the same God who engineered that victory will engineer circumstances in the lives of your friends, family, and others you know. Go to the rug for them.

Chapter 3 discusses how Jesus is the ultimate intercessor, acting as mediator between God and every Christian.

Consider the following advice when you pray for others:

- ✓ **Give it priority.** The amount of time one spends in intercessory prayer is usually a telltale sign of how strong his or her prayer life is. Therefore, give intercessory prayer priority during your dedicated prayer time.

- ✓ **Write it down.** Just as in thanksgiving prayer, writing down the names of others for whom you need to pray is an important part of having success in this area. Such a prayer log makes it easier for you to remember whom to pray for.

Looking to the Bible: Intercessory prayer

Paul writes in Ephesians 6:18–20 about persevering in your requests for your brothers and sisters in Christ:

With all prayer and requests, praying at all times in the Spirit, and being watchful to this end in all perseverance and requests
for all the saints: on my behalf, that utterance may be given to me in opening my mouth, to make known with boldness the mystery of the Good News, for which I am an ambassador in chains; that in it I may speak boldly, as I ought to speak.

Asking for Yourself: Petitionary

People often get the skewed idea that God doesn't want to be bothered with their prayer requests. That perspective reminds me of houseguests who notice that there aren't any towels in the bathroom but don't want to bother the host with such a request. So they don't ask and go without a shower during their stay. However, their suffering is needless, because hosts are usually more than happy to supply the towels if the guests ask.

God clearly wants a big part of the prayer recipe to be *petitionary prayer,* or asking God for his help. The Bible fully supports this notion: Half of the Lord's Prayer is devoted to asking; Jesus says, "ask and you shall receive" on several occasions; and even Jesus himself asks his Father for his needs.

Asking God for something in your prayer is a huge topic that involves a variety of tough issues. I only touch on it here, so see Chapters 17 and 18 for much more on this meaty subject.

Think about the ideas here when you ask the Lord for something:

- **Don't be bashful.** Some people believe that genuine saintly prayer consists of exclusively worshiping God in your prayer time. But as you can see from this book, this approach isn't consistent with what the Bible says prayer is all about. Therefore, get over being shy or bashful, and just talk to God, asking him for whatever is in your heart. Even if you're not sure whether the issue is something you should pray about, simply be honest with him about that. God finds such openness and honesty refreshing.

- **Don't be myopic.** Petitionary prayer is an important part of prayer, but if left unchecked, it can dominate your prayer life. If you find that you're praying for yourself and your immediate family and only occasionally for others outside that small circle, you're being overly focused on yourself. Personal crises aside, intercessory prayer should get the lion's share of your "asking" time in prayer.

Whether we like it or not, asking is the rule of the Kingdom.

Charles Spurgeon

Looking to the Bible: Petitionary prayer

Psalm 143 asks God for his listening ear and help as the writer goes through major struggles in life.

Hear my prayer, O Lord.

> *Listen to my petitions.*

> *In your faithfulness and righteousness, relieve me.*

Don't enter into judgment with your servant,

> *For in your sight no man living is righteous.*

For the enemy pursues my soul.

> *He has struck my life down to the ground.*

> *He has made me live in dark places, as those who have been long dead.*

Therefore my spirit is overwhelmed within me.

> *My heart within me is desolate.*

I remember the days of old.

> *I meditate on all your doings.*

> *I contemplate the work of your hands.*

I spread forth my hands to you.

> *My soul thirsts for you, like a parched land.*

Hurry to answer me, Lord.

> *My spirit fails.*

Don't hide your face from me,

> *So that I don't become like those who go down into the pit.*

Cause me to hear your loving kindness in the morning,

> *For I trust in you.*

Cause me to know the way in which I should walk,

> *For I lift up my soul to you.*

Deliver me, Lord, from my enemies.

> *I flee to you to hide me.*

Teach me to do your will,

> *For you are my God.*

Your Spirit is good.

> *Lead me in the land of uprightness.*

Revive me, Lord, for your name's sake.

In your righteousness, bring my soul out of trouble.

In your loving kindness, cut off my enemies,

And destroy all those who afflict my soul,

For I am your servant.

Part II
Turbocharging Your Prayers

The 5th Wave   By Rich Tennant

Spiritually, I believe I can manifest many good things in my life. But right now, I'd settle for being able to manifest a cab.

In this part . . .

*I*f you're going to lasso prayer, you can't do it empty handed. This part equips you with a pocketful of practical techniques that you can pull out and use at a moment's notice when you pray.

Chapter 7

Ready-Made or Do-It-Yourself?

In This Chapter

▶ Discovering the pros and cons of free-form and ready-made prayers

▶ Exploring the ACTS organizing method and other proven techniques

▶ Combining the two prayer approaches

Up until the 20th century, creating meals from scratch was the only way to prepare a meal. People roasted the catch of the day from the fisherman or hunter and ate it with handpicked corn and fresh-baked bread. However, the inventions of the refrigerator and, more recently, the microwave forever changed food preparation. People no longer had to slave in the kitchen for hours on end each day. Instead, TV dinners and microwave-ready meals enabled people to have a fully cooked meal before you could say Jiffy Pop.

For people who don't know how to cook or who simply like the convenience, these ready-made meals provide an alternative way to enjoy a balanced meal without doing everything by hand. However, these kinds of ready-made foods aren't as healthy or as tasty as meals made from scratch due to their prepackaged nature.

Prayer has two major types of approaches that mirror food preparation — do-it-yourself and ready-made. In Chapter 6, you can discover the secret ingredients to prayer. This chapter continues this discussion by combining these ingredients together to form a complete meal that uses the two approaches.

Whipping Up a Batch from Scratch

Praying from scratch (called *free prayer* or, more formally, *expository prayer*) is exactly the kind of prayer you may have read about in the first six chapters of this book. It's talking with God, pure and simple. You don't need any notes; you simply open your mouth and say whatever is on your mind.

Although this type of prayer approach is the dominant and most intuitive way that the vast majority of Christians approach prayer, you need to be aware of both its strengths and weaknesses.

Here are the strengths of free prayer:

- **Free prayer is all about a personal relationship with God.** People are hardwired with a desire to communicate with persons they like or love. With people you love (such as a spouse or best friend), a dynamic, intimate conversation is a natural extension and a proof of that personal relationship. Or with people you'd like to know, an instinctive action is to try to initiate communication with them as a way to form some type of connection that thereby makes that relationship stand out from the others in your life.

 You can apply these same truths to the spiritual realm as well. If you have a personal relationship with God, then the desire to communicate at an intimate level is natural and instinctive. Free prayer is nothing more than a response to that desire.

 Free prayer fits the real-world concept of relationships as well. For example, you don't need any romance books to talk with your spouse. Or, in the candid words of British author Malcolm Muggeridge, you don't "[make] love to your wife out of Petrarch or Donne" (two famous poets). In the same way, you shouldn't need prayers written by someone else to dictate the conversation between God and you.

- **Free prayer is real.** A second strong point of free prayer is that it tends to be honest and real. Free prayer tends to come straight from your heart because what you pray about comes directly from you and you alone.

- **Free prayer is flexible.** Free prayer allows you to tailor your conversation to where you are spiritually and emotionally. Perhaps you're having a stress-filled day and need to focus your prayer on specific concerns to help you relax. Or perhaps you received good news and want to make thanksgiving the focus of your prayer. (See Chapter 6 for more information about the ingredients necessary for complete prayer.)

 Because free prayer is unplanned, you're also more receptive to letting God lead you on a path of unexpected twists and turns. In some cases, you may end up following God to some "mountaintop experiences" that make you feel especially close to him.

Although free prayer has its strengths, you also need to consider its potential weaknesses:

- **Free prayer can lead to undisciplined spontaneity.** Undisciplined spontaneity can slowly deteriorate into a careless, ineffective prayer life. You can begin to focus on what you want instead of striving for a balanced prayer life that puts God at the center. What's more, if you're not supplementing free prayer with Bible reading or written prayers to guide your understanding of God's truth, you can start to produce a version of his will that has more to do with your personal preferences than with Biblical reality.

✔ **Free prayer can lead to casualness.** The best part of free prayer is that it promotes and strengthens intimacy with God. However, as I mention in Chapter 3, don't let that intimacy turn into casualness or a flippant attitude. Instead, balance intimacy with reverence. (See the sidebar "Is a 'good' God a pushover?" elsewhere in this chapter.)

One way to keep the spontaneous appeal of free prayer but avoid its negatives is to use a prayer organizing method or technique. These methods aren't meant to stifle your spontaneity. Instead, they're designed to provide a framework for ensuring that your prayer life stays on track and has the necessary ingredients for complete prayer. One recommended organizing method is called the ACTS method. Three additional techniques worth considering are the Five Senses Prayer, the Five Finger Prayer, and arrow prayer. The Five Senses Prayer and the Five Finger Prayer are especially suitable for teaching children of all ages.

As you look at each of these methods, don't feel that you need to pick one and stick with it exclusively. For example, you can use the ACTS method as an integral part of your dedicated prayer time and then use the other methods throughout the day.

Organizing with the ACTS method

The best, most complete organizing method I've encountered for prayer is the ACTS method. ACTS is an acronym that stands for Adoration, Confession, Thanksgiving, and Supplication (essentially a term that combines intercessory and petitionary prayer). This method includes all the active ingredients of a complete prayer (which you can read more about in Chapter 6).

To use the ACTS method, you simply need to structure your prayer in the order of the acronym.

1. **Begin by taking time to *adore* God.**

   True worship of the Lord produces a submissive and contrite heart.

2. **Contrition opens the door for you to *confess* your sins.**

3. ***Thank* God first for his grace through Jesus Christ and then move on to other things that you're thankful for.**

4. ***Supplicate* (ask) God to help with the needs of others and yourself.**

The ACTS method help ensure that you cover each of the key parts of prayer. It also helps you prioritize — making sure that you get the other three prayer ingredients added before you begin to ask God for his help.

You may want to try two noteworthy alternate versions of ACTS:

- **CATS:** Some people prefer the CATS method, in which confession is placed first so that you can get right with God before moving on to the rest of the prayer. (However, if you use the CATS method, please be aware that this approach has been known to cause a variety of side effects, including finicky behavior, a desire to sleep 22 hours a day, aloofness, and overwhelming impulses to scratch the furniture.)

- **ACTSS:** A second alternative is to add Surrender to the end of ACTS. That way, you close the prayer with an emphasis on surrendering yourself to God and his will. (The only downside is that if you repeat the word ACTSS aloud too much, people nearby may confuse you for a snake.)

Focusing on the Five Senses Prayer

The Five Senses Prayer is a technique that uses your five senses as a guide to focus your prayers:

- **Hearing:** The prayer starts off by focusing on clearing your heart and mind so that you can hear God's still, small voice as you pray. (See Chapter 19 for more information on hearing God.)

- **Touching:** One of the last words Jesus gave his disciples was what is commonly known as the Great Commission, which instructs his followers to go into all the world and share the good news of Christianity. Touching is a reminder to pray for opportunities to reach people around you with this good news.

- **Smelling:** Smelling reminds you to pray for sensitivity to any and all sin in your life so that you can recognize it a mile away and flee from the temptation.

- **Seeing:** Seeing is a reminder to pray for the needs that you observe around you, including those of your loved ones, church members, and neighbors.

- **Tasting:** Concentrating on tasting reminds you to pray for the ability to fully experience the joy that God wants each of his followers to have when they truly surrender to him.

Table 7-1 provides a summary of the Five Senses Prayer.

Table 7-1	Five Senses Prayer
Sense	*Prayer Focus*
Hearing	Hearing and discerning God's voice
Touching	Sharing the good news of Jesus Christ with others around you
Smelling	Becoming more sensitive to sin
Seeing	Meeting the needs of others
Tasting	Experiencing the fullness and joy of God

Counting on the Five Finger Prayer

Another popular organizing method for prayer is in the palm of your hand or, more precisely, just beyond the palm of your hand. In the Five Finger Prayer, which is summarized in Table 7-2, each finger on your hand serves as a reminder for a specific group of people for whom you should pray:

✔ **Thumb:** Take a look at your hand by holding it out in front of you. Notice that the extremity closest to you is your thumb. The thumb, therefore, is a remember to pray for those closest to you, such as your family and friends.

✔ **Pointing finger:** The index finger reminds you to pray for people who teach in your church (including Sunday school teachers, youth leaders, pastors, and Bible study leaders) and community (such as school teachers and college professors).

✔ **Tallest finger:** The tallest finger represents praying for government and civic leaders in your community and nation.

✔ **Ring finger:** The ring finger is commonly known as the weakest of fingers. You can use this as a reminder to pray for those who are weak and need your help, such as the elderly, sick, widowed, and poor.

✔ **Little finger:** Your pinkie finger is the smallest and reminds you to place yourself lower than others, submitting yourself to God and serving others around you.

Table 7-2	Five Finger Prayer
Finger	**Prayer Focus**
Thumb	People closest to you
Pointing finger	Teachers and leaders of ministries
Tallest finger	Civic and government leaders
Ring finger	Weak and downtrodden
Little finger	Your needs

I know, I know, a handful of people are going to be hung up on the fact that the thumb is called a "finger" in this method, when technically a thumb is not. Therefore, if your prayer life is in shambles because of this terminology error, I recommend that you refer to this technique as the Five Phalanges Prayer and eliminate any possible problems.

Shooting straight with arrow prayer

Arrow prayer isn't an organizing method per se, but it is a spontaneous prayer technique. An arrow prayer is any direct, spontaneous prayer based on a particular event that comes up during the day.

For example, suppose that you almost fall off a train but are saved at the last moment by a quick-thinking conductor. At that moment, you might say an arrow prayer like this: "Thanks, God, for your protection and for a conductor willing to risk his own safety." Or suppose that you're about to be eaten by a python in the Amazon rainforest while competing as a finalist on the *Survivor* television show. In that situation, your arrow prayer might be, "Help me, God. Please get me out of this snake's mouth and do so in a way that I won't get voted off the show!"

Arrow prayer should be part of the prayer life of any Christian who seeks 24/7 prayer (see Chapter 4). That constant, real-time communication most closely resembles the kind of relationship you have with someone close to you.

Breaking Open the Ready-Made Variety

Ready-made prayers (also called *written prayers*) are those prepared by some-one else but used as part of your private prayer time. The book of Psalms is the best example of ready-made prayers in the Bible, but many other histori-cal and contemporary prayer books are available, including *The Book of Common Prayer* that the Anglican and Episcopalian churches use.

The Jesus Prayer

The Jesus Prayer is mainly from the Orthodox tradition, although Christians of all backgrounds use it. Sometimes called "prayer of the heart," it is a simple one-line prayer:

Lord Jesus Christ, Son of God, have mercy upon me, a sinner.

The Jesus Prayer is meant to be used as a simple but substantive way to recognize your sin and desperate need for Jesus Christ to save you. It's also a reminder of the promise that Jesus made, offering salvation to those who ask for forgiveness. Many use the Jesus Prayer as a way to live out 24/7 prayer, saying it throughout the day.

Chapters 22 and 23 provide a mini prayer book for you.

Consider the strengths of ready-made prayers:

- **Ready-made prayers give you solid theological grounding to stand on.** Ready-made prayers can be helpful because they enable you to focus on sound theology, giving you "beef" rather than some low-calorie alternative. Ready-made prayers can point you to God's truth in ways that undisciplined free prayer may not always do.

  However, use good judgment and look for reliable sources for the written prayers you use, as not all ready-made prayers are necessarily sound. In searching the Web, I found several sites that had written prayers of dubious doctrine.

- **Ready-made prayers are good examples from which to learn.** Ready-made prayers show you how to apply the basic ingredients of prayer (adoration, confession, thanksgiving, and supplication) to your prayer life. They allow you to learn by example to improve the quality of your free prayers.

  Ready-made prayers can be especially beneficial for new Christians, teaching them how and what to pray.

- **Ready-made prayers emphasize reverence.** Ready-made prayers also promote a respectful and worshipful attitude when you pray. Given the focus on a personal God, modern-day people can lose reverence for him and end up treating him too casually. Written prayers reinforce a reverent attitude.

Ready-made prayers are not without their weaknesses, including the following:

✔ **Ready-made prayers can put handcuffs on God.** No ready-made prayer is customized exactly for your situation. Consequently, if you're always reading a prayer written by someone else, then you can unintentionally restrict the areas in which you're willing to let God work in your life.

✔ **Ready-made prayers can become canned.** If you've ever had canned green beans, you know how inferior their taste is compared to fresh beans. Written prayers, when you rely on them too much or say them ad nauseam, can similarly become canned and stale. As a result, they can become prayers that you utter with your mouth but have no impact on your heart. Or, as you can find out in Chapter 5, they can get a cotton-candy-like texture: You say the words, but they melt in your mouth and seem to disappear before they go inside you.

✔ **Ready-made prayers can stifle intimacy with God.** Written prayers express well the reverence you should have for God, but at the same time, they can emphasize God's glory and majesty at the expense of intimacy. This is exactly opposite of the point Jesus was trying to make when he gave the Lord's Prayer in his Sermon on the Mount. Jesus startled the people of his day when he gave the Lord's Prayer in a manner that was brief and informal and began with a simple "Our Father" rather than a long, title-filled diatribe. For more on the Lord's Prayer, see Chapter 5.

Christian author and scholar C.S. Lewis expresses it best: "It would be better not to be reverent at all than to have a reverence which denied [intimacy]." Therefore, ready-made prayers have their use, but they should never get in the way of the closeness a Christian should have with a most personal God.

Navigating the High Seas: Combining the Two Types of Prayer

Some camps within the Christian church are entirely pro free prayer, while others are all pro written prayer. However, these groups can learn a lot from each other. Prayer isn't and shouldn't be a zero-sum game like this, in which you pray exclusively in one way or the other.

When you combine free prayer and ready-made prayer, they can offset the other's weaknesses and work together nicely. Think, for example, of a ship sailing across the open seas to a faraway land. The compass guides the ship in the right direction, while the ship's wheel and rudder do the actual steering. Think of Biblical and other written prayers as being that compass to guide your prayers with sound doctrine, but view free prayer as doing the real work of steering the ship. For example, you may want to start your prayer time with a Psalm or written prayer and, after reflecting on it, enter into a time of extended free prayer.

If you use free prayer and written prayer in combination with each other, you can have the best of both worlds. Written prayers can ground you with sound doctrine and reverence for God, while free prayers can give your prayer life the intimacy that God wants to have with each Christian.

Chapter 8

Looking to the Scriptures for Help

• •

• •

"*I'm going to Disney World.*" If you've ever watched the Olympics, the Super Bowl, or the Indy 500, chances are that you've heard that ever-popular phrase uttered by the champion moments after victory. I'm sure the Disney marketing folks pay top dollar for this advertisement for one reason: It works. For causes I can't quite explain, normal folks like you and me are influenced by what celebrities and famous athletes do and what products they use.

When it comes to prayer, you may not be influenced by Michelle Kwan or Michael Jordan, but one group of people merits a special kind of attention: Jesus and the early church leaders. They may not have signed a million-dollar shoe contract, but their perspective on the Bible (the Old Testament at the time) deserves special attention when it comes to your prayer life.

Jesus was the Son of God and perhaps could have been excused for paying a little less attention to the Bible. After all, he has a very close and unique relationship with the Father. Yet, Jesus constantly referenced the Psalms and the prophets like Isaiah throughout his ministry. In fact, one of his last words on the cross referenced Psalm 22. Paul, Peter, and the rest of the early church leaders treated the Bible with the same degree of importance. They knew it backwards and forwards. This knowledge enabled them to grow closer to God and helped equip them in their prayer lives. Questions about what to pray about, how to pray, and whom to pray to are all answered in the Bible.

If Jesus and the apostles believed that knowing the Bible was important to how they lived their life, just think how critical it is for people like you and me! In this chapter, you discover how the Bible can serve as the ultimate prayer strategy guide for you.

By George, he's got it

George Patton, the controversial World War II U.S. General, offers an interesting parallel to consider when it comes to the past. Patton is considered one of the greatest strategists in the history of warfare. His tactics and battle plans that defeated Hitler's army are stuff of legend and are still studied today. Yet, one of the unique qualities of Patton that made him such a brilliant strategist was that he was a student of military history, studying the battles of the ancients to the present day. He was able to look at winning strategies from Greek and Roman wars and apply them to his modern context. Many other leaders would have looked at the past strategies and concluded that, because the Greeks and Romans didn't have machine guns and tanks, they had nothing to offer the modern field general. But Patton saw beyond that superficial difference; he recognized that some military strategies span time and technology and can be applied many years later with the same effectiveness. His success proved it.

Pairing the Ultimate Couple: Bible and Prayer

Bible study is an important component of the life of any Christian who seeks to grow in his or her faith. Yet people tend to treat reading the Bible and praying as two separate activities that are not interrelated. Although Bible study *is* important in its own right, consider integrating it into your prayer life as well. Now explore how to use the Bible as a prayer strategy guide and how to pray as you read through the Bible.

Using the Bible as the always-hip strategy guide

One of the most common objections to reading the Bible today is that it's ancient, behind the times, passé, and obsolete. After all, this is the 21st century, right? How can a book written millenniums ago be relevant to you today?

But if you feel that way, read some of the Psalms. You'd swear that they were written since Y2K, given their relevance in the world today. Jesus' words and Paul's writings are timeless as well, dealing with issues central to people no matter in which era they live.

The Bible should serve as the strategy guide for modern-day Christians; it carries with it universal truths that transcend time, fashion, cultures, nation-states, and technology. It's meant to be used and applied to your life, not treated as an ancient text that's only something studied at Princeton or Oxford. Frankly, those who regard the Bible as irrelevant are naive, as if modern thinking and technology fundamentally somehow changed the human heart.

Praying through the Bible

Reading the Bible is one matter, but knowing how to use the Bible to enhance your prayer life may seem far less intuitive at the start. However, as I introduce in this section, you can pray "through the Bible" by reading and reflecting on a passage and then praying to God about what you've read. Your ultimate goals in praying through the Bible are to

✔ Discover God's truth as you read.

✔ Pray on that truth.

✔ Determine how you can apply that truth to your life.

The following sections offer four ways to pray through the Bible.

Reading and reflecting on a Bible passage

As you read through a passage of the Bible, examine it with an eye on what God teaches you through it and how you can apply it to your life. For example, consider the story of the leper being healed in Matthew 8:1–3:

> *When Jesus came down from the mountain, great multitudes followed him. Behold, a leper came to him and worshiped him, saying, "Lord, if you want to, you can make me clean." Jesus stretched out his hand, and touched him, saying, "I want to. Be made clean."*

As I read this, I think about the faith that the leper had in Jesus. He didn't say, "If you can do it, make me clean." Instead, Jesus' ability was a nonissue to him; rather, the question was only whether Jesus was willing to do so. Therefore, you're challenged to have that same faith as the leper. You then follow that reflection with a prayer of commitment to increase your faith. For example, you might pray something like this:

> *Dear God,*
>
> *The leper in this story shows a simple, childlike faith that I want to emulate in my life. Too often I question or hesitate in my prayers, rather than simply believing in your love and your power. God, forgive me for not trusting as I should. Work in me to strengthen my faith in you. Amen.*

Or consider Jeremiah 34:8–11:

> *The king Zedekiah made a covenant with all the people in Jerusalem pro-claiming liberty to Hebrew slaves. All the princes and all the people who had entered into the covenant obeyed and let them go. But afterwards they changed their minds and forced the slaves to return.*

In reading this passage, I'm struck by the double-mindedness of these people. They made a covenant with God to free their slaves, and then the next moment, they decided that they didn't want to, and they went against their word. I began to look at my life and think about times when I made commit-ments to the Lord in a flood of emotion and then decided to go against my word later. Such a realization brings me to repentance and a commitment to be true to my word in the future.

Employing some gymnastics: Using a Bible passage as a springboard

You can also take a passage from the Bible and use it as a launching pad for praying on your own, tailoring it to your needs at that given point in time. For example, suppose that you're the victim of office politics and backstabbing at your workplace. You can use Psalm 61 (shown in bold in the following bul-leted list) as a starting point as you pray about the situation.

- ✔ **Hear my cry, God. Listen to my prayer**. My job is in jeopardy because of Toni's accusations about the way I handled Frank's dismissal. Lord, you know the truth, please help the truth to be revealed to my boss.

- ✔ **From the end of the earth, I will call to you, when my heart is over-whelmed**. You — not my job, not my home, or my family — are my only true security. You are the only source of hope that I have. I know you'll never abandon me, even if everyone else does.

- ✔ **Lead me to the rock that is higher than I.** Bring me to safety and deliv-erance from this crisis in my life.

- ✔ **For you have been a refuge for me, a strong tower from the enemy.** This promotion has been so important to me, something I've worked six years for, and now it all may be taken away. I don't know what I would do if I didn't have you to turn to, you to cry out to. I know that you're might-ier than all the lies and deceit of this world. Thanks for that assurance!

- ✔ **I will dwell in your tent forever. I will take refuge in the shelter of your wings.** When I am with you, I know I don't have to worry about office politics and jealousy. I know that I can hide out as you protect me from all the forces of evil. I pray that I'll always turn to you, and never seek solace in the temporary securities or escapes around me.

- ✔ **For you, God, have heard my vows. You have given me the heritage of those who fear your name.** When I think about the crisis I'm facing at the moment, it seems so important to me. In fact, I can't imagine anything more significant. And yet, as I read this Psalm, I realize that David faced a situation that was "the world" to him as well. His crisis of the day no longer matters today. And I realize that this crisis of mine will pass as well. And yet, presiding over all these crises, there is you. You are the same today as you were in David's time. Praise you, Lord!

✔ **You will prolong the king's life; His years shall be for generations. He shall be enthroned in God's presence forever. Appoint your loving kindness and truth, that they may preserve him.** Just as you did with David, protect me and shower me with your love and truth, so that they may act as a preservative for me, making me withstand the hardships of today.

✔ **So I will sing praise to your name forever, that I may fulfill my vows daily.** I will sing your praises and give glory to you regardless of what happens in this situation.

Leading by reading aloud or listening to a Bible passage

On occasion, you may find it helpful to listen to the words of a Bible passage with your ears instead of just studying it with your eyes. Doing so may give you a new insight into the verse or chapter you're reading. To do so, read the passage out loud yourself or listen to an audio Bible. Many audiobook presentations of the Bible are available at your local bookstore. If you're a writer type, read Chapter 9 to discover how to incorporate journaling into your prayer. Use these resources to listen to a Psalm or other Bible passage as a way to prepare your heart for prayer.

Audio Bibles you can listen to for free are available as streaming audio over the Web. The best free audio Bible I've encountered on the Web is at the Bible Gateway site (http://bible.gospelcom.net). The narrator has a riveting voice that reminds me of actor Sidney Poitier, and the site offers a great supplement to normal reading.

The water's fine: Diving deeper

A final way to pray through the Bible is to dive into the details and study it. Because you're removed from the culture and times in which it was written, you can easily miss the meaning, subtleties, and underlying assumptions of a passage. Diving into the background and context of a passage may reveal new meaning to you.

Many excellent study Bibles are available today that provide explanatory and life application notes for you within the pages of the Bible itself. Bible commentaries can be another great resource, although most tend to be more academic in nature than application oriented. The World Wide Study Bible (www.ccel.org/wwsb) provides access to numerous Bible translations and commentaries, making it an exceptional, no-cost study tool.

Scribes of the Psalms

Most people think the Psalms were written by King David, but that is only partially true. Nearly half are, in fact, credited to David, but several other authors contributed as well, the most famous of whom are Moses (one Psalm) and Solomon (two). Fifty-one Psalms are anonymous.

Psalms: The Heart of Prayer

The Book of Psalms is the most unique book in the Bible. Whereas most books provide historical narrative, prophetic teaching, or doctrinal prose, Psalms is a collection of 150 songs and prayers and nothing else. Each Psalm expresses the full range of emotions that any human goes through during the course of a lifetime: joy, sorrow, desperation, anger, vengeance, praise, peace, and thankfulness.

What's striking about the Psalms is that they're real, brutally honest outpourings of emotion along the roller coasters of life. When times are good, Psalms speak out in great thanksgiving and celebration, but when life is bad, the emotions expressed are more candid than what you hear on *Oprah*. Because of this, all of us, no matter where we are in life, can relate to the Psalms. Psalms truly expresses the *heart of prayer*.

The Book of Psalms was separated into five minibooks a long time ago: Book 1 (Chapters 1–41), Book 2 (Chapters 42–72), Book 3 (Chapters 73–89), Book 4 (Chapters 90–106), and Book 5 (Chapters 107–150). But these aren't assembled chronologically or even topically, so a much more practical way to think of the Psalms is to categorize them by topic.

You can group the Psalms into six major categories:

- **Psalms of praise and worship:** Many of the Psalms focus on praising God. As I discuss in Chapter 6, I don't think there is a better source to turn to than these Psalms to find out what adoration and worship mean. Examples are Psalms 19, 33, 103, and 109.

- **Psalms of confession:** A second set of Psalms contrasts the holiness of God with the sinfulness of man and cries out for mercy to God for his forgiveness. Examples are Psalms 6, 32, 38, 51, and 143.

✔ **Psalms of anguish and lament.** Many Psalms are written as a cry to the Lord by an individual or group for help in a crisis situation. Some of these Psalms address God boldly and even harshly because the writer perceives that God is abandoning them. However, these Psalms usually end with a confidence that God will intervene to deliver and save. Examples include Psalms 13 (individual) and 44 and 74 (communal).

✔ **Psalms of history:** Another set of Psalms focuses on incidents and events from Israelite history. Examples include 14, 44, 46, 47, 48, and 105.

Two nine-syllable terms that will amaze your friends

You can get more out of reading the Psalms when you better understand the style in which they were composed. When you think of a poem written today, you probably think of the phrases arranged in a rhyming pattern ("Roses are red, violets are blue, sugar is sweet, and so are you"). In contrast, Hebrew poetry doesn't focus on rhyming, but on the rhythm of phrases. Scholars use a fancy-shmancy term called *parallelism* to describe this rhythmic arrangement of phrases. There are several types of parallelism, but two major structures are worth exploring.

Synonymous parallelism occurs when a thought is given and then repeated in slightly different terminology. For example, in Psalm 40:11:

Don't withhold your tender mercies from me, Lord.
Let your loving kindness and your truth continually preserve me.

Both of these verses join together as a *couplet,* with the second part of the verse intensifying the first and emphasizing a cry to God to keep his grace and kindness on the author. In addition, different synonyms may be used to refer to the same person or event. Psalm 119:105 provides an example:

Your word is a lamp to my feet
And a light for my path.

The word of God is described both as a "lamp" and a "light."

Antithetical parallelism occurs when the second line contrasts the first line of the couplet. Psalm 7:9 illustrates this:

Oh let the wickedness of the wicked come to an end,
But establish the righteous;

This couplet contrasts the ending of the wicked with the establishment of the righteous.

Knowing the meaning behind these nine-syllable terms will not only make you the life of any party but will also help you develop a richer appreciation for the Psalms.

- ✔ **Psalms of anger:** As you read through the book, I suspect several of the Psalms will seem out of place in the Bible. Instead of dealing with love and peace, they sound like something you'd hear in a *Terminator* movie. An *imprecatory Psalm* is one that deals with the defeat or destruction of an enemy. (See the sidebar "Those downright nasty Psalms," elsewhere in this chapter.) Examples include Psalms 35, 37, 69, 109, and 137.

- ✔ **Messianic Psalms:** Christians believe that several Psalms make prophetic references to the coming of Jesus Christ, hundreds of years before he was born. These Psalms focus on a future ideal ruler who will defeat the enemies of Israel and stand up for righteousness and justice. Some examples are Psalms 16, 22, 45, 69, and 110.

Gospels: The Soul of Prayer

The Gospels are the first four books of the New Testament (Matthew, Mark, Luke, and John) and are separate accounts of the life and ministry of Jesus Christ. Because the Gospels are primarily narratives as opposed to the poetic Psalms, you may find it harder at first to incorporate them into your prayers.

Keep the following tips in mind as you read through the Gospels:

- ✔ **Reflect on the red.** Some Bibles use red lettering for the words Jesus spoke. If your Bible does this, read through these passages carefully and allow yourself to reflect on them in your prayers. Because Jesus is the ultimate authority, any words he says have special importance. Pay special attention to the following passages:

    - Sermon on the Mount (Matthew 5–7)
    - Garden of Gethsemane (Matthew 26:36–45)
    - The Great Commission (Matthew 28:19–20)
    - Rich Young Ruler (Matthew 19:16–26)
    - Jesus washes his disciples' feet (John 13:1–17)
    - The Last Supper (Luke 22:14–30)
    - Jesus on the cross (Luke 23:32–43)
    - Jesus as the true bread (John 6:22–40)
    - Jesus as the light of the world (John 8:12–19)
    - Jesus as the Good Shepherd (John 10:1–18)
    - Jesus is the one way to the Father (John 14:1–14)
    - Jesus as the vine (John 15:1–17)
    - Jesus claims to be God's son (John 5:19–30)
    - Jesus talks about his future return to earth (Matthew 24:26–51)
    - Jesus talks about the final judgment (Matthew 25:31–46)

Those downright nasty Psalms

When I think of the Psalms, I think first of the beauty and splendor of ones like Psalm 91:1–2:

He who dwells in the secret place of the Most High

Will rest in the shadow of the Almighty.

I will say of the Lord, "He is my refuge and my fortress;

My God, in whom I trust."

Although many Psalms are feel-good, comforting verses, my eyes about pop out as I turn the page. Some of the Psalms aren't touchy-feely at all; instead, they can be downright nasty. For example, Psalm 69:22–25 details what the author is asking God to do to his enemies:

Let their table before them become a snare.

May it become a retribution and a trap.

Let their eyes be darkened, so that they can't see.

Let their backs be continually bent.

Pour out your indignation on them.

Let the fierceness of your anger overtake them.

Let their habitation be desolate.

Let no one dwell in their tents.

The expressions of hatred that you can find in some Psalms are certainly confusing, given that Christianity is built on grace and forgiveness. What's more, Jesus called his followers to love their enemies, not spite them. Therefore, when you read these imprecatory Psalms, keep the following points in mind:

✔ First, the authors are simply being honest. They aren't trying to be holier than thou and sanitize or whitewash anything. Instead, they're showing the raw, heartfelt emotions that they have toward their enemies. When you get really angry with someone, you may feel those same kinds of emotions running through you as well. You may not be justified in feeling that way, but vengeance can be a natural emotion. The important point is that, even when you're angry, these Psalms remind you to bring that anger to God and let him deal with the solution. Don't try and take the matter into your own hands. Instead, give it to the Lord.

✔ Second, the world is different now than when these Psalms were written. Because the political nation of Israel was the people of God, enemies of Israel were, by definition, enemies of God. Therefore, people like David had a rationale for asking God to destroy their enemies, because the success of the enemies would foil God's plan on earth. However, all that changed when Jesus Christ came; the Christian church

(continued)

(continued)

> became the people of God, as opposed to a political nation of Israel. In addition, Jesus taught in his Sermon on the Mount that his followers should love and pray for their human enemies, not hate them. Paul followed up when he taught that the real enemies for Christians aren't other people but are chiefly your sinful nature and spiritual enemies (in other words, the devil).

✔ **Pick up lessons from the parables.** Jesus used stories called *parables* to teach important truths to people of all backgrounds and educational levels. The parables may appear simple at first, but packed away inside of them are important words of truth to model your life after. Therefore, when you read the Gospels and come across a parable, do the following: Read through it once and go back and pick up what the Lord is trying to teach you through it. Then say a prayer of commitment about how you can apply it to your life. Parables of special note include the following:

- Prodigal son (Luke 15)

- Four soils (Matthew 13:1–23)

- Unforgiving debtor (Matthew 18:21–35)

- Workers paid equally (Matthew 20:1–16)

- Rich man and beggar (Luke 16:19–31)

- Persistent widow (Luke 18:1–8)

- The two men who prayed (Luke 18:9–14)

✔ **Step into the stories.** The last major component of the Gospels is real-life stories that talk about what Jesus did and the people he encountered during his ministry. When you come across a story, you may find it helpful to role-play by putting yourself into the story and imagining what it would have been like if you had been there. Sometimes this role-playing can be a great way to lead into prayer.

As you read and study the Gospels with an eye on your prayer life, you discover that the Gospels express the soul of prayer. Jesus is the soul of Christianity, the whole reason for the faith. By praying the Gospels, you get to know him.

As you read the Gospels or any other part of the Bible, consider the context of the passage you're reading. Some of the worst teachings in the church occur when people take verses out of context. For example, "ask and you shall receive" is a statement made by Jesus. Without understanding the context in which Jesus said it, you might expect a Porsche to appear in your garage any day now. (See Chapter 17 for an example of how to dive into the context of this passage.)

Epistles: The Mind of Prayer

Jesus often painted broad strokes as to how Christians should live out their lives on earth. He left Paul and the other apostles responsible to fill in the practical details of the Christian life in the various letters they sent to churches. These letters (often called *epistles*) form much of the New Testament.

When you study the prayers in these books, you discover that the epistles express what you can call *the mind of prayer,* because they deal with so many practical details of what your Christian life should be about. Don't focus on only the teachings in the epistles; also look at the hidden prayers inside them.

The following prayers in the epistles serve as great tools to understanding what to pray about for those around you and for yourself:

- 2 Thessalonians 1:1–12
- 1 Thessalonians 3:9–13
- Colossians 1:9–14
- Philippians 1:9–11
- Ephesians 1:15–23
- Ephesians 3:14–21
- Romans 15:30–33
- Romans 1:8–10
- Philemon 4–7

The Bible's Ten Best Prayers

Trying to pick out the ten best prayers in all the Bible is something like trying to pick the ten best-looking apples from a fifty-acre orchard; you'll easily be able to find ten perfect apples, but who is to say which are *the* ten best?

Having said that, here are my candidates for the ten best prayers in the Bible. Some are on the list because they're examples of the spirit in which you should pray. Others appear because they express an important truth about prayer. And still others make the cut because they define what prayer is all about. (Three Psalms — 23, 51, and 91 — deserve special merit. I would have included some or all of them in this list but decided against that because I discuss each one elsewhere, either in Chapter 22 or 23.) In reverse order, here are the ten best prayers:

Samuel's Prayer of Listening

Samuel was one of the great Old Testament prophets and the prophet who anointed David as King of Israel. Early on in Samuel's life, God spoke to him one particular night, and his response is noteworthy. 1 Samuel 3:10 says:

> God called . . . , "Samuel, Samuel."
> Then Samuel said, "Speak; for your servant is listening."

Samuel's prayer was nothing profound or complicated, but remarkably direct and to the point. His simplicity is refreshing to a world in which people so often think that they need a ten-point plan in order to hear God.

Psalm 95

There are so many outstanding praise and worship Psalms that singling out just one becomes hard. However, I don't think any other Psalm packs as much into it as does Psalm 95:1–7:

> Oh come, let's sing to the Lord.
> > Let's shout aloud to the rock of our salvation!
> Let's come before his presence with thanksgiving.
> > Let's extol him with songs!
> For the Lord is a great God,
> > A great King above all gods.
> In his hand are the deep places of the earth
> > The heights of the mountains are also his.
> The sea is his, and he made it.
> > His hands formed the dry land.
> Oh come, let's worship and bow down.
> > Let's kneel before the Lord, our Maker,
> For he is our God.
> > We are the people of his pasture,
> > And the sheep in his care.

Within just a few verses, this prayer expresses God's qualities, stressing his preeminence, power over all creation, and the protection and guidance that he continually provides.

Centurion's Prayer of Faith

In Matthew 8:8–9, a Roman *centurion* (military leader) demonstrates the certainty of what faith and trust in God is:

> *The centurion answered, "Lord, I'm not worthy for you to come under my roof. Just say the word, and my servant will be healed. For I am also a man under authority, having under myself soldiers. I tell this one, 'Go,' and he goes; and tell another, 'Come,' and he comes; and tell my servant, 'Do this,' and he does it."*

Technically, this entry is not a prayer per se, but it's close enough because it is a conversation with Jesus. Jesus was amazed at the showing of faith of the centurion and even went so far as to say that he hadn't found anyone who had greater faith in all the land. The centurion represents the type of faith that you and I should emulate in prayer.

Paul's Prayer for the Colossians

Paul begins his letter to the Colossians by discussing the prayer that he continually offers on their behalf. Colossians 1:9–12 says:

> *We . . . don't cease praying and making requests for you, that you may be filled with the knowledge of his will in all spiritual wisdom and understanding, that you may walk worthily of the Lord, to please him in all respects, bearing fruit in every good work, and increasing in the knowledge of God; strengthened with all power, according to the might of his glory, for all endurance and perseverance with joy; giving thanks to the Father, who made us fit to be partakers of the inheritance of the saints in light.*

The denseness of this passage can make it hard to follow, but after you unpack it, you can see that Paul provides an excellent model for how to pray for others' spiritual growth. Specifically, pray that others will

- ✔ Be filled with an understanding of God's will.
- ✔ Live a life worthy of a Christian.
- ✔ Have success in the work they do for God.
- ✔ Become more knowledgeable about God.
- ✔ Become empowered by God so that they have endurance and patience.

Isaiah's Simple Obedience

Isaiah is usually considered the greatest Old Testament prophet. But his ministry started with but a simple one-line prayer. When God asked him whom he should send to be a prophet, instead of hesitating or recommending someone else, he said (in Isaiah 6:8):

> *Here I am. Send me!*

I want that simple obedience when the Lord calls me to do something for him.

Paul's Prayer to the Ephesians

All too often, when Christians pray for each other, the prayers focus on physical or emotional needs and fail to dive into the spiritual realm. In Ephesians, Paul starts out his letter talking about his prayer for them. And in doing so, he provides a great model for how you and I should approach intercessory prayer. Ephesians 1:15–23 says:

> *For this cause I also, having heard of the faith in the Lord Jesus which is among you, and the love which you have toward all the saints, don't cease to give thanks for you, making mention of you in my prayers, that the God of our Lord Jesus Christ, the Father of glory, may give to you a spirit of wisdom and revelation in the knowledge of him; having the eyes of your hearts enlightened, that you may know what is the hope of his calling, and what are the riches of the glory of his inheritance in the saints, and what is the exceeding greatness of his power toward us who believe, according to that working of the strength of his might which he worked in Christ.*

Paul asks God to give a spirit of wisdom and knowledge to the Ephesians and make their hearts sensitive to the Lord's hope and promises for all Christians.

Jesus' Prayer for Unity

Perhaps the best prayer for unity among the Christian church is Jesus' prayer in John 17. He spoke this in the upper room on the night he was to be arrested:

> *Not for [my disciples] only do I pray, but for those also who believe in me through their word, that they may all be one; even as you, Father, are in me, and I in you, that they also may be one in us; that the world may believe that you sent me. The glory which you have given me, I have given to them; that they may be one, even as we are one; I in them, and you in me, that*

they may be perfected into one; that the world may know that you sent me, and loved them, even as you loved me. Father, I desire that they also whom you have given me be with me where I am, that they may see my glory, which you have given me, for you loved me before the foundation of the world. Righteous Father, the world hasn't known you, but I knew you; and these knew that you sent me. I made known to them your name, and will make it known; that the love with which you loved me may be in them, and I in them.

Jehoshaphat's Prayer of Desperation

King Jehoshaphat of Israel faced a major battle against an enemy far more powerful. On the eve of the battle that looked like certain disaster, he prayed to God, completely giving God the situation and acknowledging that his soldiers could not save themselves. In remarkable candor, the prayer (in 2 Chronicles 20:12) ends with:

For we have no might against this great company that comes against us. We do not know what to do, but our eyes are on you.

I love Jehoshaphat's honesty in this prayer. He's not trying to come up with a Plan B or an escape plan; instead, he just lays out the problem before the Lord. In doing so, he provides a perfect model for you and me when facing troubles and hardship.

Jesus' Prayer of Surrender

Early in his ministry, Jesus taught his followers to pray "Your will be done" when he gave them the Lord's Prayer. On the last night of his earthly ministry, he found himself praying this same prayer as he prepared himself for his pending crucifixion. While in the Garden of Gethsemane, Matthew 26:39 describes how Jesus prayed:

My Father, if it is possible, let this cup pass away from me; nevertheless, not what I will, but what you will.

In Gethsemane, Jesus practiced what he preached, even though surrendering to his Father would result in his crucifixion and, far worse, paying the penalty for the sins of the world. This prayer is a vivid reminder that what Jesus voluntarily did was the last thing in the world he wanted to do. He was obedient, however, because it was the will of the Father. (See Chapter 16 for more on praying according to God's will.)

The Lord's Prayer

Chapter 5 is already devoted totally to the Lord's Prayer, but no list of best prayers in the Bible is complete without the famous prayer that Jesus gave to his followers. The Lord's Prayer is a model or a blueprint of what any Christian prayer should be, containing all the essentials. Matthew 6:9–13 says:

Our Father in heaven, hallowed is your name.
Let your Kingdom come.
Let your will be done,
on earth as in heaven.
Give us today our daily bread.
Forgive us our debts, as we also forgive our debtors.
Bring us not into temptation, but deliver us from the evil one.
For yours is the Kingdom, the power, and the glory forever.
Amen.

Chapter 9

Journaling the Write Stuff

· ·

· ·

You're more likely these days to get a phone call rather than a handwritten letter from a friend on the other side of the country. It's easy to see why: Dialing a handful of digits is more convenient in a busy life than sitting down and scribing a letter. But when you need to communicate deep thoughts or articulate a heartfelt message, sometimes there is no substitute for an old-fashioned letter.

Prayer too is almost always done orally, but it doesn't have to be. In fact, you may find that writing down your prayers enables you to communicate with God at a deeper, more intimate level than you can with spoken prayer. This discipline, commonly known as *journaling,* is a way to enrich your prayer life and provide a rich legacy of your Christian walk to look back on for the rest of your life.

In this chapter, you discover what prayer journaling is and why it can be so effective. You also get practical tips on how to get started.

Journaling: Don't Let Hand Cramps Stop You

As an author, I like to put ideas down on paper and then slowly, methodically transform a choppy chunk of text into a well-crafted paragraph. Yet, I'm so used to wordsmithing with my computer that I frankly don't know what I'd do if I had been born a century ago and had only a pen or manual typewriter at my disposal. Indeed, computers have made the act of writing correspondence a breeze, so much so that most people don't write much by hand anymore these days. I write quick notes all the time by hand, but whenever I try to write out a longer letter, my hand starts to cramp after the fourth sentence!

Similarly, journaling can be a hard, even painful, activity when you start out, either physically (because your hand starts cramping) or mentally (because of the self-discipline you need to sit down and write out your prayers).

The act of writing is a chore to some people, so it can become a huge barrier to journaling. People who already write letters or keep diaries have a much easier time getting started than people who rarely write. Yet, in spite of any barriers you may encounter when starting out, here are ten reasons why journaling is worth your while:

- ✔ It enables you to articulate thoughts that you may gloss over in oral prayers.
- ✔ It provides a historical record to remind you of how God has worked in your life.
- ✔ It helps you look back at your spiritual journey.
- ✔ It can prevent your mind from wandering in your prayers.
- ✔ It uproots the "buried stuff."
- ✔ It helps you sort through competing thoughts.
- ✔ It develops your worship life.
- ✔ It provides a measuring rod for your consistency.
- ✔ It helps you to apply the Bible to your life.
- ✔ It forces self-discipline.

Writing your mind

Writing words down on paper forces you to concentrate on the meaning and significance of words that can otherwise become "lip service" for you as you speak them. Try, for example, writing down the *Doxology*, a traditional Christian worship chorus:

> *Praise God from whom all blessings flow*
> *Praise Him, all creatures here below*
> *Praise Him above, ye heavenly host*
> *Praise Father, Son, and Holy Ghost*
> *Amen.*

I had sung those words in church since I was a child, but because of that familiarity, the words themselves had lost their meaning for me. But the process of writing these words down helped me understand the true significance of that traditional prayer of praise.

Journaling is more than just reading written prayers. Just like in school, my teacher made me write my spelling words out several times instead of just reading them over. Something about writing forces your brain to concentrate on the material. Similarly, the process of actually writing a prayer is more significant than reading a written prayer that someone else wrote.

Seeing how God works in your life

Everyone does some amount of financial record keeping. Even I, someone who would rather watch paint dry than take the time to balance my checkbook, still know that I need to keep certain records, especially when tax time comes along each year.

These records, however, are important for only a temporary period of time. Just how important is a 15-year-old check ledger to you today? Big whoop! Yet, if people maintain a historical record for matters of such temporary importance, why do so many people shy away from chronicling issues that are eternally important?

One of the great lessons in reading the saga of the Israelites in the Old Testament is the importance of remembering what God has done in your life. Over and over again, God commands the Israelites to simply remember. When you remember, you're far more likely to be grateful for what God has done in the past and confident about God's continued involvement in your life going forward. But when you don't, you tend to live in the continual moment, forgetting what God has done in the past. (See Chapter 18 for more on the importance of remembrance in your Christian life.)

The Hebrew term for *remember* means more than just "call to mind." Instead, it means "relive" or "experience again" in a way that you feel as though you are part of the events being remembered. For example, when Christians remember Christ's death in the Lord's Supper (Communion), this remembrance is more than just thinking about Jesus; it's being a part of the transforming power of the event. Journaling can help you "reexperience" God's presence in the events of your life.

You may be able to remember a specific time or two in your life when God has worked in your life without writing it down. But, even in major events, you forget the tiny details and the nuances of what really happened. What's more, if you don't document them, you miss the day-to-day little ways that God provided. They may seem like nothing when taken individually, but when you back up and see God working over time, then his role in your life can become quite powerful and unmistakable.

The discipline of journaling provides a natural method of recording how God is working in your life at the time a certain event happens. When you go through a difficult time sometime down the road, you can return to your journal and find strength from your words. Journaling can therefore have the side effect of being one of the best practical ways you can learn to trust God more in your life.

Documenting your spiritual journey

In addition to helping you look back at God's provision, journaling documents your spiritual journey and how you've matured in your Christian life over time.

Recently, my wife and I were cleaning out the attic and came across an old high school yearbook from our school days. We were friends even then, so I made the obligatory entry into her yearbook. Yet, when I read that same writing today, I can't believe that I actually wrote the silly stuff that I did. Only by reading this do I realize how far I've come from that goofy junior in high school.

Similarly, keeping a prayer journal over the years becomes a great way to see where you've come from spiritually. You'll be surprised at the issues that you struggled with. They may seem trivial now, yet at the time, they were significantly important. Without a journal, you can't really chronicle where you've come from spiritually.

Focusing on the task at hand

Mind wandering and other mental distractions can wreck your prayer life, as I talk about in Chapter 12. If you struggle to keep mentally focused and engaged in your prayers, journaling can be one of the most effective weapons to combat this problem. When you write, your mind forces you to concentrate in a way that you don't have to when you quickly say something aloud. Journaling breeds concentration on what you're praying about.

Revealing your subconsciousness

The task of writing your prayers helps bring to the surface issues that you've buried in the back recesses of your mind. When you pray aloud, you're more likely to stay at the surface. But over time, journaling forces you to dig down deeper and reveal what you're really thinking.

Journaling usually promotes originality, so you force yourself to deal with new issues in prayer instead of writing the same prayers day after day.

Organizing your mind

When you're making a major decision in life, journaling can become an effective way to put all the ideas in black and white and then reflect on the decision in a new light, instead of trying to juggle all the pros and cons in your mind. On paper, you may find it easier to make sense of it all and see God's will.

Worshiping on paper

Chapter 6 discusses the importance of worship and praise in your prayers. Journaling serves as an excellent way to develop this part of your prayer life. When you write down prayers of praise, you'll find it easier to consider or ponder much more who God is and who you are in relation to him. Consequently, your requests to him begin to pale in comparison to the power you feel as a child of the Creator of the universe. In so doing, journaling can help balance out your prayer life, especially if your spoken prayers focus more on requests.

Measuring your consistency

The regularity of your spoken prayers on a day-in, day-out basis are often hard to detect. Yes, you may keep an informal ledger in your head, but you can usually remember only a few days' worth of those mental entries. So, even as recently as last week, determining how disciplined you actually were in your prayer life can become hard, as one day tends to blend into the next. With journaling, you can't rationalize your consistency; it's available for you to see in black and white.

Customizing the Bible

Journaling is a great way to apply your daily Bible reading to your life. To illustrate, imagine this story line:

1. I'm reading Psalm 105 and decide to integrate it into my journaling. I might write down the first phrase:

   O give thanks to the Lord.

2. After reading the initial verse, I can reflect on what I have to give thanks to the Lord for today.

3. I list the things that I'm thankful for:

   Thanks for the safe trip I had today. Thanks for the opportunity to meet my friends at Mount Vernon. I thank you for the peace I had during the flight, and I thank you for your constant promise to take care of me.

4. I read the next phrase:

   Make his doings known among the peoples.

5. I write to the Lord of his challenge to me to share his grace and goodness to others, and I mention the people he has placed in my heart as those with whom I should share his good news:

   Give me the strength and opportunity to share your good news with George and Martha, who are really looking for something to give them meaning in life.

6. I then read:

   Sing to him, sing praises to him!

7. I write in my journal:

   In my heart, O God, I sing praises to you. For you're so wonderful. You are holy, and your name is wonderful.

Journaling helps me transform verses that I might ordinarily skim over and enables me to apply them to my life.

The Book of Psalms is a particularly good source for journaling the Bible. You'll find yourself focusing in on different parts of a psalm as you reread and journal it over successive times in your life.

Sucking in that spiritual gut: Self-discipline

In the midst of a busy schedule, your dedicated prayer time can become compressed, even without your realizing it. Because you can undertake other activities, such as jogging or commuting, when you pray orally, the other activity can begin to become the focus of the prayer time if you're not careful. However, because journaling is a more deliberate activity that demands your full attention, it forces you to slow down and focus on being alone with God.

Getting Past the Cool New Notebook: Journal Content and Style

Perhaps after reading all the reasons why you should journal, you rushed out and purchased the finest leather-covered journal money could buy. Or perhaps you took the economical route and discovered one last notebook in the house the kids hadn't yet scribbled in. Once you have the notebook, it's time to get started.

Variety is the pepper on your paper

Most journaling includes some variety of the following:

✔ Your own written prayers, consisting of one or more of the following: praise, confession, intercessory prayer, and petitionary prayer

✔ Entries about what's significant about that day (big family issues or a national crisis, for example) and a reflection on those issues to the Lord

✔ Key verses if you read the Bible in conjunction with your journaling

✔ Favorite quotes from other books, such as *My Utmost For His Highest* by Oswald Chambers

✔ Prayer request and answer list (see the section "More than Just Bean Counting," later in this chapter)

You're styling

After you make the decision to write, the next step is to figure out the style of journaling that suits your personality. You can choose from three common styles of journaling. Select the one that most suits your personality or use a mixture:

✔ **Stream of consciousness:** The most traditional method is what I term "stream of consciousness" journaling. If you use this method, you go with the flow, writing as you feel inspired, but with no set or enforced structure or length. Some days you may focus entirely on praise and worship, and other days you focus entirely on a pressing need or decision you must make. At other times, you maintain a balance between praise and requests. Some days you may write a paragraph, while on other days you may scribe several pages.

✔ **Loosely structured:** A second alternative is to keep some flexibility but divide your written prayers into four categories: adoration, confession, thanksgiving, and supplication (see Chapter 6). In other words, each journal entry has four sections. Adding this structure can help ensure that you cover each of these critical parts of prayer and don't neglect any of them.

✔ **Highly structured:** A third alternative and one that may be easier for a novice journaler is to have a structured form to fill out for each page. Instead of staring at a blank sheet of paper wondering what you should write about, you have a form that provides specifics for you to focus on. This type of form is especially helpful when you're not sure what to write about. See the ready-made journal entry in Figure 9-1 for a sample format. (You can read more about prayer logs in the section "More than Just Bean Counting," later in this chapter. There you can see an example of an entry.)

Choosing Between a Pen or a PC

Everything I've ever read about journaling treats it as a handwritten exercise. Yet, because technology infiltrates every aspect of your life, why not keep a high-tech journal as well? Explore the ways in which you can write down your prayers, depending on whether you consider yourself "old school" or "new school."

✔ **Pen and paper:** The traditional method of journaling is the low-tech but reliable pen-and-paper way. To use this method, you need to get a blank writing journal or a standard spiral-bound school notebook. Whether it's cheap or expensive is your choice, but I recommend getting something spiral bound that you can open up flat for easier writing.

When you complete a journal, label the outside with the start and end dates to make storing and retrieving them easier. (My wife says that her favorite part of finishing up a journal is picking out a new one!)

✔ **Digital journaling:** You may be thinking, "Aren't a pen and paper so 20th century?" I mean, who actually uses paper anymore unless, of course, you need to print something out on your laser jet printer? If that's your attitude, you're obviously truly hip and should try digital journaling. Use your word processor on your computer to serve as your virtual pen and paper. Digital journaling gives you the flexibility of storing your journal electronically as a series of files (on disk or in the computer's hard drive) and enables you to print journals later if desired.

Journal Entry

Date:

1. Today's Prayer Requests

Write out prayer requests that you have and then come back and fill in the answer column later when the Lord has provided an answer for that situation.

Date/Request	*Date/Answer*

2. Bible Application

Briefly write out the specific lessons you learned from reading the Bible and how you can apply them to your life.

3. Paragraph Prayer

Write out a single paragraph prayer that praises or offers thanksgiving to God based on something that happened yesterday in your life.

If you digital journal, regularly back up your journal files or even regularly print them out in the event of a computer crash or virus.

I personally prefer writing on the computer to handwriting. My hands don't hurt that way, and I also can articulate and revise my thoughts easier than when writing by hand.

More than Just Bean Counting

In addition to writing your prayers, the practice of keeping a written record of your prayer needs can be another great tool for your prayer life. You may choose to keep a written account through a prayer log or prayer cards.

> ✔ **Prayer log:** A *prayer log* consists of a simple two-column table in a notebook with a request and an answer column. It's simple to use: Just write down a request along with the date and then use it as your prayer list. When the prayer request is answered, enter how it was answered and the date. Table 9-1 shows a sample of what a prayer log looks like.

Table 9-1	Sample Prayer Log
Request	*Answer*
1/2/03 — Help Janice find a new job.	3/15/03 — Janice found one! She's now a field goal kicker for the Green Bay Packers.
1/2/03 — Mom's arthritis, making it hard to move around.	
1/2/03 — Help Dread Pirate Roberts as he seeks to pursue a more Godly career.	3/17/03 — He's been accepted as a missionary by the mission board. Leaves for Gildor next month.
1/2/03 — Stress at work. Praying for peace in all situations.	
1/3/03 — Pastor's finger stuck in tea kettle	1/5/03 — He was finally able to get it out!
1/3/03 — Help Jordan do the best he can on his quantum physics test.	1/7/03 — He got an A!

If you're unsure whether you can do a full journal, consider starting off by simply logging your prayer requests. This discipline can be a good launching pad for doing more journaling. Even if not, a prayer log is a great asset to your prayer life.

✔ **Prayer cards:** Prayer cards are another technique to use to keep track of prayer requests. A prayer card is an ordinary 3-x-5-inch or 4-x-6-inch index card that you use to write down a prayer request and date on one side and the answer on the other. The advantage of prayer cards is that you can keep the active cards handy in an index card holder. After they're answered, you can keep them in a separate archive holder or section to refer to in the future.

Keep out!

When you write your prayers down, you may put some of your innermost, private thoughts and secrets down on paper. You should feel free to share your thoughts in your journal as you feel moved by the Lord, but at the same time, be careful to keep your journals in a private place.

If you keep your journal on your computer, most word processing software, such as Microsoft Word, has password support. That feature enables you to create a digital journal without fear that someone else will read it without your consent.

If you're married, the issue of privacy can be a sensitive one. Some couples freely allow their spouses to read their journals, while others believe that a prayer journal is between God and the writer alone. As for me, I respect my wife's privacy and won't read it unsolicited, but occasionally she invites me to read a passage or section.

Chapter 10

Thinking Fast

*C*asablanca is my favorite film of all time, so much so that when my family recently got a new puppy, we named her Casablanca (or Cassie, for short). And though I've seen the classic movie 40 or 50 times, I still get more out of the story with each successive viewing. *Casablanca* blends together an intricate wartime plot, larger-than-life characters, a tragic love triangle, wry humor, patriotism, and moral dilemma, the result of which is greater than the sum of its parts — cinema at its best.

Texture is the word I like to use to describe the quality that separates the great films and novels from the rest of the pack. Whether on screen or on the page, stories with texture offer tremendous depth to the characters that are interwoven in a multifaceted story line.

I think texture is also a good word to describe what *fasting*, the practice of refraining from food for a period of time, can bring to your prayer life. As you discover in this chapter, fasting can add greater depth to your prayers and give you a deeper intimacy with God. By adding fasting as a part of your prayer life, you can surpass ordinary prayers in extraordinary ways.

Fasting isn't a replacement for your normal prayers; it's an extension of your regular prayer life.

Why Fast? It Only Makes Me Hungry

Fasting isn't a complicated business. When you fast, don't eat. You stay away from all food or refrain from specific types of food for a set amount of time. (Refraining from all food makes you the hungriest.) The duration of the fast may be a solo meal, one day, a week, or, in some cases, even longer.

Fasting from food can be done for a variety of purposes, either physical or spiritual. So abstaining from food alone doesn't constitute a Christian fast. Instead, a Christian fast is accompanied by a special focus on prayer during the fast, often substituting the time you'd spend eating with prayer instead.

In many Christian churches today, fasting has become a lost discipline, one that is rarely, if ever, discussed and practiced. Yet, in spite of its decreased emphasis, there are a host of reasons to fast:

- **Fasting has always been considered standard operating procedure for Christians.** Fasting has been a common practice by God's faithful throughout history. The Old Testament includes a multitude of examples of the Israelites fasting when seeking the Lord's blessing or direction. The New Testament records that Jesus himself fasted, as did leaders of the early Christian church.

   Jesus didn't talk too much about fasting during his ministry, but the one time when he provided specific instructions on fasting, in Matthew 6, he started by saying "when you fast," not "if you fast." So it seems logical to conclude that Jesus expected his followers to incorporate fasting into their lives.

   Although Jesus assumes that his followers will fast, he *never* instructs people on the frequency or duration of fasts. Some Christians believe that he left those specifics up to the Church to decide, while others believe he left it up to individuals as prompted by the Holy Spirit.

- **Fasting provides self-discipline in an undisciplined age.** You and I live in an age that despises discipline. I've never once seen a TV commercial with a slogan like one of these:

   - Buy this TV later, after you actually have the cash.

   - Eat just one of our chips, so you can have some tomorrow.

   - Do you really need a new car? Your old one still works fine.

   - Friends don't let friends drink. Period.

   Fasting offers a way to impose self-control in your life; it gives you a "splash in the face" to awaken you to the need for the personal strength of will that you need to grow spiritually. When you restrain yourself physically, you'll find it easier to apply this same self-discipline in your spiritual life.

   The more you practice self-discipline, the easier it is to do it the next time. With regular fasting, physical self-will has the side effect of making it easier to use this same discipline to conquer sin in your life.

- **The benefits of fasting "rub off" in your relationship with God.** Normal exercise and a good, balanced diet go hand in hand in my life. When I work out regularly, the more prone I am to eating foods that are beneficial to my health, but when I fail to exercise, I find myself craving

Twinkies and potato chips. I don't think there's anything physiological about this cause-and-effect relationship, but some real connection does exist, at least buried somewhere in my head.

Likewise, though fasting is a physical activity, the practice affects you deeply on the spiritual plane of your life as well. In other words, the amount of restraint and will power you practice physically has a tangible relationship to your willingness to submit to God's will.

✔ **Fasting fosters concentration on God and his will.** Oswald Chambers once said that fasting means "concentration," because when you're fasting, you have a heightened sense of attentiveness. Food or any physical sensation can satisfy, fill you up, and dull your senses and spiritual ears. In contrast, a hungry stomach makes you more aware and alert to what God is trying to say to you.

Fasting means concentration in order that the purpose of God may be developed in our lives.

Oswald Chambers

✔ **Fasting provides a real-life illustration of dependency.** Although modern man thrives on the idea of being independent, beholden to no one, fasting helps you put the facts in the proper perspective. It's easy to believe in your independence with a full stomach, but when you start to feel hunger pains in your belly after missing a meal or two, you awaken to your body's dependency on food to survive. Fasting reveals a physical reliance on food that points to the ultimate dependency — the fact that you're dependent on God for things far more important than food.

✔ **Fasting gives you "skin in the game."** When venture capitalists decide whether to finance a start-up company, they look for a founder who not only has a good idea but some money to put into the company himself. The belief is that the more a founder has "skin in the game" (see the "Got skin?" sidebar), the greater likelihood the company will succeed.

In the same way, Jesus calls his disciples to "die to themselves" (see Chapter 17), but it's harder to truly live that command out in your life when you're always physically satisfied. Fasting demonstrates to yourself

TIP

Hunger with a purpose

One of the most prevalent themes in all the Bible is the command for God's people to care for the poor and feed the hungry. With a fast-food restaurant on most every street corner in cities of the industrialized world, the idea of people actually going to bed hungry can seem alien. A side benefit to fasting, therefore, is that you begin to realize what hunger actually feels like, helping you better identify with people in the world who live with hunger on a daily basis.

that you do have "skin in the game," showing that you're serious and committed to Jesus' call.

Then I proclaimed a fast there, at the river Ahava, that we might humble ourselves before our God, to seek of him a straight way for us, and for our little ones, and for all our substance.

Ezra 8:21

✔ **Fasting prepares you for a big decision or an important event.** Time after time in the Bible, God's faithful spend time in fasting and prayer before a major decision or event in their lives. For example, just after getting baptized, Jesus undertook a 40-day fast in the desert as a preparation to starting his ministry. Think back to Esther, who I talk about in Chapter 1. Just before she put a plan into action that risked her life in an effort to save the Jewish people living in Persia, she calls for fasting (Esther 4:16):

Go, gather together all the Jews and fast for me, and neither eat nor drink three days, night or day: I also and my maidens will fast in like manner; and [then] will I go in to the king.

Fasting brings you in line with God to seek his will and to simultaneously show your devotion to him before the big event or decision occurs.

✔ **Fasting often surrounds God's special work in the world.** On occasion, God moves in the world in a special way. For example, consider God's interaction with the Israelites, Jesus' three years of ministry, and the formation of the early Christian church. More recently, God has moved on occasion to bring people to him in what is commonly called a *revival*, an event where large numbers of people come to the Lord. Fasting preceded the revival known as the Great Awakening that swept through the American Colonies in the 1700s. If you start to study many of these major events, you'll invariably find that God's faithful fasted before them.

✔ **Fasting empowers.** Fasting can also give you newfound strength in your spiritual life because of the intimacy you gain with God as a result. I also believe that God imparts his power in a special way when you fast for the right reasons.

Fasting is directed to two things, the deletion of sin, and the raising of the mind to heavenly things. Wherefore fasting ought to be appointed specially for those times, when it behooves man to be cleansed from sin, and the minds of the faithful to be raised to God by devotion.

St. Thomas Aquinas

The discipline of fasting can be problematic or even downright dangerous if you have experienced or are susceptible to eating disorders, such as anorexia or bulimia. Therefore, keep the following in mind:

> ✔ Don't fast beyond the time limit you originally set. If you find that you can't stop your fast, see your doctor immediately.

Got skin?

When an investor asks an entrepreneur about having some "skin in the game," the investor wants to determine how much it's going to hurt the entrepreneur if the company fails. The more the entrepreneur has invested her time and money, the more skin in the game she has. This term also is used in variety of contexts. For example, in professional golf, the "skins game" refers to a winner-take-all game of golf in which a player earns money for each hole won. When there is a tie, the money carries over to the next hole.

- ✔ If you feel yourself preoccupied with the physical aspects of going without food (such as possible weight loss), then the act of fasting may be a hindrance to your prayer life rather than a help. If you focus on the fast and have difficulty praying, break the fast immediately and pray about what you just experienced.

- ✔ If you're recovering from an eating disorder, avoid fasting altogether as a spiritual discipline. Concentrate instead on other prayer techniques, such as those discussed in Chapters 9 and 11.

Fasting in the Crossfire

The Christian church has a broad range of views on the practice of fasting, how much it should be done, how structured the fasting schedule should be, and what you should fast from.

In many churches, fasting is an optional discipline and a practice that only the most committed Christians do regularly. However, in other Christian circles, fasting is a more significant priority. For example, John Wesley, the founder of the Methodist Church, wouldn't ordain any ministers who didn't fast on Wednesdays and Fridays. Wesley tied one's ability to temper his appetite with his ability to lead a church. Additionally, in the Orthodox Church, clergymen can be deposed for refusing to obey the expansive fasting rules.

Here's an overview of how different parts of the Christian church view fasting:

- ✔ **Evangelical and traditional Protestants** encourage fasting, but they don't have regulated fasting periods during the year. Instead they believe that fasting is a decision best left up to the individual based on the prompting of the Holy Spirit. Recently, fasting has become increasingly popular among some Evangelical Christians, who see it as a way to seek God's direction and as a precursor to revival.

✔ **Catholics** in the United States have periods of fasting and abstinence on Ash Wednesday, Good Friday, and all Fridays during Lent. During these days, Catholics over the age of 14 are to refrain from eating meat. In addition, on Ash Wednesday and Good Friday, those between the ages of 18 and 59 are to eat only one full meal and two smaller meals and not eat between meals. Before the 1960s, Catholics were also prohibited from eating meat on Fridays during the entire year, but nowadays this decision is considered a personal matter.

✔ **Eastern Orthodox Christians** are far more rigorous in their observance of a structured fasting calendar than any other Christian group, believing that regular fasting is a crucially important discipline for one's spiritual growth. They point to the Old Testament tradition of fasting as the basis for their highly developed set of fasting rules. They observe four fasting seasons, several single-day fasts, and Wednesdays and Fridays as fast days. (See the sidebar "Eastern Orthodox fasting calendar," elsewhere in this chapter, for the specifics.)

When Good Fasts Go Bad

Although the importance and formality of fasting vary within the Christian church, each Christian, no matter his background, can have either a good fast or a bad fast. A good fast brings honor to God and produces a harvest of fruit, while a bad fast leaves you with a hungry stomach and nothing to show for it. Because not all fasts are created equal, you need to know what to focus on and what to avoid when fasting.

Bad to the bone

Even if you have good intentions, a fast can be detrimental to your prayer life if it's done for the wrong reasons or in the wrong frame of mind. Here are four ways to recognize a bad fast:

✔ **A bad fast is routine.** Like any activity than you do frequently, fasting can easily become the "same old thing," a practice devoid of meaning. Ritualism is an equal opportunity sin; it doesn't matter whether you're Orthodox and faithfully fast according to the church's calendar or whether you're a Protestant who fasts in an ad hoc manner. Anytime you slip into the "ho hum, here we go again" mentality, you're fasting without purpose.

✔ **A bad fast seeks to earn approval from God.** Christians easily can slip into the temptation of doing good things, like fasting, as an attempt to win God's approval. But remember, as I discuss in Chapter 3, the way to "be approved" is by believing in Jesus Christ and accepting Jesus' death for your sins, not by earning your way through religious duties. A bad fast mistakes this act of self-discipline and devotion as an act of justification, trying to earn endorsement from God.

✔ **A bad fast produces smugness, not humility.** Because fasting involves self-sacrifice, one who regularly fasts can look at other Christians who don't fast as slothful, indolent creatures. You can begin to get a smug attitude of "I fast, so I'm a better, more committed Christian than that guy over there." Don't compare yourself to others and let your pride entrap you, turning a fast that honors God into an "I'm Special" campaign.

✔ **A bad fast produces workarounds.** Almost every living creature on the face of this earth instinctively knows how to work around a problem. A mouse eventually learns how to make it through the maze to the cheese on the other side. Even tiny bacteria and viruses mysteriously adjust to the antibodies that people come up with to get rid of them. People are

Eastern Orthodox fasting calendar

The Eastern Orthodox Church has a very formalized fasting calendar that its members are called to observe. During these periods of fasting, meat, dairy products, and eggs are not allowed, with some additional restrictions on certain days.

The church observes four fasting seasons:

✔ In the spring, the **Great Lent** season, which allows fish to be eaten only on the feasts of Annunciation and Palm Sunday. It's considered long and strict.

✔ In July, the **Apostles' Fast** season has strict fast days on Mondays, Wednesdays, and Fridays, when fish is not allowed. This fast is considered short and relaxed.

✔ August brings the **Dormition Fast**, when fish is permitted only on the feast of the Transfiguration. It's to be short and strict.

✔ In the winter, the **Nativity Fast** ("Little Lent") observes Mondays, Wednesdays, and Fridays as strict fast days, when fish is not allowed. After the feast of St. Nicholas, fish is allowed only on weekends during the Nativity Fast. However, from late December until the feast of the Nativity, fish is not permitted. This fast is long and relaxed.

The church also observes several single-day fasts, including the following:

✔ Every Wednesday and Friday, except during the "fast-free" weeks. For Orthodox monks and nuns, Monday is also a fasting day.

✔ The day before the feast of the Theophany in January.

✔ Beheading of St. John the Baptist, observed in August or September.

✔ Elevation of the Precious Cross in September.

The weeks in which no fasting occurs are as follows:

✔ The holy days around and after Christmas

✔ Week of the Publican and the Pharisee

✔ Week of Cheese-Fare, in which no meats, but fish, dairy products, and eggs are allowed

✔ Bright Week of Pascha

✔ Pentecost week

the same way. When you're deprived of something, your body and mind adjust to the limitation and make do. A sacrifice that was once great can be less and less of a sacrifice the more times you do it. A partial fast of withholding certain foods is particularly susceptible to this if you allow yourself to lose concentration.

Good to the last fast drop

A good fast can turbocharge your prayer life and honors God. Consider these four ways to ensure a good fast:

- **A good fast is low key.** Jesus didn't teach much about fasting, but the one time he discussed it, in Matthew 6:16–18, he said that his followers shouldn't fast like the Pharisees did:

  Moreover when you fast, don't be like the hypocrites, with sad faces. For they disfigure their faces, that they may be seen by men to be fasting. Most assuredly I tell you, they have received their reward. But you, when you fast, anoint your head, and wash your face; so that you are not seen by men to be fasting, but by your Father who is in secret, and your Father, who sees in secret, will reward you.

  Jesus is saying that you shouldn't make it a point to tell people that you're fasting, because a temptation for people is to put on the façade of being a spiritual giant.

  Some people interpret this passage as forbidding you to tell anyone about your fast. Another perspective is that keeping a fast low key is what's important, so letting those closest to you (namely your spouse or family) know about your fast enables them to support you, so long as your attitude is pure.

- **A good fast isn't treated as an end or an accomplishment.** If you're fasting for a long period of time, you can easily let your all-consuming goal be the end of the fast — actually making it without food for an extended period of time. What's more, if you go on an extended fast, then you might actually start taking pride in what you've accomplished: "Wow, I did it! I made it seven days without food." You then become the focus, when, instead, a fast should be about God. You should view a fast as the means to a much more important end, and downplay the breaking of the fast.

- **A good fast always puts the practice of fasting secondary to the spiritual condition of your heart.** As I discuss earlier in this chapter, different parts of the Christian church differ greatly on the regulation of fasts by the church and the extent to which fasting is tied to one's spiritual growth. However, no matter whether you fast much or little, fasting should never become more important than the state of your heart's condition with God. Psalm 51:16–17 makes it clear that God doesn't want or need your sacrifices:

> *For you don't delight in sacrifice, or else I would give it.*
> *You have no pleasure in burnt offering.*
> *The sacrifices of God are a broken spirit.*
> *A broken and contrite heart, O God, you will not despise.*

Instead, what matters is your holiness, humility, and submission to him. A good fast promotes those attributes.

✔ **A good fast maintains perspective.** Although fasting should be a part of a Christian's life, the New Testament says far more about being pure in heart and mind, loving your neighbor, and denying yourself than it does about fasting. Therefore, a good fast doesn't take on an unbalanced perspective, becoming more important than other aspects of the Christian faith that are more central to living out your faith in the real world.

Getting Fast Answers to Practical Questions

If you've never fasted before, fasting can be unknown territory. Use this section to get the answers to the most common questions.

I'm fasting; now what?

As I say at the start of the chapter, simply doing without food doesn't constitute a Christian fast. Instead, a fast should be accompanied by much prayer. Here are three ideas:

✔ During any fast, plan on spending an extra amount of time in prayer and in reading the Bible. If you don't make the effort to do these things, then your fast can become a hollow exercise.

✔ Whenever you feel hungry, use that pang as a reminder to pray at that very moment about what you're fasting for.

✔ During the time you would normally spend eating, pray and study the Bible instead.

Fasting can be a time of temptation, because you're weaker physically then. Satan, for example, appeared to Jesus precisely when he was weakest, at the end of his 40-day fast. He can do the same to you, so remain diligent in prayer to be strong during any times of temptation.

What should I avoid eating during my fast?

People typically practice three types of fasts in the Christian church. To determine which one to follow, pray about the decision and make a choice from one of the following:

- ✔ **Standard fast:** A standard fast is the act of refraining from eating all food for a particular period of time. Water and juices are typically permissible, but milk products aren't allowed because they're technically a food.

- ✔ **Absolute fast:** An absolute fast is the act of refraining from all food and liquids (including water!) for a defined time. Obviously, because people need water to survive, you shouldn't undertake an absolute fast of any length of time unless you've checked with your doctor. Your body must be in good enough health to withstand the rigors of a fast, and you must feel confident that fasting is something the Lord (and not you) has placed on your heart.

- ✔ **Partial fast:** A partial fast is abstaining from certain foods for a specific time period. The Orthodox Church makes heavy use of partial fasts, usually involving denial of meat, dairy, and egg products, while sometimes permitting fish. Individuals from all Christian backgrounds can also create their own partial fasts, such as refraining from coffee for a week. (In my book, that's an ultimate sacrifice!)

How long should I fast?

After you've decided what kind of fast to undertake, you need to decide how long you're going to fast. No rules dictate the length of your fast, so pray about it and determine what seems right. If you're just starting out, I recommend starting with a single-meal fast for a time or two before trying something longer. Here are some suggestions:

- ✔ **Single-meal fast:** A single-meal fast involves abstaining from all or certain foods for one meal in a day. You may, for example, decide to fast from lunch every Monday, using that time in prayer instead of eating.

- ✔ **24-hour fast:** Perhaps the most common duration is a single-day fast, often starting out after dinner one evening and then fasting until dinnertime the next evening. This fast is long enough to provide a real sense of hunger and strong concentration for that time period, but it's still doable by most people.

- ✔ **Three-day fast:** Three days can be a long time to do a normal fast, as your body is definitely not used to going without food. However, three days of concentrated fasting can bring significant spiritual rewards.

> ✔ **Extended fast:** An extended fast may range from 7 days up to 40 days. Parts of the Evangelical Church have recently witnessed a resurgence of interest in extended fasts, using the 40-day fasts of Moses and Jesus as models.

If you're interested in finding out more about extended fasts, check out the Personal Guide to Fasting and Prayer at www.billbright.com/howtofast. This site covers the physical health and dietary issues to consider when fasting from 7 to 40 days.

The Bible makes it clear that you should treat your body well (as a temple of God), so before going on an extended fast (longer than three days), consult your doctor. Be certain that you are in good health and don't have a medical condition or take a medication that would make an extended fast potentially dangerous. If you experience any unusual physical symptoms during a fast, such as fainting, chest pains, or severe nausea, immediately see your doctor.

How frequently should I fast?

The frequency of your fasting depends on both your church background and your own personal conviction. If you belong to the Orthodox Church, your schedule is fairly set. But if not, you have a lot of flexibility. Typical examples include

- ✔ One day per month
- ✔ One meal per week
- ✔ One day per week
- ✔ No set schedule, as you feel led by God

When you first begin to fast, you may not see much spiritual impact. If so, keep at it, as learning this new spiritual discipline takes time.

If you've never fasted before, I recommend finding another person or persons who also want to fast, making a commitment to support each other in this new endeavor, and sharing how this discipline impacts your lives.

How do I break my fast?

I remember the first time I fasted for a 24-hour period. At the conclusion, I was famished and wanted nothing more than to gorge myself with a large meat lover's pizza, hot wings, fried cheese sticks, pasta salad, teriyaki chicken, and chocolate cake. But breaking your fast in this manner is bad on both the spiritual and physical levels.

On the spiritual level, overindulging yourself with food once a fast is over defeats the purpose of the fast in the first place, showing a lack of self-discipline and restraint. Physically, you can strain your body physically by going hog wild, because your body up to that point has been adjusting itself to dealing with no food. Breaking a fast isn't a big issue for a 24-hour fast, but for a 3- or 7-day fast, it becomes very important. And, after a 40-day fast, you have a weeklong process of adjusting before your body can handle normal food intake again.

When you break an extended fast, you shouldn't eat solid or cooked foods right away. Instead, begin with smaller meals of watermelon, cantaloupe, or other mild fruit, eaten several times a day. On the second day and third days, gradually introduce more foods such as baked potatoes and vegetables. After that, normal foods can be reintroduced, with strict moderation starting on the fourth day.

Chapter 11

Helping You Out: Prayer Enhancers

In This Chapter

▶ Livening up your prayers with singing

▶ Transforming your prayer life with meditative prayer

▶ Using physical prayer aids

▶ Enhancing your prayer life through special events

The Christian church is called the family of God, but I'm afraid that all too often Christians expect the church to be a family of homogenous clones just like them. And if other Christians pray or worship in a different manner than they do, they sometimes become suspicious or critical of the other group.

The reality is that the Christian church is a strange brew of folks — large and small, different colors, hip and not hip, and traditional and unconventional. In fact, I think the church is far closer to looking like the Addams Family than any other family I know.

The Christian church does need to agree on the core issues of the faith (discussed in Chapter 3), because if the church has an "anything goes" philosophy, then, frankly, it ceases to be the Christian church. However, as long as Christians adhere to the essentials of the faith, they should celebrate their diversity of prayer and worship instead of being suspicious of it. As British theologian and author C.S. Lewis says, being " 'one fold' doesn't mean 'one pool.' "

I believe much of the diversity of prayer and worship stems from the fact that people are simply "wired" differently. Certain people prefer to emphasize various parts of the Christian experience. Orthodox Christians, for example, focus on the reverence and majesty of God, while Evangelicals emphasize the personal relationship God wants with his children. Prayer too has a diversity of practices that different Christians emphasize over others. In this chapter, you explore some of these practices.

This chapter describes several techniques that some Christians will find extremely valuable to their prayer life, while others will say, "that's not for me." That's okay. The important factor is to maintain Biblical standards and then appreciate the variety in the Christian church.

Singing Your Prayers . . . Even If You Can't Hold a Tune

Some years ago, I went to an event in Washington, D.C., that brought together close to 1 million Christians for a time of worship, repentance, and commitment on the Mall in front of the Capitol building. Near sunrise at the start of the day, the event opened with the singing of *Holy, Holy, Holy.* Some half a million people belted out the classic hymn in such a gusty manner that I'm sure I saw a glimpse of what heaven must surely be like. Every time I hear that hymn today, my mind races back to that unforgettable moment when I heard hundreds of thousands of voices worshiping God in unison. As I experienced at this event, music has a quality to it that goes beyond the rational and even emotional parts of your life; it can delve into the spiritual realm in ways that are hard to understand.

Singing is a special form of prayer. St. Augustine is often attributed with saying, "One who sings, prays twice," meaning that the words you sing and your singing itself are two different forms of prayers to God. It's one of the oldest forms of prayer and can be traced back to the beginnings of the Old Testament. But nowhere is singing more center stage than in the Book of Psalms. The Psalms are more than just a collection of poems; the Israelites used them as a hymnal for hundreds of years.

Singing is evident throughout the Bible, both in worship services and in prayer. David, who is thought to have written half of the Psalms, was quite a music man: He played a musical instrument, and he even danced a fine jig, too. In the New Testament, Acts notes that Paul prayed and sang hymns while he was in prison one night. And Revelation talks about singing in heaven.

Singing can enrich your prayer life in two ways:

✔ Music has a way of turning your heart toward God with an intensity and focus that spoken prayer may not always do. I may stumble over adoration prayer for a spell, but get me belting out *Holy, Holy, Holy,* and my focus is completely on the Lord.

✔ People can much more easily memorize a song than a passage out of the Bible, so singing can provide you with a mental prayer book even when you don't have your Bible handy.

To incorporate singing in your prayers, consider the following tips:

✔ Memorize the words of your favorite hymns or praise songs that you sing in church.

   If you're trying to find the song's words, try doing a search on the Web. I've been able to find all my favorite hymns and praise choruses simply by entering in a line from the song on Google (`www.google.com`).

✔ Purchase some praise music tapes or CDs. These can be great to listen to and sing along with as you pray.

✔ Borrow a hymn book from church and read through it like a prayer book, reading and singing the words in a prayer. (Just remember to return it! You wouldn't want to be called a hymnal nabber.)

✔ Music can be a great way to start your prayer time with worship and adoration. You can then go into the normal spoken prayer.

Sing praise to the Lord, all you faithful ones.

Psalm 30:4

Freeing Your Mind

In the film *The Matrix,* in order to ensure that the evil agents aren't victorious, the rebel leader Morpheus tells the story's hero, Neo, to free his mind. As long as he does so, he won't be caught.

You may not live in a world in which you have to fight computers who take on human form, but you do live in a world that wants to keep your mind engaged and active 24/7 through countless mind grabbers, including newspapers, magazines, television, radio, computers, the Internet, the telephone, videos, DVDs, and video games. One way to offset this rush is to free your mind through meditative or contemplative prayer.

For many Christians, the word "meditation" is an instant red flag, conjuring up images of a lady sitting in the middle of a room with her knees crossed and chanting "huuuummmm" as a way of achieving inner peace. This form of meditation is part of other traditions, but that's not what I'm talking about when referring to Christian mediation. Instead, Christian meditation is not a technique or body position so much as an attempt to move your heart and mind closer to the God of the Bible by leaving the clutter of the world behind.

Practicing centering prayer

Centering prayer is one popular method of meditative prayer that has the purpose of being aware of God's presence as you pray. Instead of being active, like the prayer you read about everywhere else in this book, centering prayer is designed to be passive and restful. To practice centering prayer, do the following:

1. **Find a quiet prayer closet.**

   For centering prayer, you need to find a location that is quiet and allows you to concentrate. You can't be driving along the California coast or jogging along Chicago's Lake Shore Drive for this kind of prayer. (See Chapter 4 for more about a prayer closet.)

2. **Close your eyes and relax.**

   Let the worries and hurries of the day take a back burner, while you focus on being still with God.

3. **Pick a word of surrender and focus on it.**

   After you're relaxed, start to concentrate on a word that describes yourself surrendering to God. Focus on what that word means and how God wants you to use it in your life. Consider picking from the following "fruits of the spirit" to use as a word of surrender:

   Surrender, love, joy, peace, patience, kindness, goodness, faithfulness, gentleness, self-control, boldness, compassion, contentment, diligence, forgiveness, generosity, gratefulness, honesty, initiative, joyfulness, loyalty, obedience, perseverance, reverence, truthfulness, and wisdom.

4. **When distracted, return to the word.**

   You'll very likely have wandering thoughts come into your mind. When this happens, recenter on the word and continue to let yourself rest in God's presence. (See Chapter 12 for more tips on how to prevent your mind from wandering.)

5. **Wind down with normal prayer.**

   At the end of your prayer time, take a couple minutes to pray aloud to conclude.

Applying lectio divina

Another method of meditative prayer is called *lectio divina.* It focuses on drawing near to God through a four-step process:

1. **Lectio: Begin by reading the Bible and finding a passage to focus on.**

2. **Meditatio: Meditate on the passage for an extended period of time.**

3. **Oratio: Repeat the passage as you focus on it.**

4. **Contemplatio: Ask God how you can apply these phrases to your life.**

For more information on lectio divina, visit the following Web sites: www. lectiodivina.org and www.osb.org/lectio/about.html.

Avoiding potential pitfalls

If you practice any kind of meditative or contemplative prayer, keep the right perspective on what you carry out of your quiet times. Paul tells the Corinthians that the devil disguises himself as an angel of light, so don't automatically conclude that something you believe you heard from God was his voice. Always test what you hear, a topic I discuss further in Chapter 19.

Accessorizing Doesn't Only Make the Outfit

Prayer aids is another topic with wide differences of opinion within the Christian church. Catholics and Orthodox Christians are encouraged to make prayer aids (such as prayer beads or icons) an important part of their prayer life. The belief is that they help you grow closer to God in your prayers when you use them as intended. In contrast, Protestants tend to regard these accessories as a distraction to prayer and a hindrance to a personal relationship with God.

The following sections explain how to use prayer beads and icons as a part of prayer. You also find out about the potential problems that can surface when you use them in ways that aren't beneficial.

Using prayer beads

The Roman Catholic and Orthodox traditions both encourage the use of a string of beads called *prayer beads* to help in prayers that repeat a lot of the same phrases (known as *repetitive prayers*). More recently, some parts of the Anglican Church have started using prayer beads as well. Here's some information on different types of prayer beads and who uses them:

✔ **Catholic rosary:** The Roman Catholic rosary is a practice in which a series of prayers are said with a string of beads (called a *chaplet* or *rosary* and shown in Figure 11-1) that you use to keep track of how many prayers have been said and how many are left. The word rosary comes from the Latin word for "rose garden," a common place for prayer during medieval times.

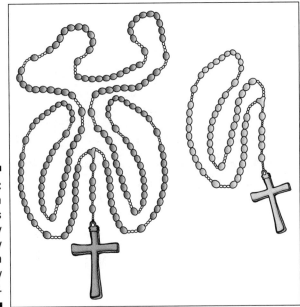

Figure 11-1:
Roman
Catholics
typically
use a rosary
bead when
they pray
the rosary.

TECHNICAL STUFF

Use what you know

The rosary's origins trace back to St. Dominic (1170–1221), who Catholics believe received it directly from the Virgin Mary to combat heresies of the day. Monks in the medieval times had a daily practice of praying the entire set of 150 Psalms. Because lay people were illiterate, they started to repeat the Lord's Prayer 150 times instead. Over time, other easily remembered prayers were added, such as the Apostles' Creed, the Hail Mary, and Gloria Patri.

Most modern-day rosaries have 59 beads and a crucifix, while a full rosary (predominantly used in medieval times) has 169 beads and a crucifix. The beads themselves may be made of a variety of materials, including wood, metal, stones, and even real berries. They're strung together on a cord, wire, or thread to form a circular loop.

✔ **Orthodox prayer rope:** Many Orthodox Christians make use of a prayer rope, shown in Figure 11-2, as a way to help focus by saying the Jesus Prayer: "Lord Jesus Christ, Son of God, have mercy on me." (I discuss the Jesus Prayer further in Chapter 7.)

An Orthodox prayer rope typically consists of 33, 50, or 100 knots and insert beads in the rope after every 10 or 25 knots. The rope not only helps you count the number of times the prayer is repeated but also serves as a focal point in your prayer to improve concentration.

✔ **Anglican prayer beads:** During the 1980s, parts of the Anglican Church invented their own prayer bead set, blending the Catholic rosary and the Orthodox Jesus Prayer. Anglican prayer beads, shown in Figure 11-3, consist of the following: four sets of seven beads to signify the weeks and creation, four cruciform beads to remind users that the central focus of Christian faith is Jesus Christ, an invitatory bead (which serves as an invitation to worship God), and a cross.

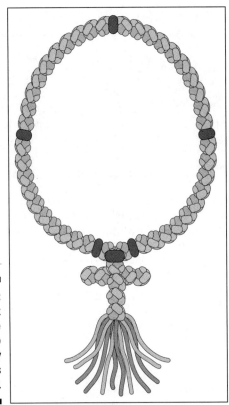

Figure 11-2:
An Orthodox
prayer rope
is used to
help pray
the Jesus
Prayer.

Figure 11-3:
Over the
past 20
years,
Anglican
prayer
beads have
become
popular in
parts of the
Anglican
Church.

For a directory of online vendors selling prayer beads, go to `directory.google.com/Top/Shopping/Jewelry/Handcrafted/Theme/Religious/Christian/`.

Communicating with icons

Icons are the distinctive paintings that are an important part of the Orthodox Church tradition. At first glance, your reaction may be simply "nice picture," but icons are meant to be more than just works of art. They communicate God's word and deepen a Christian's worship and prayer experience.

Icons were first used during the medieval times. Because few people could read, the Orthodox Church used icons as a visual way of teaching the Bible in a way that anyone could understand. Each icon represents a person or story from the Bible.

The Orthodox Church makes a point of saying that icons aren't painted or drawn, but are written. Each stroke of the paintbrush represents a prayer. Artists don't sign the icon because it's supposed to represent the word of God. According to Orthodox teaching, an icon opens a window into the spiritual for the believer. The flatness of the icon shows that it isn't intended to be realistic but to reflect the opaqueness of the material, opening into the spiritual.

Avoiding potential pitfalls

Prayer beads and icons can be aids to your prayer, but stay aware of the potential pitfalls to their use. Keep the following advice in mind if you use them:

- **A prayer aid should always be the means to God and not an object of worship or prayer.** If you go for your rosary instead of crying out to God when you need security and comfort, then doing so is a sure sign that you're placing far too much emphasis on the object itself. If so, the prayer aid can become an idol to you. The Bible is very clear in its warnings about substituting an object of worship in place of God.

- **Praying a repetitive prayer like the rosary or Jesus Prayer takes mental work to be meaningful.** If you work and concentrate on the prayer, then it can be a meaningful activity and draw you closer to God. But if you put your mind on cruise control, your prayer is only a ritual and simply empty words from your mouth.

- **A prayer aid or repetitive prayer must never get in the way of intimacy with a personal God.** If, for example, you only pray the rosary and never pray to God in a personal manner, then you're treating God like a distant deity who needs to be pleased. Your primary focus should always be trying to get to better know a personal God.

Attending Special Prayer Events: Kneeling Room Only

This book focuses on making prayer an X-factor for your daily life, but prayer at special events can also be a growth time for you and others at your church. These events include the following:

- ✔ **Prayer vigils:** Coming from the Latin word meaning "being watchful," a *vigil* is a special prayer event devoted to concentrated prayer for a particular purpose. The goal of a prayer vigil is to have people praying continuously. Prayer vigils are usually acts of preparation before a specific church or national event. They can also be a response to a special need or community crisis.

    Some prayer vigils are designed to bring people together en masse to pray for several hours, while others use the tag-team approach, in which individuals commit to praying at a specific time of the day during a 12- to 24-hour vigil at a church, a central location, or someone's home.

- ✔ **Prayer retreats:** Being alone with God out of your normal surroundings is a neglected part of the lives of most Christians, but it's something that you should consider doing periodically. After all, Jesus himself did so, most notably when he went away from everyone else to the Mount of Olives where John 8 says he prayed all night.

    If you're married, you may find it hard to justify going off by yourself rather than attending a regular church men's or women's retreat. But you should still pray about it and see whether God calls you to make a prayer retreat a priority.

    If you're considering a prayer retreat, keep the following tips in mind:

    - • Your most important objective is to find a location that will give you peace and quiet. You may want to consider a prayer retreat center, ten of which I highlight in Chapter 24.

    - • Plan at least one overnight away if your schedule permits, to provide sufficient time to unwind and then focus.

    - • Bring along a Bible, personal CD player or tape player, praise/ worship music, and a journal.

    - • Plan a variety of activities, including reading and praying the Bible, singing, walking, and resting.

- ✔ **Novenas:** In the Catholic tradition, a *novena* is nine days of prayer for a specific need or request. Catholics trace back the nine days to the Book of Acts, which describes the time between Jesus' Ascension into heaven and the time of Pentecost. A novena is intended to represent a sense of desperation and a way to demonstrate persevering prayer.

- ✔ **Pilgrimages:** Prayer pilgrimages are visits to holy places around the world as a way to grow closer in your walk with the Lord. Pilgrimages are primarily from the Catholic tradition because Catholics have holy places around the globe. However, Christians from all backgrounds visit the Holy Land as a pilgrimage each year. See Chapter 24 for a list of pilgrimage sites.

Chapter 12

Avoiding the Potholes to Prayer

L ast year, I was bicycling down a steep hill as my youngest son followed close behind. Given the steepness of the descent, I turned my head periodically to watch my son to make sure that he was handling the rapid speed well. However, as we neared the bottom of the hill, I turned around one too many times right before I approached a pothole in the road. You can guess what happened next: I hit the pothole at full speed and went headfirst over the front of my handlebars onto the pavement, cracking my helmet in the process. Although I was a bloody mess, I was somehow able to ride home, trying all the while to avoid being seen by my neighbors because I looked like I had just returned from a war zone. If you're riding a bike, potholes are more than just minor annoyances. They're dangerous spots on the road that can cause significant damage to you and your bicycle, particularly if you aren't wearing a helmet!

In the same way, the road to prayer is filled with its own kind of potholes. They can cause you to wreck and sideline your prayer life for a while or even, in some serious cases, forever. If you don't swerve to avoid these potholes, then you'll find that dedicated prayer will start to beget distracted prayer, which turns into empty prayer, then infrequent prayer, and ultimately no prayer at all. However, just as I could have avoided my bike accident by paying more careful attention to what I was doing, you can avoid potholes in your prayer life.

Hindrances to prayer come in all shapes and sizes, but you can lump them into three major categories: external, mental, and emotional. In this chapter, you explore how to overcome these hindrances to a successful prayer life. In order to avoid external hindrances, you need to adjust your priorities or modify where you're spending your time. If mental hindrances are your problem, you need to change your mind-set. Finally, to conquer emotional roadblocks — probably the most difficult pothole of all — you have to have a change of heart.

Each hindrance that I discuss in the chapter has suggested action items and a prayer that you can use if you're struggling with a particular pothole.

Reducing Distractions to Your Prayer Life

Living in this day and age does have countless advantages. I can order books over the Internet, watch a sporting event thousands of miles away inside the comfort of my home, and travel around the world and return before the week is over. Yet, I sometimes feel cursed living in this complex world because it offers exponentially more distractions to my prayer life than people like the Apostle Paul, St. Augustine, or Martin Luther ever encountered while living in simpler times.

Six of the biggest external distractions to your prayer life are the following:

- Work
- Entertainment
- Outside world
- To-do lists
- Your family
- Your church

Working your life away

Whether you work in an office, a factory, a school, or the family kitchen, the activity you do during the normal part of your day tends to dominate your time, focus, and energy. What's more, if you really enjoy what you do, then it can take over your whole life.

A few years ago, I bordered on being a workaholic; I enjoyed what I was doing in my 9-to-5 job so much that I let it permeate the other 16 hours of the day. When I got home from work, I'd problem solve in my head during dinner, work more after everyone else went to bed, and occasionally dream about my job. Then I always rose early to race off to the office for another day. Quite obviously, when I was so singularly focused on work, the other parts of my life suffered, my prayer life being chief among them.

Taking action

Paul is very clear that Christians should work hard at what they do so that they can be self-sufficient and give glory to God. But zealous work habits should never come at the expense of other priorities in your life.

Therefore, undertake the following activities:

1. **Write down your priorities.**

   Actually get out a piece of paper and make two lists:

   - Scribble down a "goal" list of what *should* be the top five priorities in your life.

   - In a second column, be realistic and write down a "reality check" list that shows where those five priorities currently rank in your life.

2. **Pray over your priority lists.**

   Take your lists and pray to God about them, talking to him about where you measure up now and where you'd like to be in the future.

3. **Take the three-week prayer adventure.**

   Chapter 4 describes a 21-day commitment that you can make to yourself and God that helps give you a kick-start to developing prayer as an integral part of your day. Use this technique as a way to break the stronghold that work has in your life as you begin to work on adjusting your priorities.

Prayer of Commitment

If you struggle with putting work in front of your relationship with God, pray the following prayer of confession and commitment:

Dear God,

I know I can bring glory to your name by doing my work with integrity and without compromise. I pray that I will continue to praise you in that manner, but I also acknowledge today that my work is getting in the way of being alone with you in prayer.

Please forgive me Lord for my skewed priorities, for letting my job become more important to me than you, and for letting it rule my life. I desire to change and ask that you'd give me strength to do so.

In Jesus' name, Amen.

Avoiding the "entertain me" trap

I'm still a kid at heart, and I love to play. I enjoy playing video games with my boys regularly, so much so that my wife is convinced that I like it more than they do. I am also a classic film buff and love few things more than relaxing with my wife watching a late-night Bogart classic on DVD. I suspect that I'm not alone in wanting to have fun, given the billions of dollars that people spend each year on entertainment. Just think of all the ways you can entertain yourself without ever leaving home:

✔ Watching television

✔ Watching movies on video or DVD

✔ Playing video games

✔ Surfing the Internet

When you do these activities in moderation, they can be good and healthy outlets for relaxation. But what often happens is that these activities chip away, little by little, at the time you should use for more important activities, such as prayer.

What's more, the two appliances in people's houses that tend to be on much of the day are their computer and television. Yet these devices suck attention away from anything else and draw you into them, and by the time you've turned them off, you've lost hours of time without even realizing it.

> *We pick out this natural pleasantness of change and twist it into a demand for absolute novelty. This demand is entirely our workmanship [and] is valuable in various ways. In the first place it diminishes pleasure while increasing desire. The pleasure of novelty is by its very nature more subject than any other to the law of diminishing returns. And continued novelty costs money, so that the desire for it spells avarice or unhappiness or both.*
>
> Screwtape, a senior devil writing to a junior devil

Taking action

If you're a Christian who wants to know God more, it's important to recognize that fun and entertainment without restraint only create a major pothole on your road to prayer.

Therefore, consider taking the following action steps:

1. **Set boundaries.**

   Limit your exposure to entertainment until after you're finished with prayer time. If you pray in the morning, consider making the computer and television off limits until after you've spent time with the Lord. Or if you pray in the evening, have a definite cutoff time for entertainment, one that still leaves you ample time and energy to pray.

2. **Put the television in the closet or trash can.**

   If your TV set is the centerpiece of your family room, you can easily get into the habit of watching more television simply because it's there. Consider putting it away in the closet for special occasions or even go one step farther and put it out for the next trash pickup.

Prayer of Commitment

As a first step to getting past this pothole to prayer, pray the following prayer of commitment:

> *Dear God,*
>
> *You created pleasure because you love us, and I thank you for that gift of being able to enjoy fun activities with your blessing. However, I confess to you that my desire to have fun has grown out of proportion to what it should be in my life. I've let entertainment rather than you become the desire of my heart. Lord, give me perspective and a foundation in your Holy Word, so that I can balance fun with what's most important. Give me the power to achieve this victory in my life.*
>
> *In Jesus' name, Amen.*

Getting out of range with communication devices

My father is a pastor, so while I was growing up, someone in the church congregation was always calling our house. Even dinner hour wasn't sacred, as he'd constantly get telephone calls while we ate. In fact, my sister and I made a regular habit of talking very loudly when one of those dinnertime calls came, saying things like "Please pass the peas!" or "Dad, your dinner is getting cold!" My mother went through the motions of scolding, but I think she was secretly rooting for us, although not too many callers took the hint.

The world beyond your door can be a distraction for your prayer life as well, because it can intrude upon your life uninvited at nearly any hour of the day. Phone calls can be something that turns your attention on a dime. Even e-mail can be the same type of distraction, especially if you have an Internet connection that gives you constant access. If so, you can have your e-mail software constantly running and set it to alert you with a beep wherever you're within listening distance. All communication devices — phones, cell phones, and e-mail — can serve as a magnet that draws you to them and away from other activities, such as prayer. Communication devices can even become addictive.

Taking action

Your prayer life can be derailed when you let the outside world interrupt your prayer time. Therefore, consider the following suggestions:

1. **Avoid the rush.**

   Select a time of day for your dedicated prayer time when you'll be unlikely to get any phone calls or face other outside distractions. (See Chapter 4 for more information on the advantages and disadvantages of morning, noon, and evening prayers.)

2. Tune out.

If the phone rings during prayer time, do what my dad would have done had technology been available at the time: Use voice mail. Then you can get back to the caller at your convenience. With e-mail, simply wait to check it until after you're done praying.

Prayer of Commitment

If you struggle with the desire to be connected around the clock, pray the following prayer of commitment:

> *Dear God,*
>
> *This world I live in today is filled with constant distractions, each vying for my attention. Lord, give me the ability to tune out the outside world when I am alone with you. Help me to realize that my time with you is far more valuable than constant communication with others.*
>
> *In Jesus' name, Amen.*

Keeping your to-do list in perspective

Whether you have a grand mansion or a one-room apartment, you probably always have work to do around your home. These household chores can intrude upon your prayer life if you aren't careful, even in your prayer closet. (See Chapter 4 to get into the closet.)

For example, suppose that your room is your regular place to pray in the mornings. But the night before, you happened to throw all your clothes on the floor and then kicked over the pile of laundry when you crawled into bed. When you get up and start praying the next morning, you soon become distracted by the general mayhem of the place. Your prayer may sound something like this:

> *Dear God,*
>
> *Thanks for the glorious morning outside, and thank you for . . . ugh, what a mess! Did I really leave my room in this shape last night? I must have been really tired. Oh, sorry, God, I thank you for your . . . yikes, I have to get these clothes picked up! My parents are coming here tonight for a visit. Oops, I'm supposed to be praying here. God please help me get this mess cleaned up before I leave for work. And, God, oh, yeah, I remember the saying "cleanliness is next to godliness." He must want me to clean my room as a sign of selflessness and obedience. Why, I bet that'd please him more than my simple prayer anyway. Yeah, that's the ticket. Thanks for being there God, Amen.*

A strong work ethic is good, but not when it impedes your prayer life. Be disciplined and stick with it, even when you're praying in the middle of a tornado disaster area (like my closet!).

The Gospel of Luke gives an excellent teaching of how Jesus views to-do lists when these busy activities get in their way of focusing on him. Luke 10:38–41 says:

> *It happened as they went on their way, he entered into a certain village, and a certain woman named Martha received him into her house. She had a sister called Mary, who also sat at Jesus' feet, and heard his word. But Martha was distracted by all her preparations and serving, and she came up to him, and said, "Lord, don't you care that my sister left me to serve alone? Ask her to help me!" Jesus answered her, "Martha, Martha, you are anxious and troubled about many things, but one thing is needed. Mary has chosen the good part, which will not be taken away from her."*

Mary made the right decision, dropping everything to sit down and enjoy being with Jesus. In contrast, Martha had her to-do list on her kitchen counter as she prepared the meal, grumbling self-righteously about Mary while thinking, "work, work, work." Martha even went so far as to ask Jesus to chastise Mary in front of her because of her laziness. She must have been flabbergasted by Jesus' response — correcting her rather than Mary.

Taking action

If to-do lists dominate your life and you see them impacting your prayer time, make the following commitment:

1. **Be a Mary, not a Martha.**

   A strong work ethic is normally a great asset, but when it comes to your prayer life, beware. That same work ethic can push you beyond what God wants you to do and can create a smugness or self-righteousness that becomes a major pothole to your prayers. Martha had a strong work ethic but came up bankrupt when it really mattered.

2. **Block out time for specific activities.**

   To prevent your to-do list from encroaching on your prayer life, block out portions of your day for household responsibilities and prayer time. If you do this successfully, you can sit still when you're in prayer, knowing specifically that you have still have time during the day to get to your to-do list.

Prayer of Commitment

To make a commitment to changing your priorities with work and to-do lists, pray the following prayer:

> *Dear God,*
>
> *When I read the story of Mary and Martha, I find myself identifying with Martha: I let my to-do list control my life, even letting busyness become more important than sitting at your feet listening to you. Lord, I confess my sin and ask for your forgiveness, made possible only through the precious blood of Jesus Christ.*

I pray that as I live each day from here on out, you'd continue to transform the bits of Martha inside me into the stuff that Mary is made of. I want that!

In Jesus' name, Amen.

Setting boundaries with your family

If you are married, live with your parents or children, or stay with a roommate, you know that it's often difficult to get peace and quiet in your home for prayer. Your family can be a potential pothole in your prayer life if you aren't careful. God does want you to give priority to your family, but with one important exception: The Lord wants you to put him first, even in front of your loved ones.

Devoted parents or spouses can have a particularly hard time with this distraction because they want to be a great mother, father, or spouse. As a result, they give their family much-needed priority but at the expense of God. The paradox is that you actually do your family a great disservice when you do this, because you're a better parent or spouse only when you're actively growing in your faith, not when you ignore the Lord.

Taking action

To prevent your family from becoming a pothole on your road to prayer, I recommend the following action steps:

1. **Go to extremes.**

   Desperate measures call for extreme actions, so your best way to prevent your family from being a distraction is to pick a time for dedicated prayer at either extreme of the day: in the early morning or later at night. If you do so, you can get that coveted quiet time that you need and still give priority to your family during other parts of the day.

2. **Get your family in the act.**

   Besides just having personal prayer time, get your whole family involved with regular family prayer. See Chapter 13 for full details on how to pray with your family.

Prayer of Commitment

If you struggle with balancing your faith with family responsibilities, pray this prayer of commitment:

Dear God,

My family is a precious gift that you have blessed me with. For that, I thank you with all my heart. And, I thank you for the desire I have in my heart to spend time with them and to serve them as I am called to do. However, I've put my family in front of you, putting something that is good in front of something that is the best. Forgive me, Lord, for doing so.

Help me to carve out a time in my schedule that gives me quality time with you and still enables me to meet my responsibilities to my family. What's more, empower me to serve them even better as I surrender them to you.

In Jesus' name, Amen.

Knowing God, not just serving him

It's ironic, but one of the greatest stumbling blocks to a growing prayer life can be the service that you give to your church or ministry. Oswald Chambers (whom you can read more about in Chapter 18) called it "actuality fever," the idea that *doing* something for God is more important than *being* with God. However, God can use you far more when your prayer life is growing, even if it means sacrificing time doing ministry work for him.

If you're an active person, *doing* comes naturally and has a certain fulfillment in its own right. Most people find that giving service to God is easier than simply being still and talking with him. After all, when you do something, you usually see visible results, whereas the fruit of a closer relationship with God, while every bit as real, may seem less tangible.

What's more, if you happen to be successful in your service efforts, such success can make it easier to justify skipping your quiet time with the Lord so that you can work even harder for more success stories. God wants a relationship with you first and foremost; service to him follows naturally after that.

> *Whether our work is a success or a failure has nothing to do with us. Our call is not to successful service, but to faithfulness.*
>
> Oswald Chambers

Taking action

If you're an active participant in your church or other ministry and you find yourself skimming your personal time with God for the sake of service, consider the following steps:

1. **Refocus on faithfulness, not service.**

   The first step is to dwell on the reality that your faithfulness is based on your growing relationship to God rather than what you're doing for him.

2. **Put on your seat belt.**

   Remember that Psalm 46:10 says, "Be still and know that I am God," not "Get off your seat and know that I am God." Therefore, if you struggle in this area, slow down, pray to the Lord, and use your time after that to do his work.

Prayer of Commitment

If you've let your service to God get in the way of your relationship with him, pray the prayer that follows:

> Dear God,
>
> Lord, heal me of this "actuality fever" that I have been stricken with, this preoccupation with doing something for you rather than focusing on simply being with you. Forgive me of this sin. I realize that I find it so much more natural to do deeds rather than being still and enjoying your company. But I desire to change and ask that you'd help me.
>
> In Jesus' name, Amen.

Clearing the Mental Cobwebs

Like all writers, I occasionally go through periods of writer's block, that frustrating time when authors can't seem to write anything on the page, no matter how hard they try. One Saturday afternoon while writing this book, my wife saw me struggling and graciously ended up taking our boys out for the day just so I'd have a perfectly quiet environment in which to be productive. After they left, the external distractions were no longer there to impede my writing, but I still had mental blocks that prevented me from writing. When my family got back, I had little besides a pair of bloodshot eyes to show for the time I had spent in front of my computer monitor.

Just as authors can get writer's block, Christians can get "prayer's block," making it difficult to pray no matter how hard they try. As you look at the types of mental distractions, remember that your mind is a battlefield, a struggle with three actors: God, Satan, and you. Here's what Ephesians 6:12 says on the subject:

> Our struggles are not against flesh and blood, but against the principalities, against the powers, against the world's rulers of the darkness of this age, and against the spiritual forces of wickedness in the heavenly places.

You face three major types of mental distractions, including the following:

- ✔ An ever-racing mind
- ✔ Superficial thinking
- ✔ A fatigued mind

Build a moat, why don't you?

Author Neil Anderson uses the illustration of your mind as a battlefield in his book *The Bondage Breaker.* Imagine your mind as a castle, surrounded by Satan who constantly shoots arrows and other armaments at it, attempting to penetrate your fortified walls. When you are distracted and have your drawbridge down, Satan is going to try and invade your fortress through these openings in your castle walls. If successful, the small invaders can distract your thought life as you pray. I think this image illustrates well how mental blocks can serve as major potholes in your prayer life. Imagine that your mind is a battlefield upon which a war for attention and focus is constantly being waged, whether you realize it or not.

A rolling stone gathers no prayers

A turbocharged, ever-racing mind is a major pothole that plagues many people today, especially those who are easily absorbed in work and other busy activities. If you have this type of personality, your mind continues to race — even when your body slows down — as you think about all the things you need to do, people you need to see, and places you need to visit.

A racing mind is usually a byproduct of an external distraction, such as work or household chores. Even when you're not engaged in those activities, your mind continues to race at a frantic pace as you think about what you should be doing instead of sitting still and being alone with God.

Taking action

To overcome the distraction of a racing mind, do the following:

1. **Apply the brakes.**

   No matter how much your mind is telling you to rev your engines and speed away, slow down by first focusing your prayer solely on that verse I've referred to before: "Be still and know that I am God" (Psalm 46:10). Too many times, I want to ignore the first half of the verse while I acknowledge the second part at 65 mph.

2. **Stick with a dedicated prayer time (see Chapter 4).**

   Do this no matter how much your engine revs in the midst of it. In time, God will work on your mind and give you the ability to ease back on that throttle.

3. **Use alternative prayer methods (as discussed in Chapters 9 and 11).**

   Adding journaling as part of your daily prayer life can be one of the most effective deterrents to a racing mind. In addition, meditative prayers can help you improve your focus.

Prayer of Commitment

If you're plagued with a mind that races when you try to be quiet, pray the following prayer:

Dear God,

The Good Book says to be still and know that you are God. Today, I acknowledge that you are God, sovereign over all and my Savior. However, I am struggling with that business of "being still."

You know how my mind races, being absorbed by the worries and activities of the day, and you know how I surrender to those scurrying thoughts and let them consume me. I'm exhausted from this mental marathon, and I yearn to simply be still and enjoy you like Mary did.

Lord, fill me with your restful, quiet Holy Spirit and give me the ability to tune out everything else and listen to your sweet, small voice.

In Jesus' name, Amen.

Stopping the cycle of thought surfing

Are you a channel surfer? If you're male, I know the answer already, but even if you're a female, you likely do your fair share of clicking the TV remote as well. (My wife won't admit it, but I'm certain that she channel surfs when I'm not around.)

Given the technology, channel surfing becomes a natural extension of one's use of the television. But what's interesting is how the technology has altered people's viewing habits. Instead of picking the best show and sticking with it, a channel surfer demands, "Entertain me now or else I'm surfing!" Therefore, when you watch TV, you're constantly inundated with sound bites and rapidly moving pictures, all of which have the express purpose of saying, "Watch me."

Unfortunately, all too often, you can take this mentality and apply it to your thought life, something I call "thought surfing." If you're a thought surfer, you have a mental remote that you click when you're momentarily bored by the current mental activity. If you find yourself doing this, you're unwilling to concentrate on anything for an extended period of time. As a result, thought surfers tend to ride a superficial wave, staying at the top so that they can quickly move to the next "big kahuna" thought that streams through their consciousness.

Too many Christians enter their prayer life with a thought surfer mentality. True prayer becomes too much work, and so they subconsciously yearn to be "choked in the shallow waters" before they dive too deep.

Taking action

If you consider yourself a thought surfer and see it impacting your prayer life, do the following:

1. **Be ready to exercise your mind.**

   Acknowledge your need for mental discipline and commitment to working at it and ask the Lord for his help.

2. **Take captive every thought.**

   As 2 Corinthians 10:5 says, "Take captive every thought, making it obedient to Jesus Christ." In so doing, you're recognizing that your mind is a battlefield, so you need to raise the castle bridge and make sure that your castle is impenetrable. When you pray and you have a "this is boring" thought, choose to not focus on it and continue on.

3. **Get a kick-start (which you can get from Chapters 7 and 8).**

   Consider starting out your prayers by reading a Psalm or a written prayer. These ready-made written prayers help ground your thoughts and direct your focus on God, who he is, and the depth of the relationship he desires to have with you. Your prayers after that kick-start should be more focused.

4. **Use alternative prayer methods (as discussed in Chapters 9 and 11).**

   Journaling is perhaps the surest way to attack a wandering mind. In addition, singing and meditative prayers are prayer methods that can help you improve your focus.

Prayer of Commitment

If you're struggling with wandering thoughts, confess this fight to God and commit yourself to lasting change:

Dear God,

I acknowledge my lack of discipline and outright laziness in my thought life. Lord, forgive me for this sin in the name of your son, Jesus Christ.

Help me fortify the fortress of my mind with your armor so that I can have the ability to take captive every thought and withstand the temptation to "thought surf" when I pray.

Lord, I also ask that you'd give me the desire to want to dive deeper in my prayers and walk with you and begin to taste the joy that comes from this closer walk.

In Jesus' name, Amen.

Pepping up a fatigued mind

A third mental pothole that you can encounter is that of the tired, fatigued mind. When you're in this state, you simply don't have the energy to pray. This hindrance, like the racing mind, can be the side effect of an external distraction, overwork, and overcommitment. Therefore, with all the commitments you have to your work, family, and church, you can find yourself with nothing left to give to God.

Taking action

To help your prayer life recover from this exhausted state, do the following:

1. **Position yourself for success.**

   Make sure that you pray in a location and posture that are optimal for alertness. If you lie in bed at night struggling to pray without falling asleep, then your problem probably has more to do with your location and posture than anything else. Instead, get up and kneel beside your bed, sit at your kitchen table, or go for a walk to get into a position that's conducive to success in praying. Chapter 4 talks more about posture, location, and timing.

2. **Give yourself a break.**

   Are you taking a Sabbath rest? God commanded humans from the very start to rest on the seventh day. I think his reason was far more than just to give out another rule; in fact, I think he intentionally designed humans that way so that they are most effective and productive when they have proper rest. In this busy world, very few people, including myself, take that command seriously anymore. "There's just too much to do" is the excuse that I find myself saying all too often. But if your prayers are hindered by tiredness and fatigue and you're not taking time off for a Sabbath rest, then you need to reset your priorities.

Prayer of Commitment

If you struggle with resting with God, pray the following prayer:

Dear God,

Just as the disciples let down Jesus in the Garden of Gethsemane by falling asleep while praying, so too do I let you down when fatigue ruins my prayers to you.

Lord, I desire a deeper prayer life and want to eliminate this roadblock. Therefore, I commit myself to praying at a time and place that I know I'll be alert, and to truly rest one day per week to recharge my physical, mental, and spiritual batteries. I can't do this on my own and need your strength to carry it out, but I ask that you'd give me the power in the name of Jesus. Amen.

Overcoming Emotional Roadblocks

The final category of potholes you face on the path to a growing prayer life consists of emotional roadblocks, which are undoubtedly the hardest to conquer. You can usually minimize external distractions by modifying your schedule or making some physical tweaking in your behavior. Mental hindrances are trickier to overcome than the external, but you can conquer them if you change your thought life through hard work and prayer. Emotional roadblocks, however, are the most daunting because they're buried deep in your heart. You can move beyond emotional potholes only through surrender to God and a patient heart.

The major emotional roadblocks are

- ✔ Fear, uncertainty, and doubt
- ✔ Pride
- ✔ Bitterness
- ✔ Tradition

Fighting FUD (fear, uncertainty, and doubt)

In the marketing world, FUD is a term that refers to the practice of using disinformation as a weapon against your competitors. For example, a salesperson who is trying to make a sale against a rival company might employ FUD by stressing the inherent soundness and safety of her company's product versus the fear, uncertainty, and doubt (FUD) that would ensue if one chose the competitor's product. In the same way, Satan runs his own disinformation campaign in a Christian's life by using fear, uncertainty, and doubt as a competitive weapon against God. He'd prefer that you trust the world's security instead of relying on God, and he'll use FUD to win. For example

- ✔ If you have money problems, Satan will aim to cause a panic so that you'll run out and manufacture any solution, even if that solution isn't what God wanted.

- ✔ If you have to wait a week to hear the results of a medical test, he'll try and use that uncertainty to drive you to despair.

- ✔ If you've lost a loved one due to illness, he'll try to create doubt in your life over why a good God would allow such sickness. (See Chapter 16 for more on this topic.)

This desperate trio of emotions can paralyze your prayer life, slowly sucking all the energy and life from it. These emotions can cause you to start looking away from God as the one to trust and looking to things of this world — things that you yourself can control — for security.

Taking action

If fear, uncertainty, and doubt are overrunning your prayer life, try the following steps to get back on track:

1. **Take a reality check.**

   Because Satan will tell you in subtle ways that God can't be trusted, you need to fortify your mind with the promises of God that you can find throughout the Bible.

   Or if nagging doubts about the truth of Christianity are creeping into your mind, don't ignore them. Instead, explore the specific questions you have to the fullest by reading such C.S. Lewis books as *Mere Christianity, Problem of Pain,* or *Miracles,* Lee Strobel's *Case For Christ,* and other great books that affirm the validity of the Christian faith. Knowing that God is on your side and in control is the essential first step towards conquering FUD. (See also Chapters 3 and 17.)

2. **Surrender your insecurities.**

   The first reality-check step focuses on your mind, but your second essential step is to take all the fears, uncertainties, and doubts that are packed in your heart and surrender them to God, asking him to change your heart from the inside out. Keep in mind that surrendering isn't just a one-time thing; instead, it's something you have to do on a daily basis for a while.

Prayer of Commitment

If you struggle with the emotional blocks of fear, uncertainty, and doubt, pray the following prayer of commitment:

Dear Father,

My life has been run over by a deep unsettledness inside of me, one that starts the moment I get out of bed and can last throughout the day. However, I realize that this is not the Christian life that is talked about in the Bible, but is a hollow shell of what it should be.

Lord, cleanse me from my fears and uncertainties. I surrender them all to you this day. And use any creeping doubts to only make my faith more solid. Fill up this void in my heart with your joy and peace that is beyond all understanding. From this day forth, empower me to resist these attacks by your enemy and stand firm in your truth and love.

In Jesus' name, Amen.

Sticking a pin in pride

God doesn't rank sins, but if I were to rank them, I'd put pride at the top of the "most dangerous" list. Pride is the source of all other sins in your life and mine. And, when left unchecked and unmonitored, pride can destroy your prayer life as well. Instead of trusting God to take care of you, you let your pride convince you that you have things under control nicely, thank you very much. Instead of surrendering all to God, you'd much prefer to hang on to some of that life yourself. The inevitable result of pride is taking your eyes off God and others and putting them squarely back onto yourself.

Taking action

If your prayer life is being squandered by a prideful attitude, take the following action steps:

1. **Come to your senses by reading the Bible.**

   Pride originates because of an inflated sense of self. To deflate that pride balloon, your best course of action is to read the Bible to get a renewed sense of your sinfulness, God's perfect holiness, and your need to be restored by him, not by your own actions. After you've done that, confess your pride and ask God to help you see the world as he sees it.

2. **Be aware of pride.**

   Masked pride is the great enemy of a growing relationship with God, but when that pride is exposed for what it is, you're already calling out the maintenance crew to fill in those potholes in your prayer walk. Simply being aware that you struggle with pride enables you to have success in this area. You may occasionally stumble, but you won't derail when pride suddenly comes out of hiding.

Prayer of Commitment

Pray the following prayer of confession and commitment if you desire to get rid of the barrier of pride:

Dear Father,

Pride caused the very first sin with Adam and Eve and continues to be a plague on every human who has walked this earth. I too have let pride impact my prayer life and relationship with you. I ask for your forgiveness and pray that you'd give me a godly perspective rather than my selfish perspective. What's more, transform me from being a self-absorbed creature into a selfless one.

In Jesus' name, Amen.

Doing battle with bitterness

Bitterness is a cancer of the heart, slowing stealing life, joy, and peace from you and leaving nothing in return. You can have bitterness toward God or another individual, but either way, it has the same cancerous effect on your prayer life.

At the root of bitterness is a holding back, a refusal to offer all that you can to God or the individual as a ransom for an injury that was done to you in the past. Such a holding back goes squarely against X-factor prayer that I discuss in Chapter 1, because a surrendering attitude is a chief component of effective prayer.

> *Create in me a clean heart, O God.*
> *Renew a right spirit within me.*
> *Don't throw me from your presence,*
> *And don't take your holy spirit from me.*
> *Restore to me the joy of your salvation.*
> *Uphold me with a willing spirit.*

Psalm 51:10–12

Taking action

If your prayer life is being eaten away by bitterness, consider the following action steps:

1. **Acknowledge bitterness in your life.**

   Because of the associated pain, bitterness is often masked by other emotions and may even exist without your realizing it. Therefore, before you can seek change, closely examine your life and identify the areas of bitterness that you struggle with.

2. **Make a choice.**

   When bad things happen in your life, you have a choice to make: You can either release those painful emotions to God and let him deal with them or else harbor them in your heart. If you bury these hurts and pains, bitterness is the inevitable result. Therefore, you have to make the deliberate choice to release them.

3. **Surrender your bitterness and heartache again and again.**

   After you decide to surrender your bitterness, the second step is to actually do so, asking God to change your heart from the inside out. Depending on how deep seated the bitterness is in your heart, the surrendering of bitterness isn't something that usually occurs overnight; in fact, months, or even years, may pass before your heart approaches a restored state. But after you take the first step, you're empowering God to begin that restorative process.

Prayer of Commitment

If you struggle with bitterness, pray the following prayer:

> *Dear Father,*
>
> *A bitter drink is displeasing to my taste buds and spoils anything I try to eat with it. Likewise, my bitter heart has ruined my relationship with you as well as with others in life.*
>
> *Lord, I don't deserve it, but I ask you in all humility and submission for your forgiveness. I know that the price of this forgiveness was Christ's death on the cross, and that only through the cleansing power of his blood can I be truly saved.*
>
> *I ask you today for your healing touch on my embittered heart, that you'd begin to create in me a clean heart and renew a joyful and humble spirit inside of me.*
>
> *In Jesus' name, Amen.*

Fiddling around with tradition

The classic musical *Fiddler on the Roof* tells the story of Tevye the Milkman, a Jewish peasant living in pre-revolutionary Russia who struggles with reconciling his family's age-old tradition with an increasingly modern world. This struggle ends up hurting his family, as he's unable to fully come to terms with the changes.

Similarly, tradition can harm your prayer life, too. Your family's prayer traditions can sometimes become a roadblock to your prayer life as an adult. Perhaps you were raised in a family that believed that prayers were to be offered only by a priest or minister, not by regular people like you and me. If so, initiating prayer on your own can be a struggle. Or suppose that your parents prayed only on Thanksgiving, Christmas, and Easter as part of holiday festivities; if so, you may view prayer as a ceremonial act, not something that's supposed to be part of your real life. Further, if your parents prayed all the time in your home but you saw them living a hypocritical life, then your attitude toward Christians who pray may be jaded. In each of these cases, the prayer traditions of your past may be an emotional pothole to a growing relationship with God, because of prayer habits, attitudes toward prayer, or the inconsistency you saw between a loved one's prayer life and real life.

Taking action

Don't let your traditions of prayer in the past that you had no control over dictate your future prayer life. Instead, take the following action steps:

1. **Break with the past.**

   Your first step is to break with past traditions that block your prayer life. Pray to God, asking him to cause that separation in your mind from your past to your future. Ask him to help you look on the past with a godly perspective, seeing it for what it was, but not letting it dictate to you anymore.

2. **Take the three-week prayer adventure.**

   Chapter 4 describes a three-week commitment to give your prayer life that turbo-boost that you need. Use this technique as a way to break the stranglehold that tradition has had on your prayer life.

Prayer of Commitment

If your relationship with God has chains of tradition dragging it down, pray the following prayer of commitment:

Dear Father,

While many honorable and worthy traditions should be upheld in today's world, any traditions that impede my relationship with you should not. Today, Lord, I confess that I've let things from the past get in the way of my prayers. I ask that you'd release me from the bonds of these traditions and give me the freedom to walk with you daily.

In Jesus' name, Amen.

Part III
Praying Well with Others

The 5th Wave — By Rich Tennant

"When did we stop giving an 'amen' and start giving the 'wave'?"

In this part . . .

Prayer is not only something you do by yourself. It's also an activity that you can do with others. In this part, you explore how you can use prayer to transform your marriage and family. You also discover how prayer in small groups is a pivotal part of your spiritual growth. And if praying in public is about as appealing as a root canal, then read on; I discuss how to overcome those fears — and you don't even need an anesthetic.

Chapter 13

Going Nuclear (Family, That Is)

In This Chapter

▶ Using prayer as your family's cornerstone

▶ Finding time for family prayer

▶ Helping your children converse with God

▶ Discovering how blessing your children can change their lives

▶ Making prayer a part of your marriage

T he Simpvers is an appropriate nickname for my family, but I'm not sure it's something I'd display proudly on a T-shirt. I think we're a combination of those most famous of TV families, the Cleavers and the Simpsons. When life is going well, I swear that Wally and Beaver are living in our house, always obedient and begging to do chores, but other times I'm sure that a crowd of Bart Simpsons is terrorizing my wife and me out of house and home.

Prayer has served as one of the key components that keeps my Jekyll-and-Hyde household sane and on the same team in the midst of this roller coaster ride. In the same way, prayer can strengthen the ties of your family as well, whether your name is Cleaver, Simpson, McPherson, or Chang.

In this chapter, you explore how to build a legacy of prayer for your children as well as how to enrich your marriage through the power of prayer.

Talking to God as a Family

Obviously, no family is perfect, and even the healthiest families experience problems living together on a day-in, day-out basis. Growing up, I was blessed to live in a nurturing, loving home, but even then, my sister and I clashed with each other on occasion. In fact, one of the sayings I spoke growing up that I remember to this day was, "Mommies are nice, daddies are nice, but sisters are shut-the-door-and-locks-its." (My sister had a bad habit of locking me out of her room when she didn't want to play.)

> *Now therefore fear the Lord, and serve him in sincerity and in truth . . . choose*
> *you this day who you will serve; whether the gods which your fathers served*
> *that were on the other side of the flood, or the gods of the Amorites, in whose*
> *land you inhabit: but as for me and my house, we will serve the Lord.*
>
> Joshua 24:14–15

Now that I have my own family, I see this saying playing out similarly with my three boys. They have tight relationships with each other, but they constantly go to battle over certain issues. Although this sibling rivalry is natural, these minor skirmishes, if left unchecked, can escalate to all-out wars between siblings or between child and parent. You can do a lot of things to keep healthy relationships on the right track or mend damaged ones, but prayer should be part of *any* solution you come up with.

If your family isn't used to praying together, everyone may find it awkward when you start. If so, take the lead and do the lion's share of the praying until the uneasiness subsides. After that, start to ask others to lead the prayer. (See Chapter 14 for small group prayer information.)

Praying together as a family is critical for three major reasons:

- **Praying helps break down walls within a family.** There is something divinely inspired about taking time out from everyday life and praying together as an entire family. Walls that are built up from hardened attitudes, rivalries, and infighting often begin to break down. Siblings who are ready to pull each other's hair out begin to respond over time to the regular practice of humbling themselves before God in prayer.

- **Sharing weaknesses with each other produces unity.** After a member of the family begins to open up and share prayer requests, major changes start to occur. This openness and humility can work magic on siblings who may otherwise tease each other over problems.

  This sharing has another benefit. Suppose that one sibling has a bad habit that annoys another sibling. If the first sibling sees that as a problem area and shares it as something he or she is giving to God to change, this sharing can improve the relationship between the two children. In my family, for example, I've noticed that one of my sons becomes less critical of his brother when he sees that his brother is trying to do something about the bad habit.

- **Family prayer develops a prayer-first mentality in your kids.** Prayer is among the most important legacies that you and I can pass down to children. Spending regular time together in prayer as a family sends the message that prayer is part of your everyday life. What's more, when a crisis occurs and your family comes together in prayer, you're teaching your children to have a prayer-first mentality — pray first and react later. Then, as your children grow older, they're likely to respond in the same way. In my family, for example, I've seen my kids turn tables and be teachers for me on occasion. When a minicrisis occurs, such as getting a flat tire or missing a plane, they've reminded me that we simply need to pray about it.

Fitting It in Between Soccer and Dessert

Soccer, Little League, play practice, piano lessons, band, gymnastics. . . . In today's world, simply trying to get a family together physically in one space in time for prayer may be your single greatest challenge. So, after factoring in your family's schedule, consider the following times to pray together:

- ✔ **Mealtime:** Praying before dinner is one of the most traditional times for families to pray together. Although it's not a time for extended prayers, it's perfect for establishing the tradition of praying together and for serving as a daily reminder to your children that God is the ultimate provider.

A memorized prayer at dinner (such as "God is great, God is good, let us thank him for our food") can be a good tradition, but I don't recommend using a ready-made prayer exclusively. If you do, prayer becomes a ritual rather than a heartfelt word of thanks to God.

- ✔ **Bedtime:** Bedtime is the ideal time to pray with your children on a daily basis because they're usually less active by this time (okay, maybe not) and the busyness of your day is usually over. Don't let a day go by without making prayer the closing part of their day (see Chapter 4).

- ✔ **Weekly family prayer-and-share time:** Consider establishing a tradition of a weekly family prayer-and-share time. The purpose of this time is to take 15 to 30 minutes from everyone's normal evening activities and spend time studying the Bible, praying together, or sharing family concerns. Tailor your agenda to what you think works best for your kids and their age levels. If you make this time together a habit, your kids are likely to look back on it years from now and treasure it as being formative to their spiritual development.

If your children are willing, let them take turns assuming the lead of the prayer-and-share time each week. From my experience, I've found that my kids get really excited and empowered by taking on this responsibility. (They even learned how to use Microsoft PowerPoint software one night so they could present their Bible study on the laptop computer.) See Chapter 14 for ideas on different types of prayers you may want to try out with your family.

- ✔ **Random moments:** One of the best ways to teach your kids the prayer-first mentality is to pray at different moments when you're all together when a need arises. For example, before you start a long car trip, take time to pray that the Lord blesses the journey. Or suppose that a hurricane or tornado hits your community. Take that opportunity to immediately pray as a family for the victims and thank God for his protection.

✔ **Special holiday times:** Thanksgiving, Easter, Christmas, and the Lenten season are all good occasions to hold special prayer times with your family. During these times of the year, concentrate your prayers together on the meaning of the holiday or season.

Teaching Junior How to Pray

My mental picture of a parent teaching a child to pray is something out of a Norman Rockwell portrait: a father kneeling together with his daughter beside her bed reciting "Now I Lay Me Down To Sleep." Although that picture is sentimental and heartwarming, parents need to go beyond simple methods of prayer. Instead, you should teach your kids the kind of prayer that will make a difference in their lives, both as children today and as teenagers and adults tomorrow.

Behold, children are a heritage of the Lord.
The fruit of the womb is his reward.
As arrows in the hand of a mighty man,
So are the children of youth.

Psalm 127:3–4

Here are several tips for teaching your children to pray:

✔ **Teach them both the "classics" and do-it-yourself prayer.** Memorized prayers are important to pass down to children, such as Psalm 23 and the Lord's Prayer. (See Chapter 23 for some excellent prayers to teach kids, Chapter 7 for ready-made prayers, and Chapter 5 for more on the Lord's Prayer.) Those ready-made prayers can be sources of great comfort to your children and help give them a solid background about prayer.

However, you should also teach your children how to pray by themselves, helping them put into words the needs they have and developing in them a simple faith of trusting in God through prayer.

✔ **Emphasize that prayer is not only a ritual but also a conversation.** One side effect of the Norman Rockwell approach to prayer that I discuss in the opening of this section is that a child can look on prayer as "that thing I do after I brush my teeth and before I get into my bed." Instead, teach your child that prayer is not simply a ritual but a constant, live conversation with God that she can have not only at bedtime but also at any time during the day.

✔ **Take turns leading the prayer.** A good practice when praying with your child is to take turns praying. When you lead, the child can learn from you how to pray. When the child leads, he can apply what he learned when you prayed.

✔ **Develop a list of things to pray about for and with your child.** An important part of teaching children how to pray is remaining faithful and persistent in prayer. Keeping a short prayer list can be an extremely helpful way to help develop faith and perseverance. You can write the list down on paper or keep it in your head, but either way, have a list that you continue to use until the prayers are answered.

When you pray about the same thing over weeks or months with your children, you develop a persistent and patient mind-set toward prayer. And when your children actually see the prayer answered, this result can significantly strengthen and encourage their faith. However, because God doesn't always answer prayers in the way you hope, be prepared to deal with that with your children. See Chapter 18 for more on this subject.

My family has a common prayer list of people we pray for. That way when we pray together at night, these people on the list are prayed for regardless of who prays.

✔ **Pray for each other.** Although you should pray for people outside your family, don't neglect your family needs either. One activity that has revolutionized my family's unity is praying for each other's character. At the start of the school or calendar year, family members pick out a character trait (see the list in the sidebar "Character traits worth praying for," later in this chapter) that they believe they need to work on in their life. (No, members can't pick for someone else, as tempting as doing so may be!) After each member chooses a trait, we all share the character trait we chose and commit to praying for each other for lasting change.

For example, my son Justy prays something like this at night:

Dear Lord,

Help Jordan to be more content, even when things don't go his way. And Jared to be more self-controlled. And mom to be more gentle. And dad to be more joyful. And help me, too, to be more obedient to mom and dad and you.

Praying for character traits has a threefold benefit:

- Each family member humbles himself or herself in front of the others by saying, "Hey, I'm not perfect. Here's something I need to work on."

- When you pray for a family member to improve in a problem area, you begin to sympathize with, identify with, and forgive a person who screws up later.

- Because prayer works, your family's character gradually grows as each member surrenders to God in new areas.

When children begin praying for each other's character, such prayer brings an intimacy and humility to relationships that otherwise may be characterized by ridicule and scorn.

Character traits worth praying for

In Galatians 5:22, Paul lists the "fruits of the Spirit," that is, character traits that Christians should make part of their lives with help by the Holy Spirit. The qualities that Paul singles out are love, joy, peace, patience, kindness, goodness, faithfulness, gentleness, and self-control.

However, you can also choose to pray for other traits, including boldness, compassion, contentment, diligence, forgiveness, generosity, gratefulness, honesty, initiative, joyfulness, loyalty, obedience, perseverance, reverence, truthfulness, and wisdom.

✔ **Pray in plain English.** Make prayer accessible to your child by talking so that it resembles a normal conversation. If you're not used to praying in front of your children, you may find yourself thinking of your pastor's perfect Shakespearean English during his Sunday prayer and trying to emulate that when you pray to your child. Instead, just pray in the same manner that you normally speak to your child.

✔ **Have patience, patience, and more patience.** Patience is a trait that you need when teaching your children to pray. When you first start praying as a family, you may have a hard time getting your children to concentrate for any extended period of time or to remain serious or quiet. In fact, they may find it "safer" to avoid the vulnerability and intimacy of prayer by mocking or avoiding it. Don't overlook this behavior, but at the same time, don't expect them to become little saints overnight, either.

If your child is reluctant to pray, encourage her to do so anyway, but without making too big of a deal of it. If she's still reluctant, you or another sibling can pray instead. Each of my kids has refused to pray at one time or another, but that reluctance eventually subsides, and each starts participating again. If the reluctance continues, talk to your child one-on-one and explore the reason for the hesitation.

Blessing Your Children

People in Biblical times had a common custom of blessing their children. A *family blessing* is a special prayer that a parent offers by laying hands on the child and asking God for his mercy, protection, and abundance for the child. This tradition of blessing your children is one you should consider practicing for three reasons:

✔ **A blessing draws you closer to your child.** The act of blessing your child creates a special intimacy between the two of you over time that normal prayer doesn't always produce.

✔ **A blessing is special for the child.** For the child, being singled out for a blessing is something special. Your child is encouraged by God's protection and abundance and is reminded of God's guidance in his life.

✔ **God honors your blessing.** A blessing is more than just a symbolic act or a nice thing to do. God will honor your blessing and make a tangible difference in the life of your child. You can see Biblical evidence of God's responding to blessings. In fact, Jesus himself thought blessing children was an important act. Mark 10:13–16 says:

> *They were bringing to him little children, that he should touch them, but the disciples rebuked those who were bringing them. But when Jesus saw it, he was moved with indignation, and said to them, "Allow the little children to come to me! Don't forbid them, for the Kingdom of God belongs to such as these. Most assuredly I tell you, whoever will not receive the Kingdom of God like a little child, he will in no way enter into it." He took them in his arms, and blessed them, laying his hands on them.*

In addition, God chooses to work in the world largely through prayers. As a result, God will work in your child's life through prayer as well.

Finally, as James 5:16 says, "the diligent prayer of a righteous person is powerfully effective." So if you're prayer ready (see Chapter 1), then God will honor your blessing.

Blessing a child may sound intimidating to you at first, like it's some magical act, but it's actually very simple. Just lay your hands on your child's head and pray a prayer of blessing, such as the one in Numbers 6:24–26:

> *Allison,*
> *May the Lord bless you, and keep you.*
> *May the Lord make his face to shine on you,*
> *And be gracious to you.*
> *May the Lord lift up his face toward you, Ally*
> *And give you peace.*
> *Amen.*

Instead of using a ready-made prayer, you may want to make up your own blessing prayer.

Blessing a child is not a one-time occurrence; you should do it frequently. If you don't do it nightly, at least do it weekly. Practically speaking, I think it often works best after your normal nighttime prayer with your child.

Es-spousing Prayer

Prayer can be an effective way to draw a husband and wife closer together. As with entire families, prayer helps bring down walls that can develop between a married couple as they humble themselves before God.

Praying together as a couple provides a practical demonstration of what a Christian marriage should be. As Figure 13-1 shows, the closer each spouse gets to God, the closer they in turn get to each other. When prayer is a permanent part of that three-way relationship, the marriage bond is strengthened.

Figure 13-1:
Prayer is
a vital
component
to the
Christian
marriage
triangle.

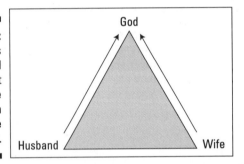

However, prayer between a married couple is sometimes easier said than done. In fact, for some screwy reason, prayer is often more difficult between a couple than it is between a parent and child. Therefore, consider the following tips for prayer between couples:

- ✔ If your spouse feels awkward, take the lead in prayer and keep the prayer short and sweet until you begin to establish a more comfortable presence together.

- ✔ If your spouse doesn't want anything to do with prayer, don't push it on him or her. Instead, in your personal prayer time, pray that God opens the door for prayer together.

- ✔ Bedtime can be a natural time for praying together as a couple. However, I recommend doing so before you turn the lights out and lie horizontal. If not, your prayer can quickly become filled with sounds of *zzzzzzzz*'s (see Chapter 4).

Dispelling myths about Biblical marriages

The spiritual roles of the husband and wife in marriage receive considerable discussion these days. The traditional view of the husband as the spiritual head of the family is often attacked, but consider what Paul says on this subject in Ephesians 5:22–28:

> Wives, submit to your own husbands, as to the Lord. For the husband is the head of the wife, and Christ also is the head of the church, being himself the savior of the body. But as the church submits to Christ, so let the wives also be to their own husbands in everything.

> Husbands, love your wives, even as Christ also loved the church, and gave himself up for it; that he might sanctify it, having cleansed it by the washing of water with the word, that he might present the church to himself gloriously, not having spot or wrinkle or any such thing; but that it should be holy and without blemish. Even so ought husbands also to love their own wives as their own bodies.

The word *submit* is a hot potato issue, because the popular idea of marriage is a marriage of equals, not a relationship in which one spouse submits to another. Yet, if you accept the Bible as truth, then it's important not to disregard its teaching on marriage. The New Testament clearly does teach that the husband is the spiritual head of the family and the wife is called to submit to his leadership. But a flip side to this issue is often overlooked: The husband is called to serve the wife *in the exact same way* that Jesus Christ served the church. (Remember, Jesus died for the church, so the husband has perhaps an even harder challenge.)

Contrary to the stereotypes portrayed in the media, a Biblical marriage is not one in which an authoritarian husband bosses around a submissive wife. Instead, it's a relationship characterized by self-forgetfulness and a focus on the other person: A husband gives up his own wants and needs to serve and lead his wife, while the wife surrenders her wants and needs for her husband.

Chapter 14

Praying in Small Groups

. . . .

In This Chapter

▶ Discovering the different ways a small group can pray

▶ Sharing prayer requests

▶ Avoiding the hazards of small group prayer

▶ Using e-mail to stay spiritually connected

. . . .

Climbing Mount Everest has always been a secret dream of mine. However, given that the highest mountain in the world claims every fifth climber, the trek up its summit is perilous beyond description. Yet, in spite of that treachery, I still have moments when I'd love to climb that peak, as I begin to think of the excitement in actually making it to the "rooftop of the world." Not quite so enthusiastic, my wife offered me a compromise: a framed picture in my office showing a panoramic view from the top of Everest.

Although only a scant few people ever climb Mount Everest, many people have their own Everests that can seem every bit as daunting as a 29,000-foot mountain. Praying in small groups used to be my personal Everest, a fear I wanted to overcome, but one that took a long-time journey to conquer.

Praying in small groups can be one of two extremes — a self-conscious ordeal to endure or an intimate encounter with God among brothers and sisters in Christ. I recall the very first Bible study I ever attended. After a Bible study lesson, we spent the last 20 minutes of the session in prayer, and each person took a turn to pray. However, because of my dread of praying aloud, I spent the whole Bible study trying to plan exactly what I would pray about rather than concentrating on the lesson.

Yet, as the years have passed, I've overcome this mountainous struggle. And in doing so, I've seen the "spectacular" view of what small group prayer can be after group members overcome that initial awkwardness and fear. I've seen not only how small group prayer encourages and strengthens me but also how it bonds a group of Christians together in ways that can't be done simply by attending church on Sunday morning. Using this chapter, you explore how small groups can avoid that self-conscious trap and take practical steps toward intimacy among group members.

The Small Group That Prays Together Stays Together

John Donne may have once written "no man is an island," but millions of modern-day Christians are living as though they are. Too many people like you and me are self-sufficient, independent creatures who regularly attend church but have little interaction with other Christians for the remainder of the week.

> *God composed the body together . . . that there should be no division in the body, but that the members should have the same care for one another. When one member suffers, all the members suffer with it. Or when one member is honored, all the members rejoice with it.*
>
> 1 Corinthians 12:24–26

Yet involvement in a small group is often an indicator of the spiritual growth of a Christian today. Of course, weekly church is central for worship and being among the general community of Christian believers. So too, personal prayer and Bible study are core to one's personal growth. But, by and large, growing Christians tend to participate in small groups as an extension of these activities.

Trying to grow as a Christian is difficult, if not impossible, if you're not involved with other Christians. Going solo is a much more difficult path to follow because you encounter many more struggles alone than you do if you have the active support of a small group and church.

Finding your niche

When I talk of a small group, I mean nothing more than a group that gets together regularly, usually weekly or biweekly, to pray and possibly do other activities, such as a Bible study.

Types of small groups include the following:

- ✔ A *prayer group* is two or more individuals who commit to meeting together specifically to pray for each other and common needs.

- ✔ A *Bible study group* (sometimes called a *home group*) meets to discuss a Bible lesson or other Christian topic and includes prayer as an integral component of the group's focus. These groups sometimes meet at a church, but many times they meet in the home of a group member. These groups may cater to couples, singles, a particular age group (such as senior citizens or college students), or a mixture of these types of people.

TIP

Looking for prayer groups in all the right places

If you're not in a small prayer group but would like to be, the best place to look for a group is at your home church. Check to see whether small groups are available to attend or, if not, ask whether other persons may be interested in starting a new group.

Men can check to see whether any local Promise Keepers (a Christian men's group calling men to live lives of integrity) small groups (which I discuss in the section "Finding your niche," earlier in this chapter) are open in their

area, while mothers can do the same with Moms In Touch (a Christian women's ministry that focuses on the needs of mothers) small groups.

If you do decide to start a new small group, don't feel that you need to limit it to people of your home church either. For example, the group I lead includes people from five different churches. Such diversity adds life and vibrancy to the group, and it enables us to get a broader perspective on the issues we talk and pray about.

✔ A *cell group* meets regularly to do an activity or study a subject of special interest to its members. The focus of a cell group can be as wide ranging as people's interests, such as tennis, classical movies, pinochle, or J.R.R. Tolkien books. Prayer is a part of the cell group's activity when it meets.

✔ A *gender-based small group* focuses on ministering to men or women by getting people of the same sex together to talk about issues related to Christian faith. These groups tend to meet weekly for prayer and sharing. (See the sidebar "Accountability: Nothing to do with your checkbook" in this chapter.)

Perhaps the best example of this kind of group is a men's Promise Keepers small group. Promise Keepers, the popular men's ministry, has small group development as a top priority for its programming because of the pivotal role of small groups in the spiritual health of men.

✔ A *Sunday school class* is another form of small group. It consists of a group of individuals getting together regularly, with prayer often a part of its agenda.

Following the leader or just popping in?

If you've read Part II of this book, you've seen that personal prayer can take many forms and styles. Small group prayer is no different. Small groups can pray in a range of different ways, but the decision of which method is the best choice for your group lies in its unique personality. As I explain in Chapter 1, these forms of prayer aren't magic. These methods are simply tools that can lead people into an attitude of earnest and humble prayer. You'll probably want to experiment by using a variety of the following methods:

✔ **Leader prayer:** Perhaps the most basic form of small group prayer is to have a single individual lead the group in prayer, praying for all the prayer concerns and requests that are offered. Leader prayer is especially useful in two instances:

  • When a group is just starting out and the leader doesn't feel that the group is comfortable enough praying together

  • When you need to keep the prayer time within a specific time constraint

  However, leader prayer also doesn't get everyone involved and help increase the intimacy of a small group, so use it only as a starting point.

✔ **Around-the-world prayer:** The opposite of leader prayer is what can be called around-the-world prayer. In this form, each member of the group takes a turn praying. This form of prayer can be good in these situations:

  • When each member of the group participates

  • When all members feel comfortable with praying

  This type of prayer, however, can force people to pray who would prefer not to pray out loud. The end result can be that, instead of listening to the spoken prayers, some people may spend all that time trying to mentally prepare what to say when it's their turn. So I recommend using this method only when all members feel comfortable praying with each other.

✔ **Popcorn prayer:** The popcorn prayer method is perhaps the best all-around form of small group prayer because it gets the group members involved but does so in a voluntary manner. With popcorn prayer, the

On the Web

Several excellent small group resources are available on the Web. Some of the best include the following:

✔ Small Group Network: http://small groups.com

✔ The Lamb's Bride Project: www.hope2 help.com/lambsbride

✔ Small Group Ministries: www.small groupministries.org

✔ The Cellular Level: www.cell-church. org (cell groups)

✔ Touch USA Ministries: www.touchusa. org (cell groups)

✔ Promise Keepers: www.promise keepers.org (men)

✔ Moms In Touch: www.momsintouch.org (mothers)

leader usually designates someone to start the prayer and another person to close, and instructs everyone else to "pop" in (hence, the name of the prayer) as they choose to. After a long pause, you'll know that everyone who wanted to pray has done so, leaving the designated closer to finish up.

The only drawback to always using popcorn prayer is that your group can get into the rut of having two sets of people: the praying folks and nonpraying folks. Without changing the form of prayer, getting the non-prayers to participate can be hard. So consider changing occasionally to the topical or single-word prayer (discussed later in this bulleted list).

If you pick people to start and end the prayer, ask people who don't feel overly intimidated by the request. You may want to have a few go-to people that you periodically select.

✔ **Topical prayer:** Topical prayer is a method in which a leader starts the prayer and then throws out a specific topic to pray about. As members feel moved, they can add a brief sentence or two about that subject. For example, suppose that you're praying for a man who just was laid off from his job. That prayer conversation might go something like this:

Leader Larry: Lord, we pray for Clark and his job loss this afternoon.

Juanita: Give Clark peace in this time of turmoil in his life.

Sue: God, we pray that you would provide a smooth transition for Clark into a new job that you have specially prepared for him.

Matthew: Comfort his wife, Lois, and their kids and help them to feel secure in your love.

Jane: Use this situation, Lord, to make Clark more like Christ.

Leader Larry: Lord, we now pray for Jane's mother-in-law.

The advantage of topical prayer is that

• You can get people who are reluctant to pray a normal free-form prayer to join in, because they need to say only a sentence or two about the particular subject.

• The leader can be sure to cover all prayer requests in a structured manner.

The only downside is that you don't always get the level of depth that you do when people are free to pray on their own.

✔ **Single-phrase prayer:** A variant form of the topical prayer is the single-phrase prayer. In this method, the leader throws out a topic, and members of the group can pop in with a single word that complements or supplements that topic. Imagine a single-phrase prayer going something like this:

Leader Linda: God, we praise you today for who you are.

Bob: Creator of the world.

Kim: A patient and loving God.

Rondell: All-powerful and all-knowing.

Leader Leroy: We are grateful in our hearts for so many things.

Phyllis: Eternal life.

Maria: Health.

Ty: This small group.

Curtis: Your Son, Jesus Christ.

This method of prayer has these advantages:

- Everyone can concentrate on the full meaning of the word that was spoken because typically pauses occur between each word or phrase uttered.

- People hesitant to pray can contribute in a nonthreatening manner.

However, given the constrained nature of the prayers, it's better to use single-phrase prayer primarily as a special occasion prayer.

✔ **Silent prayer:** Many churches have a time of silent prayer and meditation at some point during a service as a way for individuals to filter out the noise of the week and simply communicate directly to God. Small groups can do the same thing, using silent prayer as a way to

- Get people focused.

- Involve everyone, but in a nonthreatening way because individuals don't have to speak out loud.

In a small group setting, silence is often a no-no. Many people start to get uncomfortable when long periods of time go by without spoken communication. Therefore, if you use silent prayer, start out small. Go for one or two minutes and eventually expand to five minutes or even higher as you need to.

✔ **Laying-on-of-hands prayer:** The act of having one or more people place their hands on an individual during prayer has special significance in both the Old and New Testaments. The laying on of hands can be used to do the following:

- Pass on something to an individual, such as when Moses laid hands on Joshua to transfer the leadership of Israel to him

- Give a special blessing to the receiver

- Physically heal a person (see Chapter 20)

On special occasions, when someone has a special prayer need, the members of the group can gather around that person, place their hand on the receiver's shoulder, and take turns praying for that individual. Not only is this gesture in line with the teaching of the Bible, but it also brings a sense of closeness to each other.

For this cause, I remind you that you should stir up the gift of God which is in you through the laying on of my hands.

2 Timothy 1:6

Creating a tiny congregation

Many people believe they can "be their own church." Because Christianity is an individual's faith in God, the argument from these people is that they don't need to be involved with other Christians by going to church or joining a small group.

For where two or three come together in my name, there I am with them.

Matthew 18:20

Being an independent sort of person myself, I sympathize with that perspective. So when I read the Bible closely, I find myself always surprised by its group-oriented nature. The cultures of the Old and New Testaments were definitely focused more on the community rather than on the individual, but this teaching goes beyond just cultural preferences. (See Chapter 15 for a better understanding of community's role in Christianity.)

Why then is it so important that you and I get together with others in small groups?

✔ **Fellowship with other Christians builds community.** Small groups build a sense of community that is difficult, if not impossible, to get in the larger church as a whole. Except for the smallest of churches, you'll find it impossible to become personally well acquainted with many others in the congregation. If you're in a church of 50 persons, developing a bond with everyone is difficult; if you're in a church over 200 or more, don't even try; and if you're in church with more than 1,000 members, you probably won't even know most people with whom you worship regularly.

Additionally, even if you're in a church in which you know everyone, chances are that you still focus your energies on certain individuals more than others and feel more open to sharing with a select few rather than the entire group. Small groups, therefore, provide a way to join up with a smaller group of Christians with whom you feel comfortable and can open up to.

✔ **Fellowship with other Christians provides support ties.** Small groups provide support ties that help Christian brothers and sisters in times of need. When a church member is going through a crisis, a church usually takes action to make sure that that the individual or family receives assistance during this time.

Accountability: Nothing to do with your checkbook

Proverbs 27:17 says, "As iron sharpens iron, so one man sharpens another." If you aim to apply this verse to your life, you can see that Christians grow not only by sharing with and praying for each other but also by challenging and holding each other accountable.

Accountability means having a trusted, tight-knit group of people who

✔ Share successes and failures with each other. ("Tell one another the wrong things you have done. And tell God about each other's needs." James 5:16)

✔ Confront each other in love. ("Faithful are the wounds of a friend." Proverbs 27:6)

✔ Strengthen and encourage each other. ("Say something that will make them strong. . . ." 1 Thessalonians 5:11)

✔ Allow themselves to be taught by other believers. ("One who walks with wise men grows wise." Proverbs 13:20)

With this in mind, the next step beyond a prayer group is to form an *accountability group*, which has the goal of committing to pray for each member of the group and to hold them accountable for their growth in their Christian life. Without people holding you accountable, you can more easily become stagnant in your relationship with God and fall into temptation. However, because of the nature of the issues that arise, accountability groups lend themselves to being gender specific: men holding each other accountable and women holding each other accountable.

However, when you're part of a small group, people in your group will know you and your situation better. As a result, they not only can provide material needs but also can deal better with your spiritual needs. In the same way, when you hear of a particular need from a member of the group, you're more likely to respond, given the closer tie to that individual.

✔ **Fellowship with other Christians establishes an environment for growth.** Small groups provide an opportunity to grow in ways that you can't by going solo. Although Christianity is an individual's relationship with God, the Bible makes it clear that Christianity is not about holy individuals, but about a group of imperfect people gathering together.

In the early church in the New Testament, the Christian practice of meeting in small groups was a given. You never read of Christians in the early church going it alone. Even when Peter, Paul, John, or another apostle was imprisoned, another believer was often with them.

Seeking All Prayer Requests

Before your small group prays, open up the floor for members of the group to share concerns that they'd like the group to pray about.

Consider these things when sharing prayer requests:

- ✔ **Be patient.** Building closeness within your small group is a natural part of a group's growth, but just as with any other relationship, you can't gain intimacy overnight. Closeness takes time. As a result, sharing of prayer requests is a gradual process. When a new group begins meeting, it gets a few prayer requests but typically at not too deep or intimate a level. As people become comfortable with and start to trust each other, they'll gradually open up.

- ✔ **Be vulnerable.** If you're leading a group that you sense isn't really opening up to each other, consider taking the lead and sharing something that is clearly vulnerable. Many times, this honesty instantly changes the tone and fosters a new sense of closeness of the group, causing others to open up as well.

Get small to grow

A common struggle small groups have is growing to a healthy size of 6 to 12 persons. However, sometimes a small group should get smaller in order to grow larger, as illustrated in this example.

My wife and I got involved in a newly formed small group several years back. When we began, perhaps a dozen people attended regularly, but the group never really bonded. The discussions were largely superficial, and the prayer requests never reflected much openness. Over the course of several months, people gradually started to drop out, until we slimmed to just five people (including my wife and me).

But the transformation that happened next was remarkable. Instead of dwindling down to nothing, the five of us continued to meet, and in time, the group jelled and formed a special bond. After we had been meeting consistently for

about a year, new people gradually started to attend. But this time, when new persons came into the group, they were buoyed by the existing closeness of that core group of five and opened up quickly themselves.

After the group had grown to the healthy size of 14 tightly knit people, plans unexpectedly changed: My wife and I moved out of state on a job-related move, and the group gradually broke up. However, the story has a happy ending. Last year, we returned to the same area in Massachusetts, and one of the original five members of the prayer group soon asked when the group was going to start meeting again. We quickly revived the group and resumed where we left off. Today, we have not only the original five but also many of the other older members, and some new ones as well. Small groups can build bonds that last a lifetime.

✔ **Be mindful of group size.** The willingness of people to share requests is proportionate to the number of people in the group. If you have a small number of people (less than 10 or so), people tend to open up much more than in groups of 14 or more. The larger the group, the more difficult it is to retain the sense of intimacy needed for small groups to succeed.

✔ **Be confidential.** One of the most important aspects of sharing prayer requests is confidentiality. The health of the small group is built upon the trustworthiness of its members. If people trust each other, then they open themselves up, knowing that what is said never leaves the group. But if a member ever violates that trust, then the fabric of your small group could break down.

A good general rule on confidentiality is "Whatever is prayed here stays here."

✔ **Be a documenter.** Encourage members of the group to bring along a pencil and a prayer notebook to write down the concerns that people want the group to pray about. Otherwise, people tend to forget the prayer requests the moment they walk out the door. (See Chapter 9 for more details on writing down prayer requests.)

Steering Clear of Small Group Pitfalls

When praying in small groups, you definitely need to maneuver around the following traps:

✔ **Gossiping:** When people open up in small groups and share their needs and concerns, the biggest potential risk is gossip. Gossip is tricky because it happens not only in obvious cases, such as a juicy tidbit of information you share with another friend ("Did you hear about Nancy?"), but also in the form of a prayer request ("Please pray for Nancy because. . . ."). So even well-intentioned sharing can unintentionally produce gossip.

A general rule is to keep prayer requests confined to the group unless the member who shares the request agrees that you can pass the request to others outside the group.

✔ **Praying to those around you:** Another easy trap to fall into when praying with others is to pray to *them* rather than to God. This habit is far more common than what you may initially think. When you become overly concerned with your wording or how it sounds to others in the room, then you turn your prayer into a performance, "praying to the crowd." Focus on God, and God alone, and let the words take whatever form they may.

✔ **Dropping the ball:** A third trap occurs when someone shares a prayer request and then the group eventually forgets about the request. Prayer requests should not be one-time petitions; each member of the group should actively pray for the request until the request is answered, even if its takes months or even years. (See Chapter 18 for more on prayers that seem lost in the shuffle.)

If you're leading a group, write down the requests in a prayer notebook so that you can follow up on the status of requests each time your group meets.

✔ **Speaking gibberish:** I talk in Chapter 2 about the tendency to turn prayers into Shakespearean soliloquies by adding words such as "thee" and "thou" and other highly sophisticated language into your prayers. Although people praying in small groups may not be prone to start speaking like King Lear, they can find themselves falling into "Christianspeak," throwing out phrases that sound theologically deep but end up being mere gibberish if they aren't words from the heart.

Therefore, keep it simple and be real. Not only is your prayer life strengthened, but your genuineness encourages the entire group who hears your prayer.

✔ **Overemphasizing results:** A final trap to avoid when praying as a small group is focusing exclusively on praying for results rather than also praying for how God can use the situation to get the people involved to know God more and grow closer to him.

For example, John may share the need for finding a job after being laid off. Praying for God to open up a job for him is perfectly legitimate. But at the same time, group members should also pray that the Lord uses this crisis to increase the faith of John so that John trusts God more.

E-Prayer: Praying in the Internet Age

The frenzied culture in which you and I live today certainly makes it harder to get people together to meet face to face in small groups. But modern culture does provide a high-tech tool that you and I can use to buck this trend: e-mail. By using e-mail, you can form a virtual prayer group in which the group members commit to pray for each other's needs daily and keep up to date by using e-mail. (You can also expand the scope of the group to include accountability. See the sidebar "Beyond e-prayer," later in this chapter.)

E-prayer has three advantages for Christians living in this digital age:

✔ E-prayer provides a way to have daily interaction with other Christians without having it dominate your schedule. Most prayer groups that meet in person do so once a week or every other week. And face it, that's about the most frequent that a handful of busy people can get together and meet on a regular, ongoing basis. Daily face-to-face meetings are impossible, unless everyone works together in the same place or lives right next to each other. (Nor in many instances would daily in-person meetings be desirable, given family and other commitments.) In contrast, by using e-mail, e-prayer allows you to spend a few minutes each day at a time that's convenient for you.

✔ E-prayer eliminates the space-and-time factor. When you meet someone face to face, you have to be in the same location at the same time in order to meet. E-prayer eliminates those two requirements. In my group, for example, mornings are the best time for some people to check in, lunchtime for others, and evenings for one individual who can't check e-mail at work.

Geography is also a nonissue. You don't have to work or live near each other. You don't even need to be in the same state! Last year, for example, I moved from California to Massachusetts, but because of e-mail, I've been able to continue participating in my same California-based group, almost as if I never left. We may not see each other on Sunday, and we miss the face-to-face meetings, but I still can maintain a close fellowship with them, which would have been impossible without e-mail.

✔ E-prayer allows you to always stay in the loop. With e-mail-based prayer requests, you can miss a day and still be in the loop on the details of what's going on in other people's lives. With in-person prayer groups, if you can't attend a meeting, you usually miss what is shared in the discussion as well as the prayer requests.

Prayer chains: Linking to one another

A popular communication method of sharing emergency prayer requests is a prayer chain. A *prayer chain* is a group of people who commit to pass along a prayer request, usually by telephone, to the next person in the chain. Typically, one person is designated as the starting point who is responsible for calling one or more people next on the list; these people in turn call the next persons, and so on until the last link is reached.

Prayer chains are ideal for providing an immediate covering of prayer when an emergency or crisis arises. They also build true fellowship and community within an entire church body or small group.

If you do form a prayer chain, do your best to ensure that the chain doesn't have any "weak links." The biggest liability of prayer chains is the potential lack of follow-through: If one person high on the list doesn't call the assigned people, then the entire chain can break and prevent the request from making its way through the church congregation or small group.

Beyond e-prayer

For years, I struggled for much of my Christian walk trying to find consistent, quality time with God each day in prayer and Bible reading (which is commonly referred to as "quiet time"). With my ever-filled schedule and a go-getter temperament, the rush of the day all too often got the better of me from the moment the alarm clock rang. Instead of starting my morning with quiet time, I'd commonly put this activity off until later in the day. But, as you might suspect, such free time at the day's end proved elusive. More often than I would like to admit, my time with the Lord got squeezed out of my schedule.

All this changed radically for me about four years ago when I teamed up with two friends from my church to do something about this problem. However, this wasn't your typical accountability group, but one made possible only by the Internet. You see, the three of us already relied heavily on e-mail as part of our work day, so we decided to use e-mail as a way to share prayer requests and help hold us accountable to spending daily quiet time on a consistent basis.

The results were amazing. E-mail not only was an effective way to share with my buddies but also served as the springboard I needed to develop consistent quiet time habits. I'd been in weekly accountability groups before, but this one was different: I had to face these guys in my e-mail in box each morning!

Since our beginnings, we expanded our group both in number (to a total of six) and in scope (of our discussions). Today, we not only ask each other about morning devotions but also share what we're learning in our studies and explain how we're applying those lessons in our lives. When I read these messages from the others, I'm challenged to dig deeper in my daily devotions and prayers.

E-prayer is all about communicating effectively and productively with a group of trusted brothers or sisters in Christ. It enables you to encourage others, share prayer requests, and grow closer together by using a relaxed, informal medium.

E-prayer has many advantages, but you should be aware of the drawbacks as well. The first and foremost is that electronic communication is almost always an inferior form of communication compared to meeting someone in person. With e-mail, you get the facts, but you miss the subtleties, the nonverbal communication, and the tone and intimacy of a live conversation. Therefore, e-prayer is most effective when you use it as a supplement to a face-to-face group. In addition, e-mail messages are notorious for being misunderstood, so make sure that careless or incomplete wording doesn't cause confusion.

Meeting other Christians in person may be the best way to way to interact with each other. But if you can't squeeze time into your schedule or if you'd like to supplement your weekly group with day-to-day interaction, then consider e-prayer.

If you're interested in forming your own e-prayer group, here are several suggestions to get started:

- ✔ **Find a couple other Christians who are interested in making this kind of "virtual commitment."** From my experience, people fall into two camps when it comes to electronic messaging: Some live by e-mail, while others would rather just watch *You've Got Mail*. So the trick is to involve people who will use e-mail enough to make your group work.

- ✔ **Keep your group to a manageable size.** From my experience, the natural size of an e-prayer group is two to six persons. If you get many more than six people, your group will generate a lot of e-mail to pore over daily, making it easy for people to get lost in it.

- ✔ **Make a commitment to each other to keep discussions confidential.** Because e-mail is a written form of communication, discussing private struggles or prayer requests that way presents more of a threat to confidentiality than sharing them orally. So use discernment and wisdom in what you share with others.

- ✔ **Periodically recommit yourself to e-prayer.** Like everything else, you can easily get into a rut after you do the same thing over and over and find yourself going through the motions; e-prayer is no exception. Some people may participate for a season; others may be involved for a longer, extended period like I have.

Chapter 15

Overcoming the Yadda Yadda Yadda: Effective Public Prayer

Many people who listen to a public prayer have a hard time sticking with it. This condition doesn't have an official name, but statisticians may someday give this tendency some techno-sounding label like *mean zone-out rate* (or simply *MZO rate* for people in the know like you and me). I wonder whether people who zone out of public prayers do a sort of "yadda yadda yadda" in their heads, twisting public prayers so that they start to sound something like this:

> Dear God,
>
> We thank you today for . . . yadda yadda yadda.
>
> Yadda yadda yadda . . . yadda yadda yadda . . .
>
> In Jesus' name we pray,
>
> Amen.

However, in spite of this problem, praying in front of others need not be destined for ineffectiveness. I've listened to many heartfelt public prayers in my lifetime that engaged and transformed me, along with the rest of the listeners present.

Therefore, if you pray in public, don't let the "yadda yadda yadda" become a factor for you. Instead, use this chapter as a guide to explore the differences between public and private prayer and to get tips on how to give public prayers that people will actually listen to.

Praying in Public versus Speaking in Solitude

It's an age-old gag that has been played: You hold a get-together at your house and invite a crowd over, but you tell only one of your friends that it's a costume party. So, while everyone else is dressed normally, this guest arrives late, dressed like a pumpkin or King Henry VIII and sticking out like a fish out of water, much to his or her embarrassment and surprise.

Prayer too can be something like a fish out of water when you pray in a manner that doesn't make sense in the context in which the prayer is being said. Some people believe that prayer is prayer no matter where you say it, and they scoff at the idea that public prayer should be any different from private prayer. Such a perspective doesn't take into account that people behave differently around different people and in different situations.

For example, like most people, I have a different public and private face. I can be fairly reserved and appear serious in public situations, be it at church, Bible study, or the office. In fact, people who know me by my public behavior generally consider me a serious, introspective guy. Yet, this persona is 180 degrees different from the one my family typically sees, one in which I am either goofy or outright childish on many occasions. (One of my treasured gifts from my kids alludes to this fact: It's a painted plaque from my 9-year-old son with the following message: "Dad, I love you. But you are weird.") In this light, consider the different contexts of prayer that exist and the impact that praying with others has on the style and content of your prayers.

Mean zone-out rate

People listening to prayers in public have a tendency to zone out and start daydreaming if they aren't actively engaged in the prayer. Because there are statistical equations for measuring everything else under the sun, why not an equation to assess this bad habit? For all the statisticians out there, the mean zone-out rate might (nonsensically) be described according to the following equation:

$$\text{MZO Rate} = \frac{(\text{Content} + \text{Delivery}) * \text{Earnestness}^2}{\text{Duration}}$$

Climbing the five tiers of prayers

All prayer is directed to God, whether you're praying in your bedroom or Denver's Mile High Stadium filled with 80,000 people. But the manner in which you pray and the words you speak should be tailored to the people listening and the place you are. In general, there are five tiers of prayer, each of which has a different style, content, and degree of intimacy:

✔ **Personal:** Personal prayer is quite obviously your private time between you and God alone. If you've made it this far in the book, you know by now that personal prayer is a time of deep closeness between you and your loving Father in heaven. During this time, you can pray about anything and everything, anytime and anywhere (see Chapter 4).

✔ **Intimate:** In intimate prayer, you pray with the people who are closest to you in all the world. Intimate prayer partners are typically your spouse, family members, your best friend, or a small set of trusted friends. You're likely to have different levels of intimacy even within this smallest of groups, but generally you'll freely share most concerns with these trusted people. Prayer time with intimates can even approach the same level of intimacy that personal prayer does.

✔ **Small group:** Small group prayer is what takes place within a Bible study, cell group, or accountability group. The group may or may not approach the level of closeness of the personal and intimate prayer tiers, but group members share a degree of friendship, trust, and commitment. Even at this level, personal prayer needs are freely shared and prayed upon. (See Chapter 14 for more information on small group prayer.)

✔ **Church:** Church prayer consists of prayer in a church service or other Christian context, but it takes place within a larger group of people whom you may or may not know personally. Prayer at this level should be heartfelt but more reserved than the first three tiers and should focus primarily on issues that affect the entire church.

If you go to a small church of less than 30 or so members, there is much less of a distinction between the church and small group tiers. In fact, in rare cases, a small church can even begin to resemble a small group in terms of closeness. In a special scenario like this, many of the public prayer issues discussed in this chapter are less relevant, while the small group issues covered in Chapter 14 are more applicable.

✔ **Community:** Community prayer is the type of prayer said at town events that people of all beliefs and backgrounds attend. Examples include town festivities, memorial services, and graduations (depending on the latest court rulings, of course). Because people at such gatherings are likely to have different religious backgrounds, prayers should be the most formal and restrained in terms of their scope. You wouldn't, for example, want to pray for your mother-in-law's arthritis if you're called to give a prayer at the start of the World Series.

During community prayers, pray in a way that steadfastly upholds the integrity of your beliefs, while at the same time respecting the beliefs of others in attendance who have different religious backgrounds. Table 15-1 gives you an idea of how each works, at a glance.

Table 15-1	How Prayer Changes Focus Depending on Context		
Type	*Intimacy Level*	*Degree of formality*	*Focus*
Personal	Maximum	Informal	Anything goes
Intimate	High	Informal	Most, if not all, issues
Small group	Moderate	Informal	Personal and group issues
Church	Minimal	Formal	Church-level and higher issues
Community	None	Formal	Issues pertaining to community

We're not in Kansas anymore: Keeping congregation size in mind

Churches, particular evangelical Protestant ones (see the Introduction), have become more informal over the past 30 years. One side effect of this newfound relaxed approach to worship is a blurring of the traditional boundaries between small group and church prayer. The sharing and praying that used to be done only in small, more intimate contexts is now being regularly done at the church level in many congregations today.

Openness and candor within the family of God (see the sidebar "Even Christians have nicknames" in this chapter) are refreshing and healthy and should be encouraged. But, at the same time, churches should use common sense and wisdom when deciding what's appropriate when more people are gathered together.

Many churches, for example, offer a time to share prayer requests during worship. Although congregation participation is a good thing, this part of the service usually turns into a systematic listing of the current personal health problems of the church members. If you're regularly sharing your personal problems in church, you're confusing the function of the larger church (gathering as the body of Christ to worship and grow together) with your need for a smaller group with which to share deeply personal issues.

Even Christians have nicknames

The Christian church is often referred to as the *family of God* because Christians are considered brothers and sisters of Christ, with God as their father (see Matthew 12:50). The Church is also commonly called the *body of Christ* because Christians represent Christ himself on earth (see Ephesians 3:6 and 4:12).

Public prayer works best when you focus on issues that impact the church congregation as a whole. But because you're bypassing issues "too intimate" for the church at large, make sure the church has small groups and other support options so that those personal needs are appropriately and sufficiently nurtured.

Having said that, I do think that praying for special crisis or emergency needs of individuals is perfectly appropriate and desirable in the larger church context, but this practice should be the exception rather than the norm.

Public prayer shouldn't be intrusive, giving out private details about a person being prayed for that he or she may consider an invasion of privacy. For example, you probably wouldn't want to make these prayer requests in public:

"Lord, be with Al as he gets a tattoo removed from his buttocks tomorrow."

"And, please give provision to Frank, who is now 45 days behind on his Visa bill."

Finally, let the person being prayed for know before you pray for them to make sure that they don't have a problem with your singling them out in public prayer.

Keeping the Z's to a Minimum

Whether you are a pastor who prays weekly in front of others or someone who prays in public once a year, remember that public prayer is not a performance. Instead, effective public prayer recognizes that in order to get listeners to pray with you, you need to engage them, to get them to come alongside you, so to speak. Private prayer has a single goal of earnest interaction with your Father in heaven. Public prayer has a twofold goal: earnestly communicating with God and simultaneously engaging listeners to participate equally in the prayer.

Your motivation for getting people to better listen to your prayers shouldn't be related in any way to your ego or pride. Instead, if you're leading public prayer, you have a special responsibility and burden to draw listeners closer to God and not push them away because they find the prayer boring.

So with that in mind, consider the top ten list of ways to get people to actually listen to your public prayers:

✔ **Leave them wanting more.** I estimate that I've listened to at least 1,612 sermons and 2,110 public prayers since I was old enough to be able to comprehend them. And yet, of those thousands of prayers and sermons, I recall hardly any that were shorter than I expected them to be. Yes, I've loved (I had to be sure to add that qualification in case my pastor reads this book!) many of them, but I can't say that I'd describe many of the sermons and prayers I've heard as succinct.

It is better . . . that the hearers should wish the prayer had been longer than spend half the time in wishing it was over.

John Newton

I've prayed plenty of times in public and have experienced that self-induced pressure to pray a long time as well, even when I don't have much to say. I think there are two misconceptions at play:

- **"Mature Christians always give lengthy prayers."** One pressure you may experience is the notion that long-time Christians give long prayers. Based on that belief, you may assume that you need to come up with plenty to say if you're asked to pray at a public function. After all, the previous person who prayed went on and on and on. What will people think if you stop after one or two minutes?

- **"But I've got so much to say."** A second pressure is the idea that, because you finally get a chance to pray in public, you need to mention everything, including a blessing of the kitchen sink, in that single prayer.

If you follow the other nine tips in this section, people *will* listen to your prayer — at least for a while. So always quit before they start looking at their watch, falling asleep, or staring at the stained glass windows and wondering how they're made anyway.

✔ **Steer clear of using public prayer as a bully pulpit.** Remember that you're supposed to pray, not preach. Pray to God and don't use the prayer as a vehicle to preach to the listeners. Many well-intentioned people who pray publicly can fall into this trap without even realizing it. For example, notice that the following prayer is actually addressing the listeners, leaving God as a mere bystander:

Dear God,

Two-thirds of the world's population lives in absolute poverty conditions, while we in this country live in relative luxury. Why, the amount of money that we all spend on coffee or sodas each week would feed an entire family in a poverty-stricken nation for a month. May each person dwell on that fact and be moved to action. Amen.

When you pray in public, think of yourself as the people's representative to God and the one charged with expressing the praises, concerns, and needs of the people. Don't put on the hat of God's appointed spokesperson to talk to the people during that given time. If you're a pastor, save that stuff for the sermon. If you're a layperson, jump the preacher before he speaks, assume his place, and then you'll literally have a *bully* pulpit.

✔ **Avoid repetition, clichés, and safe subjects.** Public prayer can be a nerve-racking activity for even the most seasoned public speakers. Those leading public prayer often exhibit three tendencies as a subconscious attempt to compensate for being a little anxious:

- **Repetition of similar phrases or words.** Using the same words over and over can be distracting to listeners. For example, many people tend to repeat "Jesus" or "God" or use fillers such as "like" and "um" throughout their prayer, making it sound something like this:

  Dear God,

  We thank you, um, that are God. And, um, God, we thank you for being with us here today in our midst. God, you are faithful even when, um, we deliberately disobey you. So, we pray, God, that you would, um, cleanse this unrighteousness with the blood of Jesus Christ. Father God, we, um, also pray for. . . . Amen.

- **The use of a certain lingo that I affectionately call "Christianspeak."** Public Christian prayers can easily become victims of this language. You'll recognize it as soon as the speaker starts using clichés — such as "cover us with your blood, Jesus" or "we lift up Charlie to you" — that are elegant and theologically profound but may go over the heads of the people listening.

- **Avoidance of controversial topics.** Don't feel that you need to stick to safe subjects. Obviously, avoid private issues that aren't appropriate, but be bold enough to pray about new topics or pray

Teddy bears repeating

The term "bully pulpit" was coined by U.S. President Theodore Roosevelt back in the early 20th century as a reference to the unique role of the White House as an influential platform from which to forcefully advocate an agenda.

for the congregation as a whole to be challenged by God on a particular issue. When people realize that you're not praying the same old thing, they'll quickly become engaged in the prayer.

✔ **Don't press the restart button.** Are you ever almost done speaking and suddenly have something jump in your mind to pray about? Instead of ignoring it, you hit the restart button and essentially begin the prayer all over again. Anxious listeners who had been patient up to that point can suddenly turn on you and start zoning out. The best recommendation is that, after you lead listeners to the end of a prayer, you should always close the prayer at that time.

✔ **Prepare loosely, not rigidly.** People who give public prayers can often fall into two extremes. Some don't give any thought at all to the prayer before starting and end up giving a "stream of consciousness" prayer. Others prepare so rigorously that their delivery sounds forced or mechanical. Both of these extremes fail to engage listeners. A free-flowing prayer that goes all over the place may have little coherence. On the other hand, a heavily prepared prayer can sound so emotionless and stoic that people begin the yadda yadda yadda routine.

The trick is to give some thought to your preparation beforehand, sketching out rough ideas in your head as to the flow of the prayer. But don't allow the prayer to become something resembling a memorized script that sucks the life out of it.

✔ **Avoid sloppy theology.** A few years back, I invited a good friend who was looking for a church home to visit my church. After the service, I was interested in his reaction to it, because the pastor was particularly effective and challenging on that Sunday. Yet, to my surprise, his reaction was mixed. Oh, he liked the sermon all right, but he was bothered by what he thought was careless theology expressed in the morning prayer.

For example, I've heard people pray that God would "bind Satan" from the church or community. While God certainly protects Christians from the influence of the devil, the request to "bind Satan" doesn't have any Biblical foundation for Christians.

Another common mistake is to make the catchall request "forgive us for our sins," saying it so it's not in a repentant spirit, but as a way to cover any possible issues.

If you have been given the privilege to pray in public, don't get sloppy on your theology. Be precise in your wording on such issues; what might be nit-picky to you may be a major issue for others. I believe God overlooks such errors, as I discuss in Chapter 3, but some of your listeners don't.

✔ **Stay away from "pet prayers."** Public prayer should focus on the particular concerns and issues that affect the listening body of Christians. As I discuss earlier, you should avoid private issues that impact a single individual. However, this also means that you should use common sense to avoid dwelling on issues that may be close to your heart but are of little interest to the other listeners.

For example, suppose that one of your pet projects in the church is caring for the church grounds. Even though the subject may be germane to the entire congregation, you wouldn't want your prayer to go something like this:

Dear Father,

We thank you for bringing all these people here today to join with us to worship you and celebrate the resurrection of your Son, Jesus Christ.

However, we want to lift the needs we have as a congregation. I pray in particular for those shingles on the lower-left side of the sanctuary roof. They look like they may need to be replaced before the next rainstorm, so we pray for your provision before that event occurs. We also pray for those devilish weeds in the front yard that seem to be taking over the new sod we laid.

Oh, yeah, we pray for every other concern people may have here, although they couldn't be as important as those facilities issues that are so dear to my heart and yours.

Amen.

✔ **Tweak the volume knob.** Volume is a funny business. You may think that volume means only that everyone can hear you. Yes, it's true that "listenability" is the essential aspect of volume control, whether you're listening to the television or a prayer. However, even if people can hear you, your volume can still be an issue.

You have to be loud enough so people can hear you. Otherwise, people strain themselves trying to hear you pray, but they eventually get tired and zone out. On the other hand, if you're too loud, people may hear you just fine, but the excessive volume becomes a distraction, and you end up sounding unnatural and fake. Either extreme can annoy people and become an obstacle to a successful public prayer.

If speaking into a microphone, you probably can use your natural voice. If not, speak louder than usual. Pick someone in the back of room and attempt to speak to that person in a natural voice.

✔ **Be real, but don't get carried away.** When you pray in public, don't suddenly change personalities. If you suddenly switch from a Southern drawl to the King's English, you'll come across sounding artificial and turn off some listeners. Instead, use the same vocabulary, tone, and style of speech that you would use if you were having an ordinary conversation with someone.

At the same time, don't get carried away and start sounding chatty and overly informal. Doing so can come across as irreverent and disrespectful, giving people yet another reason to get distracted.

✔ **Go beyond problems.** Why do public prayers so often sound like the church is filled with a bunch of Jobs? (Job was the bad-luck guy in the Old Testament who had everything go wrong for a time in his life.) All too often, public prayer becomes a reciting of the major problems of the church members. After you've prayed for all the personal problems of the congregation, everyone feels dejected, leaving little energy for praise, thanksgiving, and adoration. Intercessory and petitionary prayers (see Chapter 6) can be part of public prayer as long as they're relevant to the context, but make sure that your prayer goes beyond a laundry list of woes, such as this prayer:

Dear Father,

Thank you for your provision for this new sanctuary that we are meeting in today. We pray that you will be glorified by everything that transpires in this place.

Lord, we as a church do have a special need. We want to ask you to help Al the construction worker who is back by the rear exit, since he accidentally glued his arm to the wall last week applying wallpaper. We pray that we can find a chemical somewhere to free him from the wall so he can go home and be with his family once again. But we do thank you he could be here to worship with us today . . .

Remembering what matters most

You may find yourself wanting to perfect your techniques of public prayer. Although doing so is important, never forget that the *most* important quality of public prayer, as with private prayer, is earnestness. An earnest prayer can compensate for a host of mistakes in delivery and still be effective.

My favorite story that illustrates this point comes from Tony Campolo, the well-known Christian author and speaker and professor at Eastern College. Years ago, Tony was asked to be a counselor at a junior high summer camp. A camper named Billy suffered from cerebral palsy and became the target of ridicule by the rest of the junior high kids. Tony describes the situation this way:

"Oh, they picked on him. As he walked across the camp with his uncoordinated body, they would line up and imitate his grotesque movements. I was irate.

"But my furor reached its highest pitch when on Thursday morning it was Billy's cabin's turn to give devotions. I wondered what would happen because they had appointed Billy to be the speaker. As he dragged his way to the front, you could hear the giggles rolling over the crowd. It took little Billy almost five minutes to say seven words: 'Jesus . . . loves . . . me . . . and . . . I . . . love . . . Jesus.'

"When he finished, there was dead silence. I looked over my shoulder and saw junior high boys bawling all over the place. A revival broke out in that camp after Billy's short testimony."

I've heard Tony Campolo speak on several occasions, and I consider him one of the most engaging and stimulating speakers I've ever encountered. And yet, in spite of his world-class speaking skills, he wasn't able to penetrate the hearts of these nasty junior high kids. Instead, the simple faith and earnestness of Billy with the stuttered speech got their attention, changing their hearts forever.

Part IV
Tackling Some Tough Issues

The 5th Wave   By Rich Tennant

@RICHTENNANT

"All of our research seems to point to one irrefutable conclusion. There _is_ a design to the universe, and it appears to be plaid with rounded gussets."

In this part . . .

*1*t's time to talk tough. This section takes you beyond the basics and stretches you as it deals with the toughest questions people ask about prayer. You get the skinny on why God may wait before he answers your prayer and why he sometimes never seems to answer it. You explore the balance between praying for God's will and asking for what you want. You find out how to distinguish between God's voice and your hungry stomach. Finally, you can read about healing prayer and the hot-potato issue of speaking in tongues.

Chapter 16

Thy Will Be Done

Did you ever listen to a song and then have the tune stick with you all day, playing over and over again in your mind? "Que Sera Sera," the old Doris Day song, is one such melody that clings to me, like gum on my shoe. Sometimes I just can't get rid of it.

You've probably heard "Que Sera Sera" before, but did you ever pay much attention to its lyrics? The song was written for Alfred Hitchcock's *The Man Who Knew Too Much* and contains a strong dose of fatalism:

> *Que sera sera*
> *Whatever will be, will be*
> *The future's not ours to see*
> *Que sera sera*

In the classic 1956 film that features the song, Jimmy Stewart and Doris Day star as a couple whose boy is kidnapped after they accidentally get caught up in an international conspiracy. Hitchcock skillfully interweaves "Que Sera Sera" into the plot, suggesting that the chaos and danger that the couple face in attempting to rescue their son are unavoidable, no matter what they do.

To many people, that same fatalism comes to mind when they start talking about God's will. Regardless of what they do, God has his own mind made up already, so whatever will be, will be. In fact, the familiar phrase in the Lord's Prayer "thy will be done" is often seen as the Shakespearean equivalent to "que sera sera."

Just what does it mean to pray for God's will to be done in your life? Does it mean throwing up your arms and resigning yourself to an uncertain fate? Or is there a deeper promise that you can hold onto when you pray for his will? In this chapter, you explore the major issues to think about when praying for God's will, specific steps to take to know God's will, and reasons why praying that the will of God be done is vital.

However, before I begin, let me apologize if you find yourself humming "Que Sera Sera" as you read through the rest of the chapter. I know I am!

Wanting Your Will Won't Get It Done

Throughout the Bible, you find examples of people obedient to God praying for the Lord's will to be carried out. I think of Shadrach, Meshach, and Abednego, who were about to be put into a fiery furnace for refusing to bow down to the gods of King Nebuchadnezzar, when they said, in effect, "We pray for God to save us, but if not, may his will be done" (Daniel 3:17–18). Or I think of stubborn Jonah, who had to get eaten by a big fish before coming to the conclusion "thy will be done," but in the end, he did. For Christians, the most famous example is found in the Gospel of Matthew when Jesus instructed his followers to pray: "Thy will be done, on earth as it is in heaven."

Praying for God's will sounds well and good until you think about the possible downside: The result may mean that *your* will not be done. Now, that's a bummer!

Yes, you and I often don't see eye to eye with God and end up clashing with him in a contest of wills: my will versus God's will. In large part, this battle is caused by the fact that you and I think differently from God in four specific ways.

Seeing the big picture

While God looks at things in the light of eternity, the outlook of mere mortals like you and me is much more focused on the here and now. We may give occasional thought to what's ahead, but the "future" is always within my or perhaps my children's lifetime. God's will is based on eternity, whereas my head starts to spin whenever I fast-forward to the time my kids will be old enough to drive, let alone to eternity.

Imagine yourself walking through a giant, life-size maze in search of the exit door. During the walk, you can see only the passageway directly in front of or behind you, and you have no real clue how your current position relates to the overall goal of getting out of the maze. Oh, on a hunch, you may make a run for what you think is the way out, but ultimately your understanding of the situation is only a guess, given your limited perspective.

Contrast that with God, who has a bird's-eye view of the entire maze, seeing the beginning and the end points. Because of this fact, if you were to let God lead you through the puzzle, he would take you around twists and turns that you might think are superfluous, unnecessary, or even in the wrong direction. But, in actuality, they would be needed steps to reach the goal of the exit.

In the same way, your will and my will are based on a ground-level, here-and-now perspective that doesn't take into account the full scope of reality. that God's will does.

Sending up a periscope to see beyond the surface

Growing up, I always wanted to be a submarine captain, the one who says, "Up periscope!" and gets the first look through the looking glass to see what's on the surface of the water around the vessel. I thought a periscope was cool because it allowed a captain to see things on the surface while the submarine remained underwater.

You and I view life in much the same way, seeing it as a snapshot of reality. Those pictures of what's in front of you help form your interests and passions as well as influence what you're concerned enough to pray for. If you're like me, your prayers are usually about you and your family, friends and acquaintances, people at your place of worship, and the occasional government leader. But when you go to God with this narrow perspective, such prayers may not factor in other people who would be affected if God answered your prayer the way that you want him to.

But once again, God sees the big picture. He has the panoramic, wide-angle lens. He knows all the ripple effects of your prayer requests and how a specific answer to your prayer could adversely affect someone you don't know.

The Lord refuses to look at your request in a vacuum like you or I probably would prefer. Instead, he looks at each request based on all of reality and responds accordingly.

Growth cycle: Pedaling through adversity

Several years ago, I rode my bicycle across the United States, traversing 3,400 miles in about a month. As I began the journey, I symbolically dipped my rear tire into the Pacific Ocean and started pedaling my bike eastward. Riding 10 to 12 hours each day over the next 4 weeks, I had but a single, all-consuming goal: to dunk my front tire in the Atlantic Ocean to complete the crossing.

When I look back today on that bicycle trip, I don't much think of that finish line anymore. Yes, I appreciate actually making it all the way across, but what I truly relish is the experiences, many of which were difficult, that I had en route: I recall that dreadful first night in the California desert, thinking I'd never survive another day; the 12-hour-straight, high-altitude climb up the Colorado Rockies; and the ride across the Kansas plains in a 40-mph crosswind, in which I struggled just to stay upright on my bike. At the time, I didn't savor these events much, given my preoccupation with the finish line. But, paradoxically, these hard times are the memories that linger in my mind as the years go by. For it was in these tough moments that I was stretched, pulled, and tugged — ultimately growing as I persevered through them.

Forgetting about the finish line

Young and old alike, people are attracted to finish lines. Something deeply rooted in men and women propels them to meet goals at all costs, striving to break the tape at the end of a race. These finish lines characterize all aspects of life, not just athletic events: landing a new job, buying a new house, finding the right mate, making enough money to retire, and so on. More often than not, much of the time you and I spend on this earth is in the hot pursuit of some goal.

Mortals can easily become consumed, even obsessed, by finish lines. Yet, God doesn't give the same importance to end goals like you or I do. He is concerned with your aspirations and helps you achieve them, but he is far more interested in the growth that occurs in your life in pursuit of these ends compared to the actual goals themselves. His will reflects that fact.

Thinking selflessly

The first three ways in which you and I think differently from God are not necessarily bad in and of themselves. More than anything, they're simply part of being human. However, the final reason you think differently from God is one that you *can* be blamed for: sin.

According to the Scriptures, every person who has walked, is walking, or will walk the earth has sinned. (Christians believe the lone exception was Jesus, who as the Son of God lived a sinless life on earth. Roman Catholics add the Virgin Mary, who they believe was born without sin and lived that way.) This sin that you have in your life invariably leads to selfishness. And being selfish means that you'd rather have what you want, when you want it, than what's part of God's plan and timing. This selfishness, when left unchecked, results in prayers that are tainted by self-interest and self-concern instead of being focused on the will of God or the needs of other people. Sin blocks your ability to see God's will and to open yourself to pray "thy will be done." (Chapter 3 dives further into the impact of sin on your prayer life.) In doing so, you put yourself in a contest of wills with God.

Knowing God's Will

When you recognize that the four ways of thinking described in the section "Wanting Your Will Won't Get It Done," earlier in this chapter, dominate your life, you won't wonder at the fact that knowing God's will can seem mysterious or even impossible to grasp. So how do you jump this chasm and begin to understand how God thinks? How can you know God's will? This question is often posed like a calculus problem or some sort of ancient puzzle that only someone like Indiana Jones can solve: If only you work hard enough, you can eventually figure out the answer.

You may be surprised to know that you don't need a calculator or fedora to find the will of God; the real answer to that mystery is surprisingly down to earth, boiling down to six basic steps:

- Know the Bible.
- Forget about yourself.
- Listen to God speak.
- Look around you.
- Pray to draw you nearer to God.
- Just do it.

These steps aren't meant to be a magical formula to knowing the mysteries of God's will, but they're definitive steps, proven by Scripture, that can greatly help you to know God's will for your life. But does it work?

Evangelist and philanthropist George Müller, who lived in the 19th century, is a good person to consider when trying to answer this question. He followed steps similar to these for much of his life. For over 69 years, whenever he sincerely and patiently sought to know the will of God, by the teaching of the Holy Spirit and Word of God, he said, "I was *always* directed rightly." But when he was not upfront with God, was impatient, or favored listening to the advice of his friends, he said candidly, "I made great mistakes." See Chapters 1 and 18 for more details on how Müller relied on prayer.

Finding a face-to-face substitute: Reading the Bible

By far, the single most important way to know God's will is to read and study the Bible. Nothing else even comes close. You may think it strange that the best thing you can do to know God's will in the 21st century is to read a book that is thousands of years old, but it's true.

Imagine that you are an architect and have a fascination with Frank Lloyd Wright's work. As a student of Wright, you want to get into his mind and understand the thought processes that led him to make the architectural decisions that he did. But Wright has long since died, so how can you get into his mind because you can't talk to him face to face?

For one thing, you can study his library of blueprints and examine the buildings that he had constructed. You can look at one blueprint or one house and start to get a grasp of what Wright thinks. When you look at all his works together, however, you can begin to construct a fairly comprehensive understanding of Wright's architectural genius. After you become a Wright expert, suppose that a real estate agent tries to convince you to buy a New England Colonial on the premise that Wright secretly designed and built it. As a student of Wright's work, you know at once that the agent is ill informed or a scoundrel.

In the same way, reading through the Bible helps give you a clearer sense of who God is by explaining what he likes and doesn't like and how he worked in the world during the Old and New Testament times. As a result, because the Lord is the same yesterday, today, and forever (Hebrews 13:8), you can better discern what his will is in today's world. The Bible is also the best litmus test for determining whether something is the will of God.

God will *never* do something that is not in line with Scriptures. You can always count on that. In reading his Word, you find over and over that God wants purity, fidelity, and honesty. So you can be certain that God never tells you to have an affair, no matter how bad your marriage is, or cheat your employer, regardless of how much you need the money. And, on the positive side, as you discover God's purpose for the world, you also realize what he wants you to focus on and be devoted to.

Reading the Bible may seem less electrifying than hearing God talk to you through dreams or visions, but most Bible scholars suggest that God's written Word is the preferred method of communication that the Lord uses for today's world.

Forgetting about yourself

You may already see pretty clearly by now that you don't think like God, so when you're seeking God's will, one of the best things you can do is to forget about your feelings or opinions on what you're praying about. Frankly, your self-interest is Public Enemy #1 to finding the will of God.

Obviously, you can't do this by simply turning on a switch and instantly being able to see God's point of view rather than your own. Instead, this act of replacing your perspective for God's is a process, one that takes time. But if you ask God to help you and are diligent in your efforts, you'll find that, over time, you become less and less concerned with your self-interest.

George Müller was a great man of prayer. As I discuss in Chapter 1, he ran an orphanage in Bristol, England, totally through prayer and trusting in the Lord. Instead of begging people for money, he simply believed that God would provide. Müller remarked that you can overcome nine-tenths of the difficulties of knowing the will of God when you forget about your will and make the deliberate decision to allow yourself to be ready and open for God's action.

When you pray to know God's will, specifically ask God to help you forget yourself!

What's that, God? Speak up!

A third way to know God's will is to learn to listen to him speak. He's not going to speak to you with a voice like George Burns did in the film *Oh God!*, but he does speak to your spirit in a way that can be just as confirming as if you heard it with your ears. What's more, you're prewired to listen to God, but whether you take advantage of this "broadband access" is up to you. Listening to God is a huge issue in and of itself, so I cover it in full detail in Chapter 19.

Taking a look around

Scottish preacher Oswald Chambers (1874–1917), a great prayer warrior who wrote the classic devotional *My Utmost For His Highest* (published by Discovery

House Publishers), always stressed that we have a proactive God, one who engineers circumstances in our lives. Chambers said that God brings people into situations so that they can learn the particular lessons he wants them to learn. Therefore, looking to circumstances can indicate God's direction in your life. (You can read more about Oswald Chambers in Chapter 18.)

Here are a couple words of warning, however:

- Never look at circumstances by themselves and make assumptions about God's will, or you'll easily be misled. Instead, look at circumstances in combination with these other steps to confirm his will. (See Chapter 19 for more on how God uses circumstances to speak to you.)

- Don't assume that all circumstances that happen, particularly the bad ones, are God's will. (See the sidebar "Is everything that happens God's will?" later in this chapter, for details on this tough issue.)

Growing closer to God through prayer

Perhaps you're reluctant to pray "thy will be done" when you're not exactly sure what the Lord's will is. But don't let that reluctance stop you from praying altogether. It's quite natural to want to understand God's will so that you can pray accordingly. The irony, however, is that the more you pray, the more you'll discover God's will in the process.

Watchman Nee, founder of the Little Flock house church movement in China in the early 20th century, once said that a person who prays not only comes closer to God but also frequently enters into his will. Imagine that! When you pray consistently and earnestly, your thoughts start to tap into God's thoughts, making his will clearer to you.

Teach me to do your will.

Psalm 143:10

Tacking on "thy will be done"

The specific words "thy will be done" aren't essential to praying for God's will. Instead, your attitude is what's all-important. When you approach God with humility and submission, don't worry about tacking on "thy will be done" to every prayer request you make.

Also, make sure that in adding that phrase on to your request, you don't harbor a lack of confidence that God will answer the prayer. For example, praying "please heal me *if it be your will*" can sometimes translate to "Lord, I'd like you to heal me, but I'm not sure you will." (See Chapter 17 for more on getting over that lack of confidence.)

Just do it

Even long-time believers expend an enormous amount of energy on the question of knowing God's will. But be careful not to make the answer more complicated than it really is. The answer is not just in front of you, but is actually part of you.

Oswald Chambers makes a good point when he says that, if you're among God's faithful, you *are* the will of God. Your everyday common-sense decisions are then God's will for you unless he gives you an "inner check." When he gives you a red flag, immediately stop what you're doing, pray, and wait on the Lord for direction before proceeding. But if not, it's like that famous slogan from that sports and fitness company: Just do it!

> *Don't say "thy will be done," but see it is done.*
>
> Oswald Chambers

Exposing an Age-Old Struggle

Even when you grow closer to the Lord and follow the steps to know the will of God, you have no guarantee that you're always going to think like he does. Don't let anyone fool you: Praying for God's will is sometimes just plain hard! It's certainly been a struggle from the earliest times through the present day.

Take Abraham, for example, who was tested by God when he was told to sacrifice his son, Isaac, as a burnt offering. Obviously, such a call would be impossibly hard for any parent, but it was even more so for Abraham. You see, years before, Abraham had been promised by God that he would be the father of a great nation, but it wasn't until he was a card-carrying AARP member that he had his son. Now, here was Isaac — Abraham's sole link to God's future promise — and Abraham was being asked to give that up.

Abraham and Isaac had about a 60-mile trip on foot to Mount Moriah, where Abraham was to make the sacrifice. The Scriptures don't give much detail of what Abraham was thinking about during that three-day journey, but I'm sure that Abraham was struggling with each step on that trek to obey what was clearly God's will but against everything he had dreamed of.

Jesus himself gives another example of this struggle in Matthew 26. He knew that the time for his death was rapidly approaching, and so he went to a quiet garden called Gethsemane to pray about the coming events.

Jesus certainly didn't want a death on the cross, but far more than that, he wasn't looking forward to the prospect of bearing the brunt of his Father's wrath when he took on the sins of all people on that cross.

Picture the scene: Jesus never sinned, was closer to his Father in heaven like no one before or since, and knew the will of God intimately enough to realize what was going to happen to him. Wouldn't you think that he, the Son of God, would calmly and effortlessly accept his Father's will? What is striking to me about this passage is that Jesus did exactly the opposite. Not once, not twice, but three separate times he prayed: "My Father, if it is possible, may this cup be taken from me. Yet not as I will, but as you will." Wait a minute, let me get this straight: Jesus *himself* struggled in seeing eye to eye with his Father? Yes! Though sinless, he was hoping for some 11th-hour alternative scheme rather than the one his Father planned for him as a way to save the world from sin.

The Apostle Paul gives Christians another illustration of this age-old struggle. Paul authored a good deal of the New Testament, was one of the pillars of the early church, and was the first world missionary. You can easily presume that whatever this saint prayed about, he surely must have always been in line with the will of God. Yet, Paul in his writings talks at length about asking God three times to get rid of a "thorn in his flesh," which scholars speculate was poor eyesight, malaria, or epilepsy. Each time Paul prayed for God to take it away, God said no, because he had a greater purpose in keeping that "thorn" in the life of Paul.

If the Father of the Jews, the Son of God, and the MVP of the early Christian church all struggled with praying God's will, then it's a given that you and I will, too. God's will may even sometimes lead to agonizing circumstances and hardship, like it did for Jesus and Paul. But in all cases, God gives you the option: You can either reject or accept it. Therefore, pray for wisdom to know God's will and the strength to do it. And, after those times your human nature takes over, pray for forgiveness and a resolve to surrender the next time around.

Discovering the Purpose of Praying According to God's Will

When you pray according to God's will, you surrender your own concerns and seek what God wants. Throughout the Bible, you find a consistent pattern of praying according to God's will. Though doing so is hard — sometimes incalculably hard, as you can see from the stories of Abraham, Jesus, and Paul in the preceding section — you're still directed to do so. I see three primary reasons to pray that the will of God be carried out:

- ✔ **You're affirming that God's in control.** When you pray "thy will be done," you're telling God you're glad that he's in control, not you. Ironically, when you turn over the car keys to the Lord, you bring glory to him and relief to yourself.

Is everything that happens God's will?

In this chapter, when I discuss God's will, I'm talking specifically about what might formally be called his deliberate will or his order. Don't confuse God's deliberate will with his permissive will.

His *deliberate will* reveals to you who God is and what he wants, while God's *permissive will* shows you what he allows to happen. God doesn't want disease, sin, suffering, or death, but he does permit them to happen as a natural consequence of the freedom he gives all people. Because you're in a world that has this permissive freedom, you have to explicitly seek out God's deliberate will to know it.

So, to answer the question, no, many things that happen today are *not* part of God's deliberate will. But all things that happen, be they good or bad, are indeed part of his mysterious permissive will.

- ✔ **You're asking God to be involved in this world.** Praying in accordance with God's will also is a plea for God to intervene in this world rather than to sit back and do nothing. You acknowledge that you're not bound by a certain fate (hear that "Que Sera Sera" tune once again?) that can't be changed by God.

- ✔ **Above all, you're surrendering yourself to God.** The most important reason to pray according to God's will is that, in doing so, you're submitting your will to his. Surrendering is hard because it goes against your nature; it means giving up what you most want for the sake of God. But this surrender is at the core of these four words: "Thy will be done."

I desire to do your will, O my God. Your law is within my heart.

Psalm 40:8

Don't confuse surrendering with being indifferent or not caring about your prayer request. No two attitudes are more unlike each other. If you're indifferent, you end up trying to distance yourself from your prayer request in a sort of fatalistic escape. But, if you surrender, you still continue to care as much about the prayer request as always, but you trust God enough to release it to him.

Waving the white flag

In a war or an athletic event, surrender means giving up, throwing in the towel, and losing. It's not much fun for the losing party. But the irony of surrendering through prayer is that while you give up yourself to God, you don't lose. Instead, you find freedom as the result.

What would Jesus do (literally)?

When Bruce Marchiano accepted the role to portray Jesus in *The Visual Bible: The Gospel According To Matthew*, he knew he had the ultimate challenge as an actor: to live and breath as Jesus did. His job was to re-create on film the Son of God as chronicled in the Gospel of Matthew. Knowing he required more than just his acting talent to rely upon, his constant prayer throughout the production was, "Lord, make me a puppet on your strings." Today, as he reflects on that prayer, Bruce says:

" 'Lord, make me a puppet on your strings.' When you hear those words, they sound like such a Mighty Man of God prayer. But the prayer actually wasn't that at all; it was utter desperation. I knew I couldn't pull it off by myself. I knew I that I didn't have the goods to play Jesus. This desperation prompted the best reaction I could have had: to simply fall on my face and cry out, asking him to do what I obviously couldn't do on my own.

"After that desperate surrender, I started praying these remarkably bold prayers, such as 'Lord, take my mouth over. Take my body over, and do what actually happened that day.'

"Throughout the filming of *Matthew*, there were many instances when the cameras were rolling that I didn't consciously know what I was doing, but the scene came together in ways you'd have to call miraculous. I say that in all humility, but it's true. I was there. For example, an actor usually tries to plan and manipulate his emotions when playing an emotional scene. But there were many times that I would explode in tears spontaneously, the emotions unveiling something deeper than anyone of us thought of, all while the scene was being filmed. I can only believe on some level God was honoring my prayers, and I know the key to it all was desperation for him.

"Beyond my own personal experience, one of the things that struck me most when portraying Jesus was that desperation was what brought people to Christ. The people whose lives Jesus touched during his ministry on earth came to him in desperation; they were sick, down and out, despised, or poor. By and large, they weren't educated or learned; all they knew was simply that they needed God. So they cried to him in their helplessness, and he transformed their lives.

"The Bible says, 'When I am weak, he is strong.' When I look back on my experience portraying Jesus and see the results on film, I see that my weakness invited his strength. For it was because of the awareness of my weakness and inadequacy that I cried out to God and he had room to move more freely in my life."

Abraham gave up what was most dear to him (see the section "Exposing an Age-Old Struggle," earlier in this chapter), and he was blessed many times over with the fulfillment of God's original promise to him. The Apostle Paul submitted his "thorn" to God and found joy and resolve even when the Lord didn't take it away, saying, "For Jesus' sake, I delight in hardships, for when I am weak, then I am strong." Jesus at Gethsemane surrendered himself with "not as I will, but as you will" and then told his disciples, "Rise, let's go. Here comes my betrayer." He didn't wait for a sign or run and hide. Instead, he carried on as normal, hoping for God to intervene but ready to surrender if not. Jesus trusted his Father and let him take care of the details.

Bruce Marchiano played the role of Jesus in *The Visual Bible: The Gospel According to Matthew* and was really struck when he played that scene in the film:

What I love most about that scene is the triumph that came with "May Your will be done" — a freshly focused Jesus, crippled in grief just a moment before, rising like a mountain of a Man, a champion, brimming with courage, ready to march headlong into whatever lay before Him. In submission to the Father, He climbs from His brokenness with granite resolve to tackle the mission before Him.

If you walk according to the will of God and don't demand your own way, then no matter what the circumstances, he'll give you peace, freedom, and resolve. Obviously, being able to fully accept that peace is a lifelong process, but God uses your surrendering attitude to transform you on the inside.

Praying in confidence for God's will

Whenever my wife and I watch an Alfred Hitchcock film, we always are on the lookout for Hitchcock to make his obligatory cameo toward the start of the film. "Hitch," as he liked to be called, was well known for making walk-on appearances in his films. These bit parts were never part of the plot but were characters such as a pedestrian passing on a street, a man getting on a bus, or a shopper browsing in a Moroccan marketplace. Hitchcock made his presence known, but the story always carried on without regard to his cameo role.

God's not a Kuzco

The film *The Emperor's New Groove* tells the wacky adventure of Emperor Kuzco, a spoiled kid who becomes king and quickly takes on the pompous self-importance nearly always associated with young royalty. Kuzco decides that he wants to build a summer home on a prime piece of real estate; the fact that the spot he intends to build on has been owned by a peasant's family for generations is a mere nuisance. Pacha, the peasant who owns the land, requests a presence with the emperor to plead with Kuzco to find another location. As you might guess, the spoiled Kuzco treats the request in a flippant, uncaring manner, throwing Pacha out of the castle without any remorse.

Some people view their relationship with God as this kind of peasant-king relationship. But, in reading the Scriptures, you can see this view is skewed. Instead, God wants you to trust him the way you would a loving parent, not as an uncaring, dictatorial emperor.

Ultimately, being able to surrender requires having a close relationship with God. Abraham's obedience with Isaac and Jesus' actions at Gethsemane both show the complete and unwavering trust of Abraham and Jesus in God, a trust made possible only through intimate walks with their Father in heaven.

If you think of God like an Emperor Kuzco, then you certainly won't have much hope or confidence when you pray to him. But if you see the Lord as someone closer than any parent, spouse, or friend, then you can have great confidence in what he says and does, knowing that he wants what's best for you.

God is sometimes thought of as behaving this same way — making periodic cameo appearances in your life and being visible just long enough to make his presence known, but being largely irrelevant to the real details of your life.

Yet, nothing could be further from the truth. Don't think of God as Hitchcock the actor, but instead think of him as Hitchcock the director. Hitch was legendary in his attention to detail when directing movies. When filming *Vertigo,* for example, he spent an entire day interviewing extras who would play only pedestrians on the street, passing in the background on camera for mere seconds. He wanted to hear from the actors about the details of their characters and why they would be passing by in that scene.

In much the same way, God is concerned about the nitty-gritty details of your life. Because you have a God who engineers circumstances, you can pray in confidence that when you ask for God's will to be done, he is completely aware of all the details of your life and takes them into account.

Striking a Balance between Asking and Surrendering

You may be tempted to conclude that, in spite of the benefits of praying according to God's will, doing so still means that whatever God wants, God gets.

God uses prayer to change you. So when you pray "thy will be done," you're transformed — exchanging your will for his, forgetting about yourself, and turning over your needs and wants to God for him to deal with. But, if you stop there, you're leaving out half the story. For the Bible talks not only about submitting to God's will but also about asking God for what you need. You find out all about the issue of asking God in Chapter 17, but the important fact to keep in mind when praying for the Lord's will is you can find both sides of the story — asking and surrendering —in the Bible. Think of the concepts "ask and you shall receive" and "thy will be done" as sort of bookends to prayer.

Most people have a tendency toward one of these extremes: Either they focus on "ask" and give little thought to surrendering to his will, or they resign themselves with "thy will be done" and seldom ask at all. But neither of these attitudes is right.

Because in the Bible God talks about asking as well as surrendering, you have to conclude that the two aren't mutually exclusive but are actually complementary ideas. In a remarkable paradox, God doesn't want either extreme — always asking or always submitting. What he wants is a dynamic mixture of the two. Therefore, ask God for anything, but do so with an attitude of genuine surrender and submission.

Chapter 17

Ask and It Shall Be Given

*J*esus says very clearly in the Gospel of Matthew, "Ask and it shall be given." On first take, this passage sounds like one of the biggest blank checks in all the Bible, much like Santa Claus would say to good little boys and girls as he packs up his sleigh with a sack full of goodies on Christmas Eve. But does life in the real world bear this promise of Jesus out? I, for one, know many long-time, committed Christians who ask God for help, but they still get sick, struggle with money problems, and have children who go astray.

So how can one reconcile Jesus' bold statement with the cold, hard reality as you and I know it? I see three possible choices as to what "ask and it shall be given" means:

✔ Jesus means that you can literally ask whatever you want and God is obligated to give it to you — no questions asked. (It follows then that Christians who have bad things happen to them must either not be asking for help or don't have enough faith.) Chapter 1 talks more about faith.

✔ Jesus means the statement figuratively, meaning that God had mankind's best intentions at heart when he created the world and watches over it, but he isn't about to deal with the pesky little details that you specifically ask for.

✔ Jesus means exactly what he said, but some conditions apply to that promise.

In this chapter, you explore this often misunderstood verse and how to apply this key principle to your prayers. I also discuss how you can balance praying in God's will (which you can find out about in Chapter 16) with asking and receiving.

I'd Like A Porsche, Please

Like many married couples, my wife and I communicate well together, but we don't always do so with 100 percent effectiveness. Suppose, for example, that I'm hard at work fixing dinner, and she's off playing Nintendo with the boys. (Okay, okay, she would be the one preparing the meal, and I'd be the one goofing off.) Obviously, nothing like this ever happens, but imagine that she were to ask me a question about how my day went and, being distracted by the game, I don't hear the question in full. I respond by answering an entirely different question, only partially related to what she wanted to know. Trying to steer back the conversation, she asks me a second question, but because I'm excited about finally beating my kid in a video game, I listen to only half of it and respond incorrectly once again.

When you attempt to apply principles that you read in the Bible to your prayers without fully understanding them, you can wind up in a similar confusing situation; you think the Bible says A, when it actually says B. A tendency for many people is to skim the Bible, pick out a verse that looks good, and run with it. Unfortunately, when you do this, you can completely misunderstand the actual point of the passage. This practice can not only make your prayer life ineffective but can also lead you down a path of resentment and a dismissal of prayer altogether.

To illustrate the danger of this type of thinking, consider the following fictional journal entries:

> *July 7*
>
> *I'm so excited! I was reading my Bible this morning and just came across John 14:14 that says: "If you will ask anything in my name, I will do it."*
>
> *Can you believe it? Jesus says that I can ask for <u>anything</u> and he'll agree to it. I kept reading just to be sure, and then a few verses later, I encountered another verse that confirmed it. John 15:7 says: ". . . you will ask whatever you desire, and it will be done for you."*
>
> *Now, I am really pumped up: whatever I <u>desire</u>. Jesus said it twice, so he surely must have meant what he said. I decided I'd better cross-check with another book of the Bible just to be certain. So, I came across Matthew 7:7: . . . For everyone who asks receives.*
>
> *Anything I desire? Everyone who asks receives? Yippee! I'm going to ask God for that new Porsche convertible that I always wanted. And, since we're in the midst of a heat wave, the sooner I get to drive it the better. I am sure God wouldn't want me to get hot in my old boring sedan.*
>
> *Wow, Jesus is better than a genie in a bottle. You only get three measly wishes with a genie. Jesus gives you a lifetime supply!*

I'm going to go pray now for that Porsche. I'll try to write tomorrow, but may not because I'll be busy driving my convertible all over town.

Deliriously yours,
Ned

* * * * * * *

July 8

I'm here again, but without a Porsche! Not sure what happened, but I woke up this morning, went out to the garage, and saw the old sedan in its place. I'm trying to think what I did wrong. My best guess is that I asked too late in the day to get a one-day turnaround. Strange . . . I'd think overnight delivery isn't too much of a problem for God, since he created the earth in a single day. But maybe cars are a special case? To prevent another mishap, I've gotten up especially early this morning and prayed just to be sure to make tomorrow's deadline.

Also, the grocery had suntan lotion on sale. With the convertible top down all the time, I'm gonna need plenty, so I bought four crates of the stuff. I certainly don't want to have to worry about running out of it later.

Speedily yours,
Ned

* * * * * * *

July 9

Still no Porsche. Bummer! Trying to think what I did wrong and came up with a theory that looks pretty solid. In rereading those verses again, I saw that John 14:14 says that you need to ask "in his name." I am not sure I did that! So when I prayed just a moment ago, I made sure and tacked on the phrase "in Jesus' name" to my request.

I have all bases covered now, so I look forward to driving it down the high-way tomorrow! Gosh, I hope it doesn't rain! And I wonder if God will give me one with a CD player? (I didn't specifically ask for that, because I didn't want to sound spoiled.)

Sincerely "In his Name,"
Ned

* * * * * * *

July 10

Still no answer! But, I realize the problem all along. Silly me. Mark 11:24 says that whatever you ask for, believe that you will receive it, and you will have it. I must have not really been believing hard enough, that's all. So, I am off to pray in order to convince God that I really, really, really do believe he's going to answer my prayer. Gotta go. I'm going to pray even harder.

Faithfully yours,
Ned

* * * * * * *

July 11

What's going on here? I prayed with total faith, prayed using Jesus' name, and specifically asked for a Porsche. When I pray like this, the Bible says very clearly that I can have what I want when I ask for it. BUT I STILL DON'T HAVE IT YET! This weekend is gonna be wasted if he doesn't answer my prayer soon!

Finally, I sold my sedan to my neighbor today for a bargain price. I figured that would be a great way to show God that I really do believe. Plus, the discounted price shows God that I am loving my neighbor at the same time. (I figure that's got to count for something.) Tomorrow will be the day.

Neighborly yours,
Ned

* * * * * * *

July 12

This whole prayer business is a fairy tale. Why did Jesus ever say all those promises and then not keep them? Now, what I am going to do with 128 bottles of suntan lotion? Maybe I can trade them to my neighbor and get my sedan back?

Nauseatingly yours,
Ned

You can see that Ned scanned the Bible verses he was looking for, but he didn't bother to go to the trouble of looking at the verses' background or circumstances in which Jesus said them: Ned tried to force the passages into *his* definition of what "ask and you shall receive" means. The end result for Ned, however, wasn't a Porsche, but false hope, disappointment, and, ultimately, unbelief in prayer.

"Image is everything" was the popular slogan of a camera maker a few years back. But when it comes to reading the Bible and applying a passage to your life, I recommend a much more significant saying: *Context is everything.*

Ned's journal was fictional, but thousands, if not millions, of Christians today share the beliefs expressed in his journal entries. Many people really do believe that a Christian can be happy, rich, healthy, and successful simply by asking God for happiness, wealth, good health, and success. (See the sidebar "Sport utility donkey: Official vehicle of the apostles?" later in this chapter.)

In order to explain exactly what Jesus means in those verses Ned referred to, I dive deeper into them. Ned should have considered these four factors when he read those passages:

✔ Jesus' promise focuses on spiritual needs, not material possessions.

✔ Praying "in Jesus' name" is not a magical phrase.

✔ "Ask and you shall receive" makes sense only when you are in synch with God. (You can find more on this in Chapter 17.)

✔ Faith, not positive thinking, is what's important.

Mounting up for a tough sermon

Jesus makes his remarkable statement "ask and you shall receive" smack dab in the middle of what is commonly called the Sermon on the Mount. The Sermon on the Mount wasn't your ordinary "20-minutes-and-it's-time-for-lunch" Sunday sermon. In fact, most people say that it's the most challenging message Jesus ever gave in all his ministry. He tells his listeners that if they're going to follow him, they need to love their enemies, turn the other cheek, and not even look upon someone with lust, or they've already committed adultery in their heart. He also says that they need to be humble, pure, holy, merciful, slow to anger, and on and on for three chapters in Matthew.

After several minutes of this, I suspect all the people listening were saying, "How can I possibly follow his commands? It's utterly impossible! I'm doomed!" As if anticipating their thoughts, Jesus then says these well-known words:

> Ask, and it will be given you. Seek, and you will find. Knock, and it will be opened for you. For everyone who asks receives. He who seeks finds. To him who knocks it will be opened.

When he said this, Jesus wasn't just giving a carte blanche to his followers to ask for any material goods or possessions. He was speaking more of how one can acquire the spiritual qualities that God requires of people who are to follow him. Following those commands would be impossible by one's own effort. But by praying for God's grace and power, everything is possible. Therefore, Jesus wants you to ask for the unattainable because, when you rely on him fully, those kinds of mountains can be scaled.

Mission impossible? Exactly

If you read through the teaching of Jesus on the Sermon on the Mount in Matthew, I suspect that you'll throw your hands up and say "impossible." Yet, I think that was exactly one of the points Jesus was trying to make in his famous message. You see, the Pharisees, the religious leaders of the day, were trying to attain God's favor by following strict rules and regulations that they had invented that went beyond what

God gave the Jewish people. Jesus fires back, saying that those rules, as severe as they may be, aren't good enough for God. So, instead, Jesus lays out what is really required to be acceptable to God, and this standard is far harder than anyone imagined. In so doing, Jesus made it clear that that the way to God was not by human effort, but *only* by trusting in God.

Saying more than "Open sesame"

Some people add on "in Jesus' name" to their prayers, almost treating it as a magical expression like "open sesame." They are correct in praying in the name of Jesus, but they totally misunderstand the significance of the phrase. John 14:14 says:

> *If you will ask anything in my name, I will do it.*

You can easily gloss over or minimize the phrase "in my name," but those three words pack a powerful punch. When you pray "in the name of Jesus," you're not simply adding a trite saying to the end of your prayer. On the contrary, when the disciples around Jesus heard those words, they knew exactly what he meant. You see, in the culture of Biblical times, a person's name represented more than just a word shouted to get someone to come home for dinner. Instead, a person's name symbolized everything that person was about and stood for. Therefore, when you pray in the name of Jesus, you're saying that your prayer request is completely in accordance with the person of Jesus Christ and is something that honors his name.

Let me put it in a different way. Consider an ambassador of a country. When on foreign soil, he is the chief envoy or voice of the country being represented. When the ambassador says something to the government of the host country, the message carries the full weight of the ambassador's country. An ambassador would never conceive of speaking out of line on official business, because careless words risk the reputation of the country being represented. In the same way, when you pray in the name of Jesus, you claim yourself as a spokesperson or representative of Jesus. In effect, you're putting Jesus' reputation on the line with your prayer.

Getting in synch with God

Like most people, I enjoy watching figure skating during the Winter Olympics, but what amazes me the most (besides, of course, the sometimes tacky outfits and questionable judging) is the way the top-notch pairs skaters float across the ice in unison, with perfect precision and synergy. I shudder watching them do side-by-side camels, each spinning on one leg, with their other leg extended in the air, parallel to the ice, inches from their partner's head. I fear someone is going to get his face cut by the blade, but amazingly the skaters always seem to pull off the move without a hitch. Even when something goes awry in a routine, such as a fall, the pair seems to instinctively know how to continue, usually without missing a beat.

This same synergy is what God wants to have with you and me. He desires you to be in synch with him so that what you ask for is in line with his plan, not your own agenda. John 15:7 speaks to this synergy:

> *If you remain in me, and my words remain in you, you will ask whatever you desire, and it will be done for you.*

You can focus on "ask whatever you desire," but if you do, you would also neglect the qualifying phrase earlier in the verse. When you remain identified with Christ and let his teaching permeate your life, then you are in total synch with the Lord and can see his will. Rather than obsessing about a new car or luxury vacation home, you'll instead be focused on what God desires in your life, such as being holy and serving others. And then and only then, when you're in such a position, does he give you the proverbial blank check.

Strengthening your faith, not psyching yourself out

During junior high, I loved to play basketball, but I was never very good at it. To be honest, I was pretty lousy. No matter how much I practiced, I just didn't seem to improve. One day, I decided that what I needed was a way around this talent problem, so I resolved to ask God to make me grow to be seven feet tall. I pleaded with God, suggesting all the good I could do for him if I was the world's best basketball player. I distinctly remember going to bed one night in 8th grade, totally psyching myself into thinking that God was going to make me grow a foot and a half that night.

My focus wasn't whether or not such a request was in line with God's will (see Chapter 17 for more on that topic); instead, it was on believing that my pending height change was absolutely, positively going to happen. All that upbeat energy may have given me championship-quality basketball play in my dreams that night, but when I awoke the next morning, I was still my same old 5-foot-something-reject-of-a-ballplayer.

You could take Mark 11:24 out of context:

Therefore I tell you, all things whatever you pray and ask for, believe that you receive them, and you shall have them.

On quick take, those words are strong indeed, especially because Jesus doesn't appear to qualify these words as clearly as he did all the verses I talk about earlier in the chapter.

However, consider these three factors before you start praying faithfully for selfish wants:

✔ Jesus is *not* saying that a positive outlook determines the result of your prayer, as if positive thinking can will something to happen. God is not going to be swayed by your psyching yourself out. Instead, Jesus is saying that a steady belief in God is what's important to your prayer life. He's got everything under control, so believe that truth when you pray. Otherwise, why pray at all if you don't believe God is trustworthy to handle your request?

The Book of James talks more on this subject when it says in 1:6:

Ask in faith, without any doubting, for he who doubts is like a wave of the sea, driven by the wind and tossed. For let that man not think that he will receive anything from the Lord. He is a double-minded man, unstable in all his ways.

When you first read this verse, it sounds pretty ominous, doesn't it? Who hasn't had moments of weak faith or genuine intellectual struggles with answered prayer? But James really isn't talking about this kind of occasional doubting. Instead, he is speaking of something much more insidious, a situation in which people are divided in their minds about God and end up riding a prayer roller coaster. One moment, in a flood of emotion, they're full of faith and shouting from the mountaintop, but the moment something goes wrong, they're in the pits of despair, doubting whether God even cares about them at all. You and I may have an occasional meltdown like this, but James is speaking of a life characterized by this double-mindedness.

✔ The more faith in God you have, the greater the likelihood that your will is aligned with his will. When you have a solid faith, you know that God is going to take care of you, so you don't need to stress over or become preoccupied with matters that you know God will handle.

✔ While Mark 11:24 (see the verse earlier in this section) seems more open ended than the other verses, you have to look at this passage within the context of the whole Bible. So in case anyone is tempted to run hog wild with this verse, I would simply pull the harness in by pointing them to James 4:3, which says:

You ask, and don't receive, because you ask with wrong motives, so that you may spend it for your pleasures.

This single verse can save you a lot of trouble. For when you pray out of selfishness, James makes it clear that God won't have anything to do with your request.

If God had granted all of the silly prayers I've made in my life, where should I be now?

C.S. Lewis

Sport utility donkey: Official vehicle of the apostles?

Certain segments within the Christian church today actually promote the idea of God being a vending machine (see the section "I'd Like a Porsche, Please," earlier in this chapter). Many popular terms are associated with this type of belief, such as *health-wealth gospel, name-it-claim-it,* and the *word-faith movement*. But whatever it's called, whenever I hear anyone proclaim this promise, not only do I reflect on the Biblical verses discussed in this chapter, but I also consider Jesus' disciples and the early leaders of the church, such as Paul, Luke, and James.

If any Christians deserved to have everything they asked for, don't you think it would've been these folks? After all, they were closer than anyone else to Jesus, wrote the New Testament, and were instrumental in the explosive growth of Christianity in the 1st century A.D. If a blank check existed, I imagine that each of them would have driven a sport utility donkey, owned a summer beach house on the Mediterranean, enjoyed early retirement — complete with a daily round of golf — and lived a long, healthy, and carefree life.

Yet, the lives of the Apostles and early Christian leaders show that God indeed answers prayer, but he wasn't concerned about these cushy things that humans crave. Each of them lived remarkable, significant lives, but they did so with little money in their pockets, no home to speak of (except maybe prison cells), and just a worn pair of sandals to take with them on their travels. To cap it all, nearly all of them died gruesome martyrs' deaths.

Dietrich Bonhoeffer, who was one of the few German pastors in the 1930s to speak out loudly against the Nazis and who himself died a martyr's death, said it best when he said, "When Jesus calls a man, he bids him 'come and die.'"

Staying within the Lines: Sticking to God's Will

If you took the time to dive deeper into the Bible passages about "ask and receive," this question may come to mind: Do Jesus' promises amount to anything or are they hollow, given the major constraints imposed when you look at what Jesus really means?

On the surface, these conditions may seem imposing and burdensome, but as I consider how I interact with my own children, then Jesus' words start to fit together quite consistently with reality as I know it. My wife and I have what we call a road map that we want our family to follow. If we follow it perfectly, then the plan is designed to make each family member the happiest, most complete person that each can be. I'm not just talking about collective happiness, but the fulfillment of each individual as well.

However, because our three boys didn't come up with this road map, we established a set of boundaries that govern our household to help keep the boys in line with the plan. We don't impose those restrictions arbitrarily or simply for the sake of showing who is boss; we impose them to protect them from falling off the map, which would hurt their own well-being and happiness.

When the boys ask for something, our decision is straightforward when we keep one eye on the road map. Suppose, for example, that they ask for a new Star Wars toy; I may on occasion grant that request, as a way to express my love for them. However, if I comply every time they ask, then I would only

REMEMBER

Surely my request is inside God's will

In this world that you and I live in, you may occasionally have a prayer request that you're convinced is inside of God's will. You may have diligently prayed about this request according to Jesus' teachings. Yet God still doesn't answer the request as you expect. Sometimes a loved one dies for no apparent reason. An accident leaves someone permanently scarred. Or a marriage ends in a tragic divorce. This subject of "unanswered" prayer is perhaps the thorniest of all issues of prayer and is the focus of Chapter 19.

There's no point in dancing around the subject: Those seemingly "lost" prayers are difficult for even the strongest of Christians to deal with. Often you can make a seemingly airtight case why such prayer requests, if answered, would be inside of the will of God.

I'm afraid no answers this side of heaven can fully explain why this happens. But when it does, the key is surrender. Surrender your request to God and let him have his way, no matter how much you don't understand it. God is asking you to trust him enough to recognize that he knows what he is doing, even when it doesn't appear so to you and me.

spoil them, letting them satisfy their short-term wants at the expense of their longer-term character development. Or suppose they plead to stay up late to watch a movie on DVD; I may agree on occasion if it's a weekend and part of a family fun night. But I wouldn't agree on a school night, because they'd be too exhausted in the morning to perform well in school (thus taking them off the road map).

When the kids focus on staying within the boundaries, their requests often (surprisingly) fall within the road map. Even when they know the boundaries but their requests don't fall within them, they respond with an attitude of acceptance. But when they stray from the plan by totally ignoring the boundaries, their requests quickly turn into demands, and our no's are met with stormy protests.

In the same way, God wants you to be inside the boundaries of his will. When you are and you ask for things in accordance with that road map, then he will give them to you. But if you ask for things that will get you or someone else off track, then God can't answer your prayer in the way you want. Always look at his desire to bless you in light of his will.

Praying according to God's will means surrendering yourself and your desires for what God wants instead. (Chapter 16 details this journey.) In this chapter, you discover that as long as you ask for things that are inside of the will of God, Jesus invites you to petition God for anything.

These two concepts form the bookends to prayer:

- ✔ Praying in God's will
- ✔ Ask and you shall receive

Ultimately, true Christian prayer is the stuff that lies between those bookends. Your objective when you pray should be to keep within these boundaries, and you'll never go wrong. Unfortunately, many Christians get distracted and go outside of those borders. Some people may become preoccupied with God's will and his sovereignty, and they begin to give up on prayer, thinking it is of no use. On the other side, others may ignore God's will altogether in a self-absorbed quest of their own, seeking fame and fortune by using God as the means.

To make sure that you stay within these bookends, consider the following questions when you pray:

- ✔ Is your prayer in line with God's mission in the world? (See Chapter 3.)
- ✔ Does your request honor God?
- ✔ Is it in line with God's eternal perspective? (See Chapter 3.)

✔ Is your prayer an extension of a life of obedience and holiness?

✔ Do you believe that the Lord will answer your request and wants to do so in the way you petition as long as this is within his will?

✔ When you pray in Jesus' name, would you stake the reputation of Jesus on your request?

✔ Do you trust God enough to accept his answer, even if it's not in accordance with your desires?

Chapter 18

Lost Prayers

● ●

In This Chapter

▶ Facing the challenge of lost prayers

▶ Understanding God's promises about prayer

▶ Playing the waiting game

▶ Dealing with a "no"

▶ Disagreeing with God

▶ Struggling with a lost prayer

● ●

My sister-in-law Teresa recently had an interesting experience with lost mail. Back in grade school, she was to have received a letter from a friend during a school bus ride, but the envelope slipped down the side of a bus seat and remained there for over 35 years. When the bus driver was cleaning out the bus during his retirement, he came across the old lost letter addressed to her. He made it a personal mission to track Teresa down to deliver the lost letter to her. I can only guess that he considered the letter of possible grave importance — perhaps an early marriage proposal, a secret note with vital Russian secrets, or a surprise correspondence from an unknown relative. After making a series of attempts to contact Teresa and driving hours from his home, he finally was able to reach my in-laws, who promptly delivered the letter to her.

Sometimes prayers can seem like Teresa's misplaced letter, falling in between the cracks of a bus seat and remaining there indefinitely without God's notice. In this chapter, you find out about "lost prayers," or prayers that appear to be either ignored or not answered altogether. In so doing, you explore what God promises when you do pray, why God sometimes waits to answer you or even says no, and what to do when you disagree with God's answer.

Some prayers are followed by silence because they are wrong, others because they are bigger than we can understand.

Oswald Chambers

Considering Prayers That Looked Misplaced and Forgotten

Have you prayed about something in earnestness and humility and then had the result be the exact opposite of what you expected? Lost prayers can be some of the fiercest challenge to your Christian faith if you experience them, and can leave you grasping for answers. Before I start talking about what God promises in prayer, first look at several prayers that seemed lost for a time or even a lifetime.

A most preventable tragedy

Unless you've jumped directly to this chapter, you've probably already encountered the name Oswald Chambers quite frequently in this book. Born in Scotland in 1874, Chambers was a gifted pastor and teacher who had energy, charm, and wisdom beyond his years. He headed up a small school called the Bible Training College in London, but when World War I broke out in 1914, the 43-year-old pastor felt called by God to travel to Egypt and serve as a chaplain to the British troops stationed there. So he left London and had his wife, Biddy, and young daughter follow shortly thereafter. Chambers was an immediate hit with the soldiers and generated strong attendance at the church services he held each night. Biddy helped out by playing the piano during worship time, and she used her secretarial skills to take shorthand notes of Chambers' sermons to keep herself engaged.

All was going as planned until an October night in 1917, when he suddenly came down with severe abdominal pain and had to stay in bed for several days. Because the wounded soldiers needed all the beds, Chambers refused to go to the hospital for his sickness for over a week, until the pain got so severe that he finally relented. The doctor performed an emergency appendectomy that was initially deemed successful.

Biddy and many of the troops who loved Chambers prayed constantly for his recovery. And for almost a week, Oswald appeared to be getting better. But then he took a turn for the worse from a blood clot in his lung. Biddy, however, remained steadfast by his side and felt a quiet assurance from God that Oswald was going to pull through. And, in fact, over the next week, Oswald was on the road to recovery, when he suddenly started bleeding internally once again. Two days later, Oswald died, leaving a wife, a 4-year-old daughter, and decades of ministry unfulfilled.

If only Chambers had sought medical attention sooner for his appendicitis. If only God had intervened and healed Chambers to continue his ministry and raise his child. If only . . .

The forgotten prayer of a prayer warrior

George Müller was one of the prayer warriors that you may have read so much about in other chapters in this book. George was the founder of several children's orphanages in 19th century England, running them solely by the power of prayer. For decades, Müller trusted fully in the Lord to provide everything in his life and for the orphans, and God never failed to supply their needs.

Yet, there is one prayer spoken by this champion prayer warrior that went unanswered for more than 63 years: that his friend would be converted to Christianity. Year after year, while other prayers were being answered, this prayer seemed to have been lost between the cracks. Even through his final days on this earth, Müller continued to pray expectantly for answer, but the prayer remained unanswered as Müller died and his friend remained "unsaved." Why did God, who answered thousands of Müller's prayers throughout his life, turn a blind eye to this dearest prayer of his heart?

A missionary that never was

Kaboo was a boy prince living in West Africa who grew up in the latter part of the 19th century. His father was the chief of the Kru tribe, which evidently could have been nicknamed the Bad News Krus, as they were lousy warriors. His father was forced to give Kaboo up as a hostage three times to a rival conquering tribe until he could pay off the ransom.

However, after the third time this happened, Kaboo's father was broke and had no money to pay off the debt, causing the victorious tribe to plan Kaboo's execution as a response. Yet, on the day of the planned killing, Kaboo escaped in a miraculous manner when a bright light and voice confused his would-be executioners, causing them to run away and leave Kaboo free to go. Kaboo didn't understand what happened, but he knew enough to realize that returning home wouldn't be safe, so he eventually made his way to Monrovia, the capital of Liberia.

Coming across a plantation, he met a boy his age who worked there, and helped Kaboo secure a job as a laborer. The boy was a Christian and invited Kaboo to church, where he met an American missionary who taught the Sunday School class. On that first Sunday, the missionary was sharing the story found in the Book of Acts of how Saul (later called Paul) saw a bright light on the road to Damascus, heard the voice of Jesus, and was transformed by it. Kaboo couldn't believe his ears: This account of Saul's had many striking parallels to what happened to him during his escape! More than a little excited, Kaboo relayed his recent experience to the others and ended up becoming a Christian on that day.

Over the next two years, Kaboo stayed at the plantation and grew rapidly in his faith, spending considerable time at church, learning more about Jesus, and developing a very strong prayer life. Around this time, Kaboo changed his name to Samuel (Sammy) Morris, in honor of one of the American sponsors of the nearby mission.

As Sammy's faith grew, he felt increasingly drawn to return to his parent's tribe and share his "good news" to the Bad News Krus. However, he became convinced that he first needed an education in order to serve God effectively as a missionary. Learning of the mission's contact with a learned preacher in New York, Sammy hopped aboard a merchant ship with empty pockets but a faith-filled heart and made his way to America in six months. After spending some time in New York, Sammy enrolled at Taylor University, a Christian college in Indiana.

Sammy had a charisma and infectious enthusiasm that seemed to rub off on everyone he met. The rough sailors with whom he crossed the Atlantic went from mocking and treating him cruelly to being totally won over by his steadfast, enthusiastic faith. The professors and students at Taylor University went out of their way to help Sammy catch up on his years of lost schooling. He'd often go to local churches and offer to speak. The ministers would initially treat this young African skeptically, but after a few minutes, they'd be swept away by Sammy, and he'd be given the pulpit to speak on Sunday mornings.

Sammy's future as a missionary to his people back in West Africa seemed certain. When he prayed, he'd envision himself back in Africa sharing the message of Jesus to the tribal children and could almost taste the impact he'd have not just on the Kru tribe but perhaps on neighboring tribes as well. However, the harsh Indiana winter soon arrived and had a deteriorating effect on his health. Fighting a cold, he neglected to tell anyone about it and continued on in his studies and preached like normal. Sammy's body had a hard time fighting the cold, and it continued to get worse and worse, until he became deathly sick before help was sought.

The entire university was shocked and prayed diligently for his healing; even the university president stayed with Sammy and prayed with him by his bedside. Doctors were unable to do much, because the sickness had become too serious. As he lay contemplating what seemed a certain death, Sammy was astonished: Why had God spared his life back in Africa only to have him die so young, before he'd had even had a chance to be a missionary? Despite prayers to the contrary, God did not spare Sammy, who died on a cold winter's morning in Indiana at age 20.

Revoking an answered prayer

A good friend of the family I'll call Rachel was going through a particularly difficult time. As a single parent, she'd been struggling to make ends meet with her part-time position and desperately needing a full-time job in order to provide for her family. My Bible study group was praying that the Lord would take care of Rachel's needs by supplying her with a better employment opportunity.

Finally, a full-time opportunity was handed to her when her boss quit; she took over this new position. Talk about a prayer seemingly answered with a divine exclamation point: Rachel got not only a full-time position but also a much-needed raise and promotion!

Yet, after just three weeks in this new role, Rachel's answered prayer appeared to have been revoked. She was unexpectedly laid off, along with almost half the others in her company. On hearing this news, I was dumbstruck. What seemed like a very clear and obvious answer to prayer now looked like a cruel hoax. When I read 1 Corinthians 14:33, I'm reminded that God is not a God of confusion, yet Rachel's situation looks terribly confusing to me.

Cornering Confusion, Ousting Doubt

Lost prayers can be perplexing. But lost prayers can go beyond confusion. When you don't deal with them directly, they leave doubt and resentment, building up a formidable wall between God and you.

Therefore, when you have what you consider a lost prayer, the first thing to do is to come back and remind yourself of the basics of what God promises concerning prayer:

- ✔ God is willing and able to answer prayers.
- ✔ God hears your prayer provided that you're "prayer-ready."
- ✔ God will answer your prayer according to his will.

God is not a God of confusion, but of peace.

1 Corinthians 14:33

Ready, willing, and able

God demonstrates throughout the Bible that he is ready, willing, and able to answer prayers. Jesus gives a good illustration of this fact in Luke 18:2–5: A judge in a certain city didn't fear God and didn't respect man. A widow in that city often came to him, saying, "Defend me from my adversary!" For a while, the judge wouldn't defend her, but afterward he said to himself, "Though I neither fear God, nor respect man, yet because this widow bothers me, I will defend her, or else she will wear me out by her continual coming." Jesus goes on to say that if this unjust judge is willing to answer the request of this poor helpless widow, just think of what your loving heavenly Father is eager to do for you.

In this simple parable, Jesus contrasts both the judge and widow to the reality of the true situation. First, God is completely the opposite of this corrupt government official; whereas the judge was disrespectful and had a spotty reputation, God is the very definition of honor, integrity, and truth. Second, whereas the widow was utterly powerless in her situation, Christians are empowered with 24/7 access to God through prayer. What's more, the Lord welcomes Christians literally as his sons and daughters, not pesky "bothersomes." In this parable, Jesus clearly exhorts people to pray, because God is willing and able to answer them.

> *Wake up! Why do you sleep, Lord?*
> *Arise! Don't reject us forever.*
> *Why do you hide your face?*

> Psalm 44:23–24

Getting ready with Be's

In Chapter 1, I talk about the Five Be's, or attitudes, you need for an effective prayer life:

- ✔ **Be aware.** When you pray, be aware of exactly whom you're praying to, acknowledging the Lord.

- ✔ **Be real.** Don't put up a front or say words you think God wants to hear; simply be honest and open to God.

- ✔ **Be repentant.** If you have a sin that you brazenly continue to practice or have something in your past that you don't want to confess to God, you're not going to have an effective prayer life. Sin in your life can be a major block to your prayers, so always approach prayer with a repentant heart. (See Chapter 3 for more details on repentance.)

- ✔ **Be dogged.** In the parable of the widow and the judge (see the section, "Ready, willing, and able," earlier in this chapter), the widow didn't just ask once and then drop it. Instead, she was tenacious in her requests to the judge. In the same way, you and I should be diligent in prayer — praying, then praying some more, and, when you think you're all done, praying more about it.

- ✔ **Be expectant.** You should have certainty that God will answer your prayer. God may not necessarily always answer your prayer in the way that you desire, but anticipate that God *is* going to answer it somehow.

You always get an answer when you ring his phone

An unanswered prayer is an oxymoron. God promises to answer your prayers. End of story. He may not do so necessarily in the way you request, but he guarantees an answer nonetheless.

Therefore, for all prayers, God replies in one of three ways:

- ✔ **Yes:** If your prayer is inside the boundaries of his will and you're prayer ready, then God promises that he will answer your prayer with a yes. (See Chapter 17 for more details on praying in God's will.)

- ✔ **No:** If your prayer falls outside of his will, God is going to answer no, not because he doesn't love you or want your prayer answered, but because he has a specific reason why he won't do so. (See also Chapter 17.)

- ✔ **Yes, but wait:** The third possibility is that God will answer your prayer, but you'll have to wait to see the result of that answer for a while longer.

Yanking Your Chain? No Way

I hate waiting. Patience is one of those qualities that is so difficult to attain. I suspect that patience is even more of a challenge in today's world than in ages past, given the speed at which society moves. When you face a major crisis, significant life change, or insecurity, your natural tendency is to simply want the ambiguity to be over and done with so that you can get on with your life in one way or another. For some, this waiting game can even be worse than actually receiving an answer they don't want because not knowing is so very difficult to live with.

> *Never give up [praying] until the answer comes.*

George Müller

When you pray, like it or not, delay happens. God may wait to answer your prayer or may not reveal the answer to you right away. But keep in mind that God's not just yanking your chain when he does this. He has two primary reasons for keeping you waiting:

- ✔ **God is answering your prayer by triggering a chain of events.** The first explanation is that God is indeed answering your prayer, but he's doing so by causing a series of events to happen first to set up the answer. This chain of events may be visible to you, or it could be completely hidden from you until the last moment. Therefore, be patient and let God do his thing.

Uncertainty certainly effective

Uncertainty is perhaps the least popular of all the tools that God uses to mold Christians into being like Christ. But the unknown is an effective instrument that God uses to strengthen believers and produce a robust faith in his children. In my life, I believe that uncertainty probably works better than anything else does for capturing my attention.

When you're in a secure situation, this stable environment inevitably makes you master of your own fate. You no longer need to rely on God for providing for your basic needs, making your mortgage, or saving for your kid's college education. Your conscious attitude may not necessarily be one of independence, but God isn't able to cause you to grow in those parts of your life. In contrast, when you're unsure of what's next, you're forced to go to God daily in prayer and depend on him as you weave your way through the dark forests of uncertainty.

✔ **God is working on your heart before answering the request.** God sometimes waits because he's using this interim period as an opportunity to change you. When you're in the midst of a crisis, the resolution of a particular problem can naturally become the security for you, so you're not trusting in God in the midst of the process.

As a result, this waiting game should be seen not as an ordeal but, paradoxically, as a gift from God. No, I'm not trying to be a masochist, but I am starting to realize that these times are precious opportunities to make choices: Are you going to grow closer to the Lord and trust him more or follow your own path? Are you finding more of your security in the Lord or in your own crafted solutions? Are you going to force a solution today or hold out for God's prize at a later time?

"Beware of praying for patience" was a half-comical warning I once heard from a beloved Christian elder from whom I've sought wise advice for years. And I think he's right, because God always seems to answer that prayer when I've prayed it during my life. Don't get me wrong: You *should* be praying for patience if it's a quality lacking in your life, but if you do, just be prepared for the answer.

I Can't Believe He Said No

Delays are one thing, but sometimes God gives a flat-out no to your request, refusing to answer your prayer in the way that you desire. However, as you begin to ask "why?" consider these two possibilities when God declines your request:

✔ **Never:** If your prayer is fundamentally at odds with God's will, then he will never, ever answer affirmatively. Fortunately, you can almost always figure out your mistake the more you read the Bible and get to know God more intimately.

Is your prayer selfish? The Book of James says very clearly that God won't answer selfish prayers. Does your prayer go against God's plan for the world? God reveals his plan for the world in the Bible; if you're praying for something that goes against that plan, he's not going to answer it in the manner you desire.

✔ **Not this time:** The second possibility is that nothing in your prayer request contradicts God's revealed will, but for some reason, God is saying no this time because he has a different plan. This response is the tough possibility, because you may never exactly figure out why God is saying no in this particular instance.

Each of the lost prayers I talk about in the section "Considering Prayers That Looked Misplaced and Forgotten," earlier in this chapter, fall into the "not this time" camp. All of them were worthy prayers that would have seemed to have been in line with God's will, but in each case, he said, "not this time."

Seeing Eye to Eye Isn't Always Possible

Because you're a free moral agent with the ability to make your own judgments based on what you experience in life, chances are that you're not always going to agree with God's will and his answers to your prayers. Even while writing this book, I've struggled with the news of Rachel concerning her job loss (which I discuss in the section "Revoking an answered prayer," earlier in this chapter). My initial reaction was that I flat out disagreed with God on how he answered that prayer. Such disagreements can cause you and me to react in one of three ways, which I discuss in the following sections.

> *There is a difficulty about disagreeing with God. He is the source from which all your reasoning power comes: you could not be right and he wrong any more than a stream can rise higher than its own source. When you are arguing against Him, you are arguing against the very power that makes you able to argue at all: it is like cutting off the branch you are sitting on.*
>
> C.S. Lewis

Thinking that God blew it

When something really bad happens, you probably find it hard to see any good coming from the situation. In such cases, you may think, "God, you blew it. Nothing good can come of this." Yet, as I talk about in Chapter 16, as humans, you and I have a limited, here-and-now perspective compared to God's broad, eternal point of view. So, because I can't see what's around the next corner, I make instant judgments based on bits of information in front of me. In contrast, God has the complete information before him.

Above all else, most people value the preservation of earthly life for themselves, their family, and their friends and loved ones. And so when tragic events occur, people find them especially hard to understand and often fail to see any good coming from them. Inevitably, you question why God either caused the tragedy or, if he did not, why he allowed it to happen without intervening and stopping it. (See Chapter 16 for a discussion on why God allows tragedies to occur.)

However, God's perspective is quite different than yours and mine on matters involving tragedy and death. Although preservation of earthly life is our mantra, God very clearly doesn't value this "earth now" campaign as *most* important. He does give long life to many people, but many great saints, such as Oswald Chambers and Sammy Morris (see the section "Considering Prayers That Looked Misplaced and Forgotten," earlier in this chapter), all died at very young ages. Many people who die young could have done wonderful things for God had they been given more years on this earth.

Clearly, then, you have more to factor in than meets the eye. Despite the impact that many "saints" could have made if they had lived longer, God had a better idea, a better plan. C.S. Lewis offers a clue when he said that God views human birth "important chiefly as the qualification for human death, and death solely as the gate to that other kind of life." With such an eternal perspective, you can see that God sometimes makes different decisions than I do with my "earth now" penchant. He views today's tragedy in light of eternity and so can reconcile the temporary pain and suffering with the lasting purpose of his actions.

Therefore, when bad things happen, your best action is to remind yourself of the fact that you see the world from a very limited point of view compared to God's eternal viewpoint. Give God the benefit of the doubt until you know the full story. In Rachel's case (see "Revoking an answered prayer" section), for instance, I need to give God the benefit of the doubt even if the present situation looks confusing from my standpoint.

Questioning why God is doing nothing

The second reaction to a lost prayer is to begin to question God and speculate on the following:

> ✔ God is impotent and can't change the situation.
>
> ✔ God doesn't really love you, so he isn't going to get his hands dirty taking care of the situation.

This response is often natural, even for long-time Christians. The Bible has examples of these honest questionings in the Book of Psalms (such as Psalm 44) and the Book of Job. When you're tempted to react in this manner, your best response is to immerse yourself in the Bible, picking out the verses that demonstrate both his power and love (see Chapter 8). Use these verses to feed your mind and spirit with these promises of God.

One key reason for being grounded or rooted in your knowledge of the Bible is that you have a foundation to fall back on when these natural feelings of displeasure with God surface in the midst of a crisis.

Demanding an explanation from God

A final reaction that you may experience when you disagree with God is accepting God's answer at face value but, in so doing, expecting God to satisfy your curiosity by telling you the reason behind it. Somehow knowing the reason behind his response makes things more palatable when you're disappointed.

Even tragedies become easier to accept if you can see the reason that they occurred. That's why you often see the surviving members of a family attempt to piece together the reason behind a tragedy, hoping to find that missing piece of the puzzle to give them peace.

I sometimes wish God were more like Hercules Poirot, the master sleuth of the Agatha Christie mystery stories. When I read an Agatha Christie book or watch the film adaptation, I know that after Poirot has pieced together the clues of the crime, he invariably gathers all the suspects together in a room, takes them through a step-by-step account of what happened, and ultimately identifies the guilty party. In the same way, why doesn't God do the same thing: gather up everyone involved in a mysterious situation and give a play-by-play account of what happened and why?

When you feel that God owes you a complete justification for the way he answered your prayers, I recommend taking a lesson from the classic comedy film *The Princess Bride*. In one particularly funny scene, a character tells another to get used to disappointment.

My kids can tell you that I use that phrase — "Get used to disappointment" — around our house all the time when they don't get something they want. In the same way, I think that phrase is a good reminder that sometimes you and I need to simply accept the fact that our curiosity isn't always going to be satisfied. In this life, you and I should get used to disappointment.

God asks you to trust him always, even when you don't know the reason for his actions.

> *There will come one day a personal and direct touch from God when every tear and perplexity, every oppression and distress, every suffering and pain, and wrong and injustice will have a complete and ample and overwhelming explanation.*

> Oswald Chambers

Finding Your Lost Prayer

Because God never fails to answer a prayer, a lost prayer is misplaced in name only, not in actual fact. (See the section "You always get an answer when you ring his phone," earlier in this chapter.)

And so, if you're struggling with a lost prayer, put the responsibility back onto yourself and don't blame your frustration on God. Instead, focus on the following activities:

- **Wrestle with God.** The Book of Genesis talks about a very strange encounter between Jacob and God: During a pivotal time in his life, Jacob wrestled with an angel all night, not quitting until the stranger would bless him. God rewarded Jacob's persistence, and he was blessed. In fact, Jacob became known as "Israel" after that night, a name that literally means "he struggles with God."

  Remain diligent in your prayers, showing the same persistence that Jacob did, not giving up until you're certain that the prayer is answered and can be checked off your list. In Müller's (see the "The forgotten prayer of a prayer warrior" section) case of praying for his friend, even 63 years wasn't too long a time to keep at it.

- **Don't run and hide.** If you are in the midst of a crisis and don't see God moving, one of the worst steps you can take is withdrawing from him and masking your true feelings in your prayers. Because God already knows how you feel anyway, doing this only hurts you and your relationship with the Lord.

Dealing with sorrow and heartache is an extended process, and one of the natural reactions is a time of anger and of questioning, no matter whether you are a new or a long-time Christian. British author and scholar C.S. Lewis, for example, was author of *The Problem of Pain* and knew better than most people why pain exists in the world and God's triumph over it. But for years after his wife died, Lewis too went through a time of anger and despair as the true reality of pain flooded his heart, not just his intellect. He was able to work through this pain and have his faith strengthened as a result, but it was a process he had to go through.

If you're mad, don't force a smiley face on the situation; the best thing you can do is to tell God that you're angry. He craves that honesty and will help you through the rough times — if you let him.

✔ **Learn — and quickly!** As I discuss earlier in the chapter, one reason that God may not answer your prayer right away is that he's using the present time to teach you something. A quick word of advice: Learn quickly! The sooner you learn God's lesson, the easier it will be for you.

✔ **Remember, remember, remember!** As I read through Deuteronomy in the Old Testament, I'm struck by how frequently the word *remember* is repeated throughout the book. Time and time again, the Israelites are exhorted during their journey to the Promised Land to remember specific events that the Lord engineered in their lives. This constant reflection was intended to reassure them of God's faithfulness and provision in the past and his promise to do the same in the future.

Obviously, God must believe that remembrance is essential for people like you and me in order to maintain trust in him. Without such constant reminders, you and I get spiritual amnesia and start complaining to God in something that sounds much like a Janet Jackson song: "What have you done for me lately?"

In reading the story of the Israelites' desert journey and their incessant whining along the way, I find myself calling the Israelites idiots for having such short memories. After all, if you saw the Red Sea parted, would you ever have a hard time trusting God again? Yet, no sooner do I heave that insult than I find myself convicted as well as I look honestly at my life. No, I haven't seen a body of water divide itself in half lately, but I have undeniably witnessed God's work in miraculous ways in my life. Sadly, like the Israelites of old, I so easily discard these past blessings in times of crisis.

When you face trials, remembrance can be one of the most effective tools to reinforce your trust in God. You may want to try using a prayer technique that works for me in these situations: After I reflect on specific, practical examples of God's action, I'm learning to say, "Just as God worked in that circumstance, so he is working in this situation as well, even if I can't see it now."

Revisiting the Lost Prayers: The Rest of the Story

As I close the chapter, let me return again to the lost prayers that I chronicle at the start of the chapter, and provide the "rest of the story" after each prayer was given up for lost.

- ✔ **Oswald Chambers:** The story of Oswald Chambers doesn't end with his death. In fact, it was very likely *because* of his premature death that the idea of the classic devotional *My Utmost For His Highest* was born. Biddy, his wife, had hundreds of shorthand copies of his sermons that were literal word-for-word versions of what Oswald spoke. Convinced that his messages should live on, Biddy transformed them into daily readings for *My Utmost For His Highest*, a book that has been read and treasured by millions since it was first published over eight decades ago.

  Had Chambers lived on, he may have had an impact on hundreds or even thousands of people, but his devotional and life story has impacted the spiritual growth of millions of Christians worldwide because of his premature death.

  It wasn't a storybook ending for Biddy and their daughter, as they struggled financially for years after Oswald's death and just barely scraped by. Nonetheless, their faith and joy in Christ remained constant throughout their lifetimes.

- ✔ **George Müller:** Müller died before he could see the result of his 63-year-prayer for the conversion of his friend, but it most certainly wasn't a lost prayer. For no sooner was Müller dead than his friend made the decision to accept Christ into his heart, even before Müller's funeral.

- ✔ **Sammy Morris:** Sammy may have died before his missionary career got off the ground, but God's plan with Sammy didn't end on his deathbed. Shortly before his death, he told the university president that he was beginning to realize that the work he was setting out to do wasn't his work at all, but Jesus' work. As a result, he became content with the fact that he had fulfilled his purpose in life. His words rang true, because soon after Sammy's death, three Taylor University students decided to go to Africa as missionaries in Sammy's stead to minister to the Kru tribe. Not long after, more students followed the trio. In hindsight, you can see that the Lord was able to do far more in Africa than if Sammy had gone back flying solo as a missionary.

✔ **Rachel:** In the previous three stories, I have the benefit of hindsight to look back and assess how lost prayers from a century ago were in fact answered, but in a far different manner than what anyone expected. Unfortunately, for Rachel's case, I don't have that luxury and so am forced to look at the situation in this current space and time with very limited information.

I wish I could report on a miraculous answer to prayer, but nothing miraculous has happened yet, despite our continued prayers to the contrary. What's more, while the tragedies of Oswald Chambers and Sammy Morris later revealed a positive side effect, that's not the case every time. Many times you and I may never see a benefit or reason when tragedy occurs. Therefore, when something bad like this happens, I have a choice to make: Will I trust and surrender to God, even when no explanation can be made? Or will I become embittered because God hasn't graced me with a full explanation? God uses lost prayers in your life to bring you closer to him, causing you trust him even more. But the question is, will you let him?

Chapter 19

Hearing That Voice in the Cornfield

"*I*f you build it, he will come." Those seven words, uttered by a mysterious voice in an Iowa cornfield, have become one of the most memorable lines in all cinematic history. The film *Field of Dreams* tells the story of Ray Kinsella, a struggling 36-year-old farmer who hears this other-worldly voice and chronicles the actions he takes in response to that command, often to the amusement of his neighbors, alienation of his in-laws, and risk to the well-being of his family.

When people think of God talking to someone, many of them think the experience is something akin to Ray's peering over the cornstalks straining to hear an omnipresent voice. Yet God himself would surely scoff at such an image. I can imagine him saying, "Too Hollywood" (or "too Iowan," as the case may be). While his modus operandi today is far more subtle, his voice can still be perfectly clear, even if your ears can't hear a peep. In this chapter, you explore how God talks to people today and discover how you can get ready to listen to him.

Suffering from the "God Told Me" Syndrome

Too many people have the "God told me" syndrome, so much so that they're starting to give God a bad name. You hear the phrase on TV by some lunatic after he blows up a building or performs some other notorious act. Or you may innocently hear it from your sweet churchgoing friend after she takes an uncharacteristic action. It's to the point now that whenever I hear someone say, "God told me," sirens and buzzers immediately go off in my head.

> *He who has ears, let him hear.*
>
> Matthew 13:9

Don't get me wrong. I do believe that God does speak to Christians today, but I also know that a lot of well-intentioned folks mistake the words of their emotions, friends, or Satan for the words of God. When they fall into this trap, the actions they believe God told them to do are never something that the God of the Bible would endorse.

Sadly, I believe that the words "God told me" are so often misused that many people have become jaded to the very possibility of hearing God. If you have that same attitude, this chapter's for you and designed to help you identify what God's voice is and is not.

Waiting for God to Speak: Expect a Peep, Not a Roar

The people who lived in Biblical times sure had it easy, didn't they? While I struggle with the issue of trying to hear God in a nonverbal manner, the traditional interpretation of the Bible is that many Biblical people actually heard God in the same way that Ray Kinsella heard the voice in the cornfield — with their ears: Adam walked and talked with God; Moses heard God from the burning bush; Elijah had several one-on-ones with the Creator; and the disciples of Jesus Christ walked with him for three years before he died and then saw and ate with him many times after he was resurrected. Not to be left out, Paul saw a bright light and heard Jesus' voice coming from heaven.

I read in the Bible that God is the same yesterday, today, and forever. If that is the case, why would he change midstream the method of interacting with humans? Why doesn't God talk to you and me aloud in this day and age?

Bulletproofing your faith?

If only I could hear the voice of God clearly with my own ears like some of the special folks in Biblical times. If so, I'm sure that I could be the most faithful, trusting person ever! Truth be told, as much as you and I might think so, hearing God speak directly to them was no bulletproof method for strengthening one's faith indefinitely. People who heard from God directly, such as Elijah, Moses, and the disciples, still had the same periods of doubt that you and I go through today, in spite of their special talks with the Lord.

Inadequate communication mediums can't be the reason, because he has more options available today than ever before. Who needs a burning bush when you have telephones, faxes, e-mail, FedEx, and videoconferencing!

On first take, this change in plan seems inconsistent to me, almost fishy. And for years, this issue was one that troubled me, but I was finally able to make sense of it all. I think a modern-day example can help explain the reason behind the change.

George Lucas is best known as the creator of the *Star Wars* saga. Lucas had the vision to originate the classic sci-fi adventure and bring it to the big screen as the director and producer of the many films in the series. Because Lucas's mission was to tell a story, he had two ways to achieve that goal: (a) He could go to each person in the world and spend an evening telling every person the same story; or (b) He could make a series of movies depicting the tale and then show the films in theaters. Being a filmmaker and a sane person, he chose the second option.

Because Lucas was directing the movies, he needed to enlist the help of a team of actors. In order to perform as Lucas needed them to, the actors needed a special relationship with Lucas; they wanted to be able to talk directly to him on a daily basis during filming so they knew what to do and what to say in their roles. Notice that Lucas interacted with people in two ways. He talked directly with the actors, but he relied on the movie to "talk" to the rest of the people. He did treat the actors differently than the general public, but not because he liked them more or because he changed his mind about how to tell the story. He treated them differently because the actors played a special role in the story and they needed a different style of communication.

Although this analogy obviously has flaws, you can still learn several lessons from it when you consider how God interacts with people today compared to times past. Like Lucas, God is the author of the story of the

Differing views on hearing God

Within the Christian church, there are a variety of different views on how God speaks to people. The traditional view held by most Christians is that God speaks through the Bible and by the Holy Spirit. While evangelical and mainstream Protestants believe that these are the only two ways God speaks to Christians today, other parts of the Christian church differ. Roman Catholics believe that God also speaks through papal decrees and church councils. Charismatics (see Chapter 21) believe that God also speaks through Christians with special spiritual gifts, such as the gift of prophecy. Finally, the Seventh-Day Adventist Church believes that founder Ellen White was a true prophet of God and her writing and teaching, while not equivalent to the Bible, should be paid attention to as if it were.

human race as well as the "executive producer" of the Bible. God spoke directly with certain people in Biblical times, but only on an as-needed basis because of their special role in the story. God needed to deal with these people more directly to ensure that his vision was carried out. However, after the New Testament period was over and the Christian church was established, he'd already revealed his full saga — both its beginning in Genesis and conclusion in Revelation — in the Bible, so he didn't need to communicate as visibly as before.

God wants people to live by faith, not by sight or audible words from him. He had a few exceptions, but I get the feeling that he was reluctant to do so and would have preferred to use the faith method throughout history.

Today, God speaks to people through the Bible and also provides the foundation by which all words from him can be checked against: the Holy Spirit, who dwells in all Christians. (See Chapter 3 for more details on the Holy Spirit.) Before Christ came, people didn't have the indwelling gift of the Holy Spirit, except in certain specific situations. So God evidently believes that having a Bible in hand and the Holy Spirit on your inside is actually the preferred way of dealing with him while you live on earth.

Fine-Tuning Your Ears

Radios and televisions tune in to specific frequencies in order to pick up and receive the right channels. However, in order to do this, these receptive devices must be equipped to do so, because a radio isn't suddenly going to tune in a TV channel. Similarly, in order to hear God speak to you, you must fine-tune your ears so that you can hear God's voice.

Before we can hear, we must be trained.

Oswald Chambers

Before listening, make sure that you're prayer ready. See Chapters 1 and 3 for more on the steps you need to take before you're ready to pray. These same steps apply when listening to God as well.

To prepare yourself to listen to God, perform the tasks that I describe in the following nine sections.

Snooping in God's journal

You can get to know a lot about a person by reading his diary or journal. Suppose that you picked up a stranger's diary and read through it cover to cover. You'd begin to have an insight into that person's dreams and plans in life. And if you ever had to try and pick out this person in a crowded room, chances are that you could use that inside information to select the exact person from the pack.

The Bible is something like God's diary. It provides all the details you and I need to know about God and his thoughts, expectations, and plans for the world. Therefore, if you're trying to pick out God's voice within a crowded group, your single best way to know his voice is to read his diary.

God's voice is always in line with the Bible. So if you ever think you hear God telling you something that goes against something written in the Bible, you can be certain that you have some earwax built up, because you're not hearing him correctly.

Martin Luther challenged Christians to listen to the "Word in the words," discovering God's truth within the words of the Bible. When you are listening for God's direction, be mindful of preconceived notions and then turning to the Bible for a verse that seemingly supports or justifies your position. As Chapter 17 discusses in greater detail, passages in the Bible have to be understood in context.

Spotting a fake

To be able to recognize counterfeit money, new bank clerks typically spend time studying genuine currency. That way, when they come across a fake bill, they'll know it instinctively simply because it looks and feels different from what they know to be the real thing. In the same way, the closer you begin to get to God, the less of an issue hearing God becomes; you can begin to know his "still small voice" (1 Kings 19:12) and differentiate it from counterfeit ones.

Studying the art of hearing God's voice

If you come across someone who tells you a foolproof method of knowing God's will or hearing his voice, then look to see what else they're selling, because hearing God is never cut and dried. Instead, listening is an art, not a science.

In thinking through God's plan for the world, I think the reality of listening as an art is by God's deliberate design. First, this method leaves me more reliant on him for wisdom. Second, this method teaches me humility; I know that if I take my ears off him, then I'll stumble, mistaking another voice as his.

> We always hear the thing we listen for, and our [character] determines what we listen for. When Jesus Christ alters our [character], he gives us the power to hear as he hears.
>
> Oswald Chambers

Listening to the rules

When you listen for God's voice, you need to listen in three ways:

- ✓ Actively listen, with focus and energy spent in prayer and anticipation. Don't just passively wait for God to talk to you; go to him with expectant ears.

- ✓ Listen to *all* God's message, not just parts of it. My kids are famous for being selective listeners around the house, hearing what they want to hear ("Kids, it's dinner time!"), but somehow not quite catching the other stuff ("Hey, it's your turn to set the table for dinner."). Likewise, not all of what God says to you may be what you want to hear, but obedience requires that you to do just that.

- ✓ Listen attentively so that you don't miss something God's trying to say to you. You may hear words other than what you expect. Don't ignore them, waiting for what you want to hear — God may want you to move and do something before you're ready for the next thing.

Shhhhhh

When God communicates with you, he usually does so with a whisper, not a yell. He did this with a literal whisper in 1 Kings 19:11–13 to Elijah when he was running for his life, fearful of King Ahab and Queen Jezebel. God told Elijah:

Go forth, and stand on the mountain before the Lord. Behold, the Lord passed by, and a great and strong wind tore the mountains, and broke in pieces the rocks before the Lord; but the Lord was not in the wind: and after the wind an earthquake; but the Lord was not in the earthquake: and after the earthquake a fire; but the Lord was not in the fire: and after the fire a still small voice. It was so, when Elijah heard it, that he wrapped his face in his mantle, and went out, and stood in the entrance of the cave. Behold, there came a voice to him, and said, What are you doing here, Elijah?

You may expect the Creator of the world to bang you over the head when he communicates, but in this example with Elijah, he specifically didn't, even though he could have. In the same way, he speaks with you in a "still small voice."

The instinctive thing to do when someone is whispering a message to you is to physically move your ear closer to the person's mouth so that you don't miss the message. Similarly, because you know that God's going to whisper to you, get closer to him.

Getting an unexpected message

When God communicates with you, he's going to say something that makes sense in your situation. This doesn't mean that what he says isn't going to be unexpected, but it often fits your reality, availability, or financial situation. But if it doesn't, then perhaps he's asking you to take a step of faith and rely on him to work things out for you.

Patterns begin to make more and more sense as you learn how to listen to God. He's not going to tell you after you've felt a call to be a doctor to become an ice cream taste tester when you've finally graduated from medical school. However, he could throw you a loop and call you to be a missionary doctor. God's ways are not your ways, so they aren't always going to make sense at the time, though they will later on.

Watching the tone

Another key way to determine whether God is speaking to you is to identify the manner and tone in which the message is delivered. God's messages are patient and ordered, even if unexpected. Satan or your own tendency towards sin will speak to you with an emotional, impulsive, and pushy tone, telling you to do something *now* in an impulsive or rushed manner, without adequate reflection. God's a patient God and wants his followers to be patient, too, so make sure that the tone of the voice is calm and composed.

If God is telling you to act this very moment ("Act now! Operators are standing by for the next 15 minutes!"), this rushed tone is an almost certain red flag about the true origin of that message.

Circumstances speak louder

When your ears are plugged and you don't listen to him, God may be forced to speak to you through circumstances. Remember, God engineers circumstances and sometimes needs to use them to get your attention. Consider Isaiah 30:20–21:

> *Although the Lord gives you the bread of hardship and the water of suffering, your teachers will be hidden no more; with your own eyes you will see them. No matter where you turn, your ears will hear a voice behind you, guiding you, saying, "Walk this way." (Paraphrased)*

Sometimes when bad things happen to me, I can naturally blame God and say, "Why me?" But I also should prayerfully evaluate such circumstances to determine whether the Lord is actually speaking to me through the situation, trying to get my attention.

Putting the prayer before the horse

More than anything else, listening to God is a lifestyle, a byproduct of how you live your life. Those most frustrated with not hearing God are typically those who want easy answers and don't want to take the effort to get close to God to hear him. However, your success at hearing God is always directly proportional to the health of your relationship with him. (See Chapter 4 for more details on this subject.)

> *For as many as are led by the Spirit of God, these are children of God.*
>
> Romans 8:14

Questioning That Inner Voice: God or My Empty Stomach?

The Christian life may not be easy but, for most of it, you can at least gauge whether you're doing a good job of it. You can accurately figure out your consistency in daily prayer and Bible reading. You can effectively evaluate how you're treating others around you. However, perhaps the one mystery that eludes most Christians is how much they're actually hearing God.

Undoubtedly, one of the most difficult aspects of the Christian life is listening to God and figuring out whether what you think God said is actually him or not, even after you've prepared yourself fully.

> *For we walk by faith, not by sight.*
>
> 2 Corinthians 5:7

If you're a Christian, God speaks to you. He does so by planting a thought in your mind, usually so quickly that you'll wonder where it came from. All of a sudden, it's just there. In addition, quite often, the message will impact your heart as you begin to focus on it.

Oswald Chambers speaks of God's voice in this manner:

> *When we hear a thing is not necessarily when it is spoken, but when we are in a state to listen to it and to understand. Our Lord's statements seem to be so simple and gentle, and they slip unobserved into the subconscious mind. Then something happens in our circumstances; up comes one of these words into our consciousness and we hear it for the first time and it makes us reel with amazement.*

After you believe that you heard God speak, ask yourself a few questions:

- ✔ Is the message in line with the Bible?

- ✔ Does it pass the "gut check" test? Does it seem like something God would say?

- ✔ Does the message fit your reality, availability, and financial situation? If not, could it possibly be something God wants to use to stretch your faith?

- ✔ What is the nature of the voice? Is it pushy or impulsive?

- ✔ If God's message is something you agree with or want to do, are you certain that it's not just wishful thinking on your part? Is it wise caution or a dread over what you may have to sacrifice?

- ✔ If God's message is telling you something you don't want to do, what are the reasons behind your hesitation?

The practice of hearing God is a process. Like any other discipline, he starts out slow with you and, as you have success, he continues to talk more and more.

Identifying False Voices

When you sit down on the couch with a TV remote in hand, you can click through hundreds of different channels. Some of the channels are always ones that you shouldn't tune to, while others may have good or bad content, depending on the particular hour of the day. When tuning in to God, you can draw a parallel.

Be alert for several false voices that can fool you or at least hinder you from hearing what God wants you to hear. Some voices are always false, while others may or may not be, depending on the exact situation.

Could it be . . . Satan?

A few voices that you may hear will *always* be false. It's important to recognize the following four false voices so that you're sensitive to them:

- ✓ **Impatience:** An impatient heart can cause you to rush God, making you mistake God's call for the first message that comes along. God runs on his own timetable, not yours, so don't confuse your impatient self for God talking.

- ✓ **Rationalization:** If you want something in your heart, that desire can easily become a false voice when you listen to God. In fact, you can psych yourself out so much that you begin to believe your own propaganda, convinced that God is telling you to do it. Therefore, when listening to God, be honest with yourself and make sure that you're not twisting his message to suit your own ends.

- ✓ **Competing priorities:** If you have other priorities that compete with God for that number-one spot in your life, they can easily become a false voice, allowing you to confuse their message with God's. For example, suppose that you put your work in front of God and your family on the priority ladder and a job promotion comes your way. Initially, that promotion may seem like God's blessing and something you should accept. Instead, it could be an entrapment to get you to focus even more of your attention on work rather than on what's most important.

- ✓ **Satan:** Of course, I'd be remiss not to mention Satan. He may use any of the previously mentioned false voices, or he may choose simply to impersonate God, hoping to fool you in the process.

Protesting too much: Perhaps false

Other voices you may hear can be true or false, but really depend on the exact situation. These are as follows:

- ✔ **Other people:** Beware of other people who tell you, "God told me to tell you to do such and such." In such a situation, run away as fast as you can, because God doesn't work in that manner. God may work through people around you, but it's usually in one of two ways:

  - He may communicate his message through an unknowing but obedient person in your life. God's message is almost said accidentally and unknowingly by that person, not because of a revelation given to that person.

  - More often the case, God may use a person to confirm a message that God has already spoken to you. (I discuss this later in the section "Testing What You Hear.")

- ✔ **Christian teaching:** The finest Christian books, such as the one you're holding in your hand, can be great resources and help equip you in your Christian life. Pastors or well-known Christian speakers and teachers can steer you toward God through their teaching. However, no author or talking head, no matter how spiritual and Christlike he is, is infallible. (I'm sure this may come as a big shock to you, but even I have been known to make a mistake or two from time to time.)

Reaching a guilty verdict

Guilt is a feeling that can haunt you for years, even decades, both before and after you've asked for forgiveness for a particular deed. But it is important to differentiate between the remorseful pangs that originate from God and the guilt that comes from Satan. Paul explains the two types of guilt in 2 Corinthians 7:9—10:

I now rejoice, not that you were made sorry, but that you were made sorry to repentance. For you were made sorry in a godly way, that you might suffer loss by us in nothing. For godly sorrow works repentance to salvation, which brings no regret. But the sorrow of the world works death.

Therefore, *godly sorrow* originates from God and has the sole purpose of bringing about repentance for a specific sin. Although the consequences of the sin may cause you grief for a lifetime, godly sorrow has definite closure to the guilt feelings associated with it. In contrast, *guilt,* the "sorrow of the word," is a vague, uncomfortable feeling inside of your belly that is defeatist and allows for no closure.

Therefore, if you have a guilty conscience, make sure that you have repented for the sin, but then give up that guilty feeling to the Lord. Know that God isn't going to keep going back and sticking your face in your sin after you've repented.

Therefore, even a well-intentioned message from a Christian book or teacher, if not in line with God, can be a false voice. This doesn't mean that you shouldn't read Christian books or listen to Christian teaching. It does mean that your only truly reliable source is the Bible. Recognize the possibility of fallibility in anything you read except the Bible.

✔ **Counselors:** Christian counseling has become a booming ministry over the past 20 years, but don't mistake the "Christian" label to mean that everything you hear is endorsed by Jesus Christ. Many great doctrinally sound Christian counselors are out there, but all too often, counselors can confuse the latest theory with the word of God and, in so doing, can threaten to become a false voice.

Testing What You Hear

After you've prepared yourself properly, listened to God speak, and filtered out any obvious false voices, your final step is to test what you hear. Follow these steps to do so:

✔ **Immediately pray about the message.** When you hear God speak, your first action should be to immediately go back to God to confirm what you just heard. You should pray something like this:

Dear God,

I truly want to seek your will on this new job promotion. In listening to you, I'm almost certain that I heard you say that I shouldn't take that promotion because of what the time demands would do to my family.

I'd love to have this promotion, but I know I have to follow you first and have my priorities in order. Lord, was that truly your voice or was that just a sense of ill-founded guilt that surfaced?

I'm going to proceed as if you said no, but please throw a roadblock and thwart these plans if these aren't pleasing to you.

In Jesus' name, Amen.

✔ **Write it down.** Chapter 9 outlines the importance of journaling to your prayer life. Journaling can also be an important part of listening to God. When you hear God talk, one of the best things you can do is to document it by writing it down in your journal. Writing it down enables you to form a track record of how well you listen to God. You can look back at times when you've heard God speak and then go back months later and see the result and whether you were accurate. When you see a pattern, you begin to know whether you're headed in the right or wrong direction.

✔ **Confirming with another trusted person.** Although you shouldn't look to other people as being the initiator of God's message to you, another person can be a great way to confirm a message of God's. If you ask advice from someone else about God's talking to you, be sure that you're close enough to that person to know that he or she is grounded in the Bible and is obediently following Jesus Christ. If not, you'll very often get that person's opinion rather than what God wants.

✔ **Be aware that you're fallible.** I shudder over the certainty and confidence of people who say, "God told me to do this" and then are proven wrong later. Even if you're confident that the voice you heard was genuine, always realize that you just may be mistaken about God's words, no matter how convinced you are in your heart. But don't let this fact lead to "analysis paralysis" and inaction. Instead, continue to have a healthy, reflective attitude. Or as Oswald Chambers used as his life motto, "Trust God and do the next thing."

Test all things, and hold firmly that which is good.

1 Thessalonians 5:21

Chapter 20

Healing in a Modern World

In This Chapter

▶ Facing the facts about healing prayer

▶ Using healing prayer techniques

▶ Knowing what to do when God doesn't heal

*T*he M word. You know the word I'm referring to; it's one term that can be so offensive to people's ears today that I'm reluctant to write it out fully. This is a family-oriented book, after all. But when it comes to the subject of Christian healing prayer, the word is impossible to avoid: miracles.

Skeptics and even some Christians replace the M word with a much more palatable sounding term, such as "coincidence," to explain away any active role by God in earthly matters. St. Augustine, one of the greatest Christian thinkers of all time, lived for much of his Christian life without much thought to the M word. He thought God's healing went away at the end of the New Testament era.

Yet, after personally witnessing a healing in his church and talking with the healed man afterwards, Augustine changed his mind. The power of God working in that situation was unmistakable to him, something he couldn't write off as mere happenstance. In fact, from that point on, he devoted a considerable amount of time and energy looking into miraculous claims in his church and documenting the ones that could be verified as a way to strengthen and encourage believers.

The question of how much God heals in today's world will always be present, whether it's Augustine's 5th century or your 21st century. In this chapter, you begin by looking at the issue through real-life stories and then go on to explore Biblical principles that point to God's continued healing role in the world. You'll close out by looking at the tough issue of when God doesn't heal.

Before reading this chapter, read Chapters 16, 17, and 18. Don't explore healing prayer until you have a solid foundation in how to pray for God's will, why you should pray in Jesus' name, how faith works into God's response, and how to cope with lost prayers.

When God Heals

The New Testament is filled with stories of Jesus and the Apostles healing the sick, making the blind see, and enabling the crippled to walk. God continues this healing work today, as shown in the following two real-life stories.

> *The fitness of the Christian miracles and their difference from mythological miracles lies in the fact that they show invasion by a Power which is not alien. They are what might be expected to happen when she is invaded not simply by a god, but by the God of Nature; by a Power which is outside her jurisdiction not as a foreigner but as a sovereign. They proclaim that he who has come is not merely a king, but the* King, *her King, and ours.*
>
> C.S. Lewis

In the nick of time

Nancy gave birth to a 10-pound 3-ounce baby boy named Nicholas. The pregnancy was normal, and the delivery seemed to be going routinely. However, during the birth, Nicholas aspirated his own first bowel movement, causing a condition known as meconium aspiration syndrome (or MAS), which, in severe cases, can be fatal. Nancy knew that something was seriously wrong when Nicholas turned blue while he was trying to eat for the first time, causing the nurses and doctors to whisk him away and begin running a series of tests on him.

In the ensuing weeks, doctors took an X-ray that clearly showed that Nicholas had a severe case of MAS. Because normal therapies weren't being effective, they recommended a treatment called ECMO, which uses a heart-lung machine similar to one used for open heart surgery. ECMO can be very risky, however, and therefore is tried only after the doctors have exhausted less-severe remedies.

Because the ECMO treatment looked like the only chance for Nicholas to survive, Nancy resigned herself to the fact that she had no choice but to go forward with it. The day before Nicholas's scheduled surgery, Nancy and her family gathered at the hospital to pray for his healing and to lay hands on him.

Nancy was terrified, and in spite of all the prayers that afternoon and night, she continued to feel little peace or comfort. Finally, by morning, Nancy didn't know what else to do and felt called to do so something much like Hannah from the Old Testament did with her son, Samuel: give her child back to God. She prayed, "God, Nicholas is your son before he is mine; I give him back to you. Please heal him or take him home to be with you. Just make the pain and sickness stop, Lord."

Later that morning, new X-rays were taken as a routine measure prior to the surgery. Much to everyone's amazement, the X-rays showed a 180-degree turnaround from the previous day; they showed no more signs of MAS! Nancy knew that the only change agent during the previous 24-hour period was the prayers offered by her and her family to a healing God.

The midnight miracle

Lynne suffered strokelike symptoms as a side effect of a new medication, leaving her paralyzed on the entire right side of her body. She was confined to a wheelchair after returning from the hospital, unable to move anything more than her fingertips.

One night, about ten days after returning home, Lynne had fallen asleep. Her husband, Peter, was lying in bed beside her, tossing and turning, unable to get to sleep. Usually a sound sleeper, Peter thought this sleeplessness odd and knew that it seemed to happen only when God prompted him to pray for someone who really needed it.

Looking at the pillow beside him and seeing his semiparalyzed wife, he started to lay his hand on the right side of Lynne's head, but he immediately felt directed to put it on the other side instead. Peter was initially puzzled until the thought came to him that the left side of the brain controls the right side of the body. He began to pray several times for her healing as Lynne slept soundly.

Afterward, he fell into a sound sleep but woke up a couple hours later, sensing the need to pray again. Praying the same words as before, Peter continued for several minutes and then went back to sleep. He awakened once more that night to pray and then fell back asleep until morning.

As was the norm, Lynne had already gotten herself up by the time Peter awoke. (She'd figured out a way to get into the wheelchair and wheel it into the kitchen.) As Peter walked into the kitchen for breakfast, he was amazed to see Lynne in front of him exclaiming, "Look at this!" She proceeded to move her arm, wrist, fingers, and toes and extend her leg! By the end of the day, Lynne was up and walking again.

A doctor's confirmation

Doctors who witness the effects of healing may not be able to explain what happened from a scientific perspective, but they're almost always reluctant to use the M word to credit God for the physical transformation. In his book, *The Practice of Christian Healing* (InterVarsity Press), Roy Lawrence tells the story of an exception to that norm.

At a healing conference that Lawrence was leading, a man told the crowd that the power of Jesus healed his wife of terminal cancer. The vicar of his church and a local doctor both laid hands on her in the name of Christ, and X-rays later showed that the cancer was gone. The woman's doctor was present at the conference and confirmed that she had indeed had cancer but was healed after the laying on of hands.

Just the (Healing) Facts, Ma'am

Christian healing is often discussed in anecdotes of healing from the Bible and from modern times. Although stories of healing encourage and strengthen your faith, don't try to imitate the same steps or techniques that were used in a successful healing, like it involves some kind of magic. Instead, healing stories should cause you and me to focus on the God who did the healing as well as to consider how healing fits into his overall plan for the world.

> *These are cases recorded in the Bible, and in our own day, of people who have been marvelously healed, for what purpose? For us to imitate them? Never, but in order that we might discern what lies behind, namely, the individual relationship to a personal God.*
>
> Oswald Chambers

Consider these seven truths about healing prayer:

✔ **Healing is a big deal to God.** Many churches low-ball the concept of healing prayer today, but healing is something that God consistently saw as important throughout the Biblical period. God miraculously healed time and time again in Old Testament times. Jesus certainly thought healing was significant, as he did more healing than almost anything else during his ministry. The early New Testament church records many instances of healing miracles in the Book of Acts. Your physical well-being and your emotional well-being are a big deal for you. Because God loves you, they're a big deal for him, too.

> *For I am the Lord, who heals you.*
>
> Exodus 15:26

✔ **It's not always God's will to heal.** Some healing ministries today claim that God's will is for everyone to be healthy and that Satan is always at the root of someone's illness. They contend that God always heals a sick person and never deliberately sends or allows sickness to enter a person's life. Therefore, when someone isn't healed, a blame game must be played to explain why God didn't heal: The sick person lacks faith, the people praying for healing lack faith, or the sick person has a sin that's causing the illness to stick around.

As popular as this "health gospel" may be in some circles, you won't find it consistent with the teaching of the Bible or the life of Jesus and his disciples. (See Chapters 17 and 18 for more discussion on the problems with this perspective.)

God looks at the present sickness in light of eternity, so what makes perfect sense from your limited perspective may make no sense at all from God's longer-term viewpoint.

If it was God's will to bruise his own Son, why should it not be his will to bruise you?

Oswald Chambers

✔ **Healing prayer is a temporary solution, not a permanent fix.** Christian author C.S. Lewis had a close friend with a sick son who was feared to have a terminal disease. However, when this report turned out negative, Lewis wrote to his friend upon receiving the good news:

Thank God. What a mare's nest! Or, more grimly, what a rehearsal!

Lewis, in his dry wit, gets to the heart of the matter when it comes to Christian healing. If the person you pray for is healed, you can and should rejoice, but the fears and concerns you had before the healing took place are nothing more than a dress rehearsal for what will inevitably happen someday. You, I, and that person just healed are still going to die at some point.

Consider healing prayer from the proper perspective. Jesus came to heal the sick, but he came for something far more permanent than curing leprosy or blindness: to reconcile sinful humans with God for eternity. Unfortunately, some people get so wrapped up in faith healing and healing services that they replace a focus on eternity with a preoccupation with temporary health.

✔ **The faith of the person praying is important, but it's not the source of healing.** Throughout this book, you can discover the many ways that prayer is the X-factor for how God chooses to work in the world. But in order for prayer to be that vital link, it should be done in a spirit of faith and anticipation. James 5:15 makes this connection when it says, *"The prayer of faith will heal him who is sick."*

Should you go to the doctor?

A minority of Christians shun medicine, believing that you should rely on God, not a doctor, to heal. If you go to the doctor to seek treatment, according to this perspective you are showing a lack of faith in God. But how consistent is this approach with how you live the rest of your life?

You're called to pray in faith to the Lord for healing, but you're also to pray in faith for your daily bread and his provision for your financial needs. Therefore, if you take an inactive role in treating the sick, shouldn't you be required to take a passive role in other areas of your life as well? If you were to follow that lifestyle consistently, then I suspect that you would never go to the grocery store for food. Instead, you would sit at home and wait for God's miraculous provision to show up on your doorstep. You wouldn't work for pay; you'd sit at home and pray for his check to arrive in the mail.

I'm not saying that faith and trust never play a part in healing prayer, but here's an illustration to point out the difference between trust and recklessness: Suppose that I think my job is in jeopardy and that I could be laid off at any time. However, as I pray about it, I specifically feel called by God to trust for his provision in this matter. Because I have a wife, kids, and a mortgage, I have a big decision to make: Do I immediately take matters into my own hands and interview elsewhere? Or do I wait for God to save my current position or open up a spot elsewhere? If I feel God's call to trust him, then he very well may be asking me to stay put and trust that he'll engineer the circumstances. However, suppose that I do get laid off and have little money to support my family. In such a desperate situation, is it being obedient or reckless to sit at home watching *Oprah* while I wait on the Lord to get me a job? God wants your faith, but he wants you to respond to him by living a life of faithfulness coupled with wisdom and responsibility. God wants you to pray to him for healing when you're sick, but he wants you do to so in conjunction with following the doctor's orders.

God is not at our service. To claim to penetrate his secrets, know his signs, and have his power at our beck and call is not faith, but magic.

Paul Tournier

The target of your faith is God himself, not the certainty of a favorable response from him. A prayer of faith isn't "God, I know you're going to heal my aunt tonight." Instead, it's "God, I know you love my aunt and have the power to heal her, so if you so will it, I am certain that she'll be healed by morning."

Your faith should, therefore, always lie in the confidence you have that God listens to your prayer and will answer it according to his perfect will. In addition, an effective healing prayer is related to the faith of the person praying, but don't confuse it as the causal factor. God himself is the sole cause and power behind any healing.

- **Healing prayer doesn't shut out the doctor.** Healing prayer works in conjunction with modern medicine and should never be seen as a substitute for it. The Bible always shows that treating and praying for the sick go hand in hand with God's works. The Good Samaritan, for example, didn't only pray for the healing of the injured man on the road. He also treated his wounds and cared for him. God works both through the doctor and the M word. Let the decision on which to use be God's.

  In addition, the Bible talks about anointing the sick with oil as a part of the healing prayer. However, oil was also one of the primary medicines used during that time to treat people who were ill. Therefore, when James 5:14 tells the leaders of a church to pray for the sick and "anoint their head with oil," this text very well may suggest that prayer accompanied by treatment is what is needed.

- **Any Christian can offer healing prayer.** In 1 Corinthians 12:9, Paul writes that some Christians have a special gift of healing, so their healing powers go beyond those of ordinary Christians. However, even if some people have this gift, these people don't have a monopoly on healing prayer. In the same way, Paul says that certain people have the gift of evangelism, but the people with that gift shouldn't be the only ones to talk about their faith. Instead, God wants all Christians to be empowered to pray for healing.

- **Healing prayer is best done as a body of Christians.** The one instructional teaching on healing prayer in the New Testament is in James 5:14–15:

  Is any among you sick? Let him call for the elders of the assembly, and let them pray over him, anointing him with oil in the name of the Lord, and the prayer of faith will heal him who is sick, and the Lord will raise him up. If he has committed sins, he will be forgiven.

  James talks about the leaders of church praying over an individual, and he isn't talking only about healing prayer done in private. Although this teaching doesn't preclude an individual from praying for another's healing, it does show that an emphasis on healing prayer in groups is important. Having the leaders of the church make a house call, so to speak,

---

Sinfully sick

Ever since Biblical times, some people immediately suspect foul play when someone gets sick. People often want to believe that the root of a person's illness is due to some hidden sin in that person's life. Examples in the Bible do show that sin can cause physical sickness, but Jesus made it perfectly clear (in John 9) that this isn't always true. In fact, many times, illness is simply a consequence of living in a fallen, imperfect world.

However, if you find yourself sick, use your illness as a reminder to examine your life and ensure that you've confessed any sins you've been harboring. That's good medicine, whether the sin is the source of your sickness or not.

emphasizes the dependency that exists within the church — something that is so often minimized in today's individualistic culture. See Chapter 1 for more details on the role of prayer in physical and emotional healing.

Applying the Techniques of Healing Prayer

When you pray a healing prayer, keep in mind two techniques that are used often in the Bible and should be a regular part of healing prayer today:

- ✔ **Laying on of hands:** In many instances, Jesus and other disciples laid their hands on the sick person who was being prayed for.

- ✔ **Anointing with oil:** Jesus instructed the disciples to anoint the sick with oil, and James tells the elders of a church to anoint with oil as well.

Because the act of prayer isn't what heals a sick person, you may wonder why these ceremonial techniques are important enough to have been included in the Bible and continue today. I think healing prayer techniques have proved to be valuable through the ages because they do the following:

- ✔ **Demonstrate active participation.** When you lay your hands on someone or anoint someone with oil, you take a physical step of participation in the healing process. You're not just sitting by and praying about the healing.

- ✔ **Enable you to become God's representative.** To a sick person, your direct physical contact can seem like a touch from God's representative. Human touch can be a catalyst that helps the sick person feel God's healing and comforting touch.

- ✔ **Enable you to identify with the sick person.** Prayer healing techniques help demonstrate your identification with the sick person, in the same way that Jesus touched the leper. The physical contact serves not only as a healing gesture but as a way to draw closer to the sick person.

- ✔ **Add an exclamation point.** Watching a football coach interact with his players on the sidelines is revealing. He talks to different players in different ways, depending on the emotion and flow of the game. Sometimes he may behave stoically while, at other times, he may rant and rave. However, during those special times when the coach really needs to get a player's attention, he often stands in front of the player, puts his hands on the player's shoulders, and speaks directly into his face. His nonverbal communication adds an exclamation point to his spoken words, saying in effect, "Listen closely. This is important." Similarly, the laying on of hands and anointing with oil go beyond a normal prayer and add that exclamation point that conveys the message that this act is important.

Reflecting on healing in the good ol' days

No Biblical evidence is convincing enough to conclude that God stopped healing people once the Bible times were over. At the same time, healing is probably not as common today as it was during that peak period during Jesus' ministry and the start of the New Testament church. God used healings in a special way during the ministry of Jesus to provide tangible evidence of his role as the Son of God, and in the New Testament church, healings were a way to help kick-start it. By the end of the New Testament period, these miracles became less prevalent in the life of the church. That isn't to say that Christian healing didn't occur anymore after that, but at the same time, you and I shouldn't be looking to re-create the "good ol' days of healing" of the 1st century.

Don't think of healing prayer techniques as a magic touch that causes the healing to occur. They're simply inspired acts of obedience that help open up the power of God to heal.

When God Doesn't Heal

While God often heals people in today's world, he doesn't always do so. If you read Chapter 19, you saw that even some of the most God-fearing Christians with vast potential at doing great things for God died early due to sickness. I experienced this first hand. Lori was a lifelong friend of my wife and me from Indiana. In her early teens, Lori developed cancer in her eye, requiring months of treatment that ultimately caused her to lose her left eye. She recovered fully from this traumatic event, however, and went on to live a typical teenager's life as she grew in her Christian faith.

My wife and I got married when we were in college, and we kept in only occasional touch with Lori for several years after we moved away from Indiana. However, a few years later, she was traveling in the Boston area on business, and we rekindled our friendship. She quickly became a close friend of our family once again.

Several years ago, we learned that she had once again developed signs of cancer. Our family, her home church, and scores of other family and friends prayed diligently for her healing.

The doctors felt confident that they caught the tumor early enough and thought it was treatable by surgery. As Lori's family and friends prayed for her, she underwent the surgery that seemed initially successful. However, a respiratory condition known as ARDS (Acute Respiratory Distress Syndrome) unrelated to the cancer, arose from the surgery itself and sent her to intensive care. She fought for over a week and seemed to be getting better for a while, but her health slowly deteriorated and the complications from ARDS claimed her life.

In this case, no last-minute heroics saved the day, and no miraculous healing touch cured the infection. Only the pain and sorrow that come from losing a loved one far too soon remained.

God engineers circumstances in your life based on prayer — but not always as you expect. And God heals — but not every time.

It's natural for any Christian to go through times of questioning and doubt when a prayer isn't answered the way that they expect, particularly when a loved one is sick or passes away prematurely. When you go through these times, remember that God remains unchanged through all life's blessing and tragedies. Your faith is what goes up and down like a roller coaster, depending on how well things go in life.

As a result, healing prayer that doesn't cure the sick must never turn you against God. Instead, it's a reminder pointing you back to him. A lost prayer of healing reminds you that God has far more to offer you and me than just a clean bill of health for this temporary life. Instead, he's offering an eternity with him for those who believe.

Chapter 21

Getting Tongue-Tied

. . . .

In This Chapter

▶ Discovering what speaking in tongues means

▶ Exploring what the Bible says about tongues-speaking

▶ Looking at the critical issues of the tongues debate

▶ Deciding whether to make tongues-speaking part of your prayer life

. . . .

Do you love hot potatoes? I sure do. My mouth waters when they come piping hot out of the oven, covered with butter, sour cream, chives, and bacon bits. In the culinary world, hot potatoes are nothing more than good eatin' but, in every other context, hot potatoes are those nasty issues that leave you with nothing but a bellyache.

Within the Christian church, the hot potato for centuries was the chasm between Catholics and Protestants. Big differences still remain, of course, but the steps that Catholics and Protestants have made toward unity over the past 40 years have significantly bridged that age-old gap. However, because nature abhors a vacuum, the issue of speaking in tongues quickly filled the void and became one of the major hot potatoes in this day and age.

All Christians agree that everyone should speak *with* tongues, because the enunciation of words is infinitely more difficult if you don't use that vital piece of equipment in your mouth. But Christians are quite contentious about whether speaking *in* tongues is a valid way to pray in this modern age.

With every hot potato issue, you have a choice: You can pass it off as quick as you can or hold it in your hand and risk being burned. So, with that thought in mind, get your oven mitt on and get ready to handle this sizzling topic.

Unwrapping Spiritual Gifts: "Whatchoo Talkin' about, Willis?"

I grew up in a very ordinary, mainstream church that thought it a big deal when someone shouted "Amen" or sang too loud during a service. And so when I first heard about people speaking in tongues, my response was probably something like the classic line from 1970s sitcom *Diff'rent Strokes*: "Whatchoo talkin' about, Willis?" I could handle doctrinal differences, but this notion of someone speaking in a weird alienlike language was quite another thing. Certainly this was something quite unlike anything I'd experienced in my Christian life. If you've never been exposed to the issue before, it may sound strange to you as well.

Speaking in tongues can refer to two different types of phenomena, both of which have fancy-shmancy sounding names:

- ✔ *Glossolalia* is the phenomenon of an emotionally intense spiritual experience that prompts a person to start talking in an unrecognizable speech. The tongues speaker believes that the words spoken are an angelic language given by the Holy Spirit (see Chapter 3 for more on the Holy Spirit) so that he or she can pray spontaneously as directed by God. To a bystander, the words won't resemble any humanlike languages and, from a purely human standpoint, could be clinically described as "gibberish" or "babble." When you hear people talking about tongues-speaking in today's world, they're almost always referring to glossolalia.

- ✔ *Xenoglossia* is the supernatural ability to speak a foreign human language without ever having learned it before. If you read Chapter 3, you already know about my meager French-speaking abilities, in spite of several years of French lessons. An example of xenoglossia is my ability to go to Paris and start talking fluent French to the surprised Parisians. Viva la France!

People who experience speaking in tongues are usually called *charismatics,* a term that stems from *charisma,* the Greek word for "gift." Charismatics believe that speaking in tongues is but one gift that Christians receive from the Holy Spirit. Other gifts include the ability to prophesy (or highlighting Biblical truths for a specific context), seeing visions, and physical and emotional healing. (See Romans 12:6–8 and 1 Corinthians 12:27–31 for Paul's listing of spiritual gifts.)

The charismatic movement, which refers to those churches that emphasize spiritual gifts, has rapidly increased in popularity over the past four decades. Once deemed a fringe activity in Pentecostal churches, the charismatic gift of tongues-speaking is widely practiced today by a growing number of Catholics and non-Pentecostal Protestants and even some members of the Orthodox church.

TECHNICAL STUFF

I think, you think: Views on tongues-speaking

The Christian church has four major views on tongues-speaking:

- **"Huh?"** Many people today turn a blind eye to the issue or don't know anything about it.

- **"That gift is so passé."** Tongues-speaking occurred in the early New Testament church but ended after the New Testament books were completed.

- **"Just do it!"** Tongues-speaking is central to what Christianity is all about and is a required sign of true believers.

- **"Proceed with caution."** The Holy Spirit can still give the gift of tongues today, but an emphasis should be given to the strict limitations that the New Testament places on their use and relative importance.

Tongues Spoken in the Bible: News at 11

All Christians who believe in the authority of the Bible do agree on the fact that the phenomenon of tongues-speaking did exist in the New Testament church. So the best place to begin looking at this hot potato issue is to turn to the Bible. Then you can then start to draw some conclusions as to what it says about speaking in tongues in today's world.

With all this hubbub about tongues, you may find it surprising that the New Testament contains a mere four instances of Christians speaking in tongues. To provide an account of what happened in each of these cases, I stumbled across some old copies of the *Jerusalem Daily Gazette* in my attic and found the following news clippings describing what happened in each case.

Multilingual Christians amaze visiting foreigners

Jerusalem, A.D. 33 (RW) — In an exclusive interview, visiting Jews told the *Daily Gazette* that they overheard a group of local Christians miraculously speaking in their native languages yesterday morning.

The incident occurred as Jews from over a hundred nations were at the Jerusalem Convention Center celebrating the annual Feast of Weeks, when they reportedly heard Christians in the neighboring Willow Crack conference room begin to speak fluently in dozens of their home country languages.

"I can't believe it! These guys rule!" Al Carbonia of Cappadocia told reporters yesterday afternoon. "They're all local rednecks with little formal education. But once I came into their room to see what was happening, one of their leaders named John started speaking Cappadocian with me, telling me all about their Jesus. Wicked cool! They got my attention, and I'm going to their next meeting to learn more about who this Jesus the Messiah really is."

However, another eyewitness, who asked not to be identified, simply made fun of them, suggesting that the Christians must have had "too much wine to drink."

To dispel any rumors, Peter, the leader of the Christians, told the perplexed visitors, "These men are not drunk. Why, most of us haven't even had our morning café lattes, since it is only nine in the morning. Instead, these linguistic miracles are signs to you revealing the truth of what we speak."

Independent lab reports released late yesterday evening confirm Peter's statement. The blood alcohol levels of all Christians present were negligible, far under the legal limit of 0.05 percent.

The claimed supernatural event was an effective attention getter for the young Christian church, as over 3,000 of the Jewish visitors became followers of Jesus Christ as a result.

Apostle Peter: Christianity is an equal opportunity faith

Jerusalem, A.D. 38 (RW) — The Apostle Peter, leader of the fast-spreading Christian church, urged fellow Jewish Christians today to welcome Gentiles into the faith alongside them as brothers and sisters.

Peter recently came under attack from Jewish believers of Jesus Christ when he reportedly met and ate sushi with Gentile Christians. At a church gathering held this morning in Jerusalem, Peter surprised attending churchgoers when he recounted his experiences at a house of a Roman centurion named Cornelius.

Said Peter, "During our meeting, the Holy Spirit came upon us, and then the Gentiles instantly began to speak in tongues." Upon hearing this news, the Jewish Christians recanted their protest and had no further objections.

After the conference, Al Galilee, a local Jewish follower of Christ, agreed with Peter and told this reporter, "Jewish-only rules are so B.C. It's the first century now, so we need to be open-minded and progressive. Why, I'm gonna invite some of those Gentiles over for bingo tonight!"

"Clueless" Christians get inside scoop

Ephesus, A.D. 51 (RW) — Twelve new Christians who live in the Ephesus metro area discovered today what Christianity really means during a visit from the Apostle Paul, one of the key Christian missionaries who is in town this week as part of his two-year Asian tour.

"I love those guys, but they sure were clueless," said Paul. "But I think we've got them on the right path now."

In a television interview to be broadcast tonight, Al Elphenzo, the self-appointed spokesman for the group, revealed, "We believed in Jesus as Messiah, but we didn't realize what his death and resurrection really meant. We were as thick as two short planks; we didn't even know anything about the Holy Spirit."

"Paul found this out after talking with us and then went ahead and baptized us with the Holy Spirit. All of a sudden, we started talking in a different language and prophesying. It was, like, really awesome, dude!"

Eyewitnesses to the event have mixed views of what language they were speaking. Some contend that it was a foreign language, while others thought it was mere babble.

Due to the controversy, the local authorities have formed a commission to determine the exact origin of the language in question. However, in order to pay for the investigation, they voted 4 to 1 to increase the local capital gains tax on camels and chariots.

Reforms will be made, says Pastor Al

Corinth, A.D. 53 (RW) — The First Church of Corinth, located on the city's upper east side, has long had a reputation among the local Corinthians of holding wild and disorderly church services. In a handwritten correspondence, the Apostle Paul, world-famous Christian missionary and key authority on doctrinal matters, called the local parish to task, urging reforms and discipline.

"Paul rightfully hammered us on our behavior," said Pastor Al Corinstopolus, speaking at an impromptu news conference earlier today. "Before we became Christians, many of us worshiped pagan gods and were into some pretty wild stuff. As a result, we ended carrying over some of that behavior into our worship services."

What's the point?

The Bible gives three primary purposes for speaking in tongues:

✔ **A road sign pointing to God:** Tongues-speaking was used to lead nonbelievers to the Christian faith, the best example being Pentecost. Paul also talks about this role in the church at Corinth. However, he points out that the *act* of speaking in tongues by itself was not a sign, because the nonbelievers present just thought the Corinthian church was crazy. Instead, Paul indicates that the *interpreted truths* coming from the tongues would lead people toward God. In many ways, interpretation is a gift even

more important than the gift of tongues by itself.

✔ **Proof of one's faith:** The other accounts in Acts indicate that tongues-speaking was given as a proof of the speaker's Christian faith to other Christians.

✔ **Builds up the speaker:** Paul writes that tongues-speaking "builds up" the one who does this and helps confirm one's faith. But at the same time, he is quick to point out that without a translator, public tongues-speaking does no one else any good.

"However, Paul pointed this out in no uncertain terms, but he provided constructive steps for us to take to remedy the situation. In fact, we formed a committee to begin implementation right away."

"The jury's still out, but I am encouraged by this news," said Petri Dishwalla, a local merchant who has been an outspoken critic of the church. "I went there last year with my wife and kids and couldn't make sense out of anything in the service. They were all talking in some strange language that I couldn't make out. Perhaps they thought all that crazy stuff would make me believe in their God, but it just gave me a migraine. I was down the rest of the day."

When asked if he'd return for a second try, Mr. Dishwalla revealed, "If the reports from others are good, I'll return. But I'll be bringing some aspirin just in case!"

Taking a closer look

Although the stories above are loose interpretations of the actual Biblical accounts, they are an attempt to capture the true newsworthiness of the tongues stories depicted in the New Testament. Look at each of these individually:

Pentecost (Acts 2)

In this instance, the type of tongues spoken is clearly of the xenoglossia variety, because foreign speakers could understand their native language being spoken by the Christians present. The purpose of the miracle was to serve as a sign of the evidence of Christianity's miraculous power. As a result, it got the attention of the visitors, many of whom became Christians on that day.

House of Cornelius (Acts 10)

The Gentiles who spoke in tongues on this occasion did so as a spontaneous response to being "baptized in the Holy Spirit." It was a visible demonstration to Peter and the Jews present that the Gentile Christians were equal and on the same level as they were; just as they spoke in tongues at Pentecost when they received the Holy Spirit, so did these Gentiles.

Peter alludes to the similarity of this event and Pentecost when he said that the Holy Spirit "came on" the Gentiles in the same way that he had at Pentecost. You could infer that the Gentiles spoke in xenoglossia as well, but the text never clarifies this issue.

Ephesus (Acts 19)

The Christians that Paul encountered in Ephesus had received bits and pieces of what Christianity was, but Paul filled in the missing details for them and then proceeded to baptize each in the Holy Spirit. Here too, when the Holy Spirit came on them, they began to speak in tongues and prophesied.

The text is not specific as to whether xenoglossia or glossolalia was spoken.

Corinth (1 Corinthians 12 and 14)

Tongues-speaking at Pentecost led to understanding, because the tongues speaker was understood by a listener who spoke that language (and perhaps the speaker as well). At Corinth, however, the church was evidently giving an inordinate amount of attention to speaking in tongues during worship services, which caused bewilderment and disorder, turning off visitors rather than leading them to the Christian faith. This situation prompted Paul to call for significant reforms if public tongues-speaking was to occur.

While the text is not definitive, most scholars contend that Paul is referring to glossolalia here rather than xenoglossia.

Table 21-1 summarizes these four occurrences.

Table 21-1	Biblical Occurrences of Tongues		
Instance	*Reference*	*Type*	*Likely Purpose*
Pentecost	Acts 2:1–13	Xenoglossia	A sign for non-believers
Cornelius house	Acts 10:44–48, 11:15–18	Inconclusive	A proof showing the faith of Gentile Christians to Jewish Christians
Ephesus	Acts 19:1–7	Inconclusive	A sign of the Holy Spirit's presence in a Christian's life
Corinthians	1 Corinthians 2–14	Most likely glossolalia	A sign of the Holy Spirit's presence in a Christian's life

Practicing Tongues Today . . . or Not

This hot potato issue raises several key questions concerning the practice of speaking in tongues today, but most center around three topics:

- ✔ Their validity in the modern era
- ✔ Tongues' relative importance compared to other gifts
- ✔ The rules for their usage

Questioning the expiration date

Although Christians on both sides of the fence acknowledge the practice of speaking in tongues in the New Testament church, considerable disagreement remains over whether the phenomena is valid today — whether its "best if used by" expiration date has long since passed.

The Bible contains no definitive statements that tell you without question whether tongues are valid today or not. However, one passage that could allude to it is 1 Corinthians 13:8–10:

> *But where there are prophecies, they will be done away with. Where there are various languages, they will cease. Where there is knowledge, it will be done away with. For we know in part, and we prophesy in part; but when that which is complete has come, then that which is partial will be done away with.*

Unfortunately, Paul is particularly vague in this verse, leaving open to debate what "that which is complete has come" is referring to. Opponents of modern-day tongues contend that Paul is referring in this passage to the New Testament, so that when it was completed, the gift of tongues was made obsolete. However, others believe that Paul is actually speaking here about the return of Jesus Christ, leaving open the door to the continued practice of tongues-speaking prior to that event.

The Biblical evidence for any expiration date for tongues-speaking is highly suspect at best and remains unconvincing to me. But, at the same time, the practice of speaking in tongues diminished after the early New Testament church for over a thousand years. By the second century, speaking in tongues within the Christian church didn't appear to be practiced. Justin Martyr, for example, wrote in that era about several types of gifts, but he didn't mention speaking in tongues at all. In fact, the practice wasn't recorded again until the late 17th century, when a group known as the Huguenots reportedly practiced this gift in southern France. However, not until the 20th century did the practice receive any attention at all from the Christian church as a whole. The rising influence of Pentecostal and other charismatic churches helped bring the issue to the forefront.

In summary, based on the Biblical evidence, speaking in tongues shouldn't be seen as obsolete today, but at the same time, the New Testament and church history show that tongues-speaking has not been an integral part of the experience of the vast majority of Christians either.

Evaluating the role of tongues in Joe Christian's life

If tongues-speaking is permissible today, just how important or critical is it that you and I speak in tongues? Here are the three general viewpoints on this question:

- A visible sign of being a true Christian, so if you don't speak in tongues, you aren't really a Christian

- A sign of spiritual maturity, so immature Christians may not practice the gift, but mature Christians do

- A spiritual gift given to some people but one that isn't as significant as other gifts

To determine which view is most backed up by Scripture, look at the key questions that I discuss in the following three sections.

Baptism of the Holy Spirit

The term "baptism of the Holy Spirit" is a term that often causes considerable confusion among Christians. Jesus used the term in Acts 1:5, when he said, "For John baptized in water, but you will be baptized in the Holy Spirit."

Baptism refers to being immersed or submerged, just as people are today when they're baptized in water as an outward sign of their decision to become a Christian. The idea of baptism of the Holy Spirit is then equated with being immersed in the Holy Spirit.

As Jesus says, John the Baptist's baptism was a sign of repentance from sin and cleansing, but the baptism of the Holy Spirit goes beyond that; when you receive the Holy Spirit in your life, he gives you power to live a new life. According to Romans, every Christian receives the Holy Spirit, but the Book of Acts doesn't have a set pattern or specific teaching for when they receive it.

Is there a relationship between speaking in tongues and the baptism of the Holy Spirit?

The relationship of speaking in tongues with the baptism of Holy Spirit (see the sidebar "Baptism of the Holy Spirit," later in this chapter) helps indicate whether all Christians should be speaking in tongues or whether it's a gift only for some people.

The Bible clearly suggests that a relationship existed between tongue-speaking and baptism of the Holy Spirit in a few specific cases that I discuss in the section "Tongues Spoken in the Bible: News At 11," earlier in this chapter. Charismatics emphasize this fact and associate being "filled with the Spirit" as synonymous with speaking in tongues.

However, noncharismatics correctly point to several examples of people being filled with the Spirit or baptized in the Spirit without any reference whatsoever to tongues being spoken. As a result, you can't sweep these references under the rug if you're going to objectively look for an answer from the Bible.

Although a connection does exist between the tongues and Spirit baptism, it's a loose relationship at best. You can find precedent, but when you look at the New Testament as a whole, speaking in tongues is a relatively rare occurrence and not the general rule when Christians received the Holy Spirit.

TECHNICAL STUFF

A higher language or gobbledygook?

Critics of tongues-speaking tend to downplay or ridicule the speech as babble or gibberish. Charismatics, on the other hand, contend that the sounds may not make sense to humans, but that's because it's an angelic language that only God can understand.

Linguistic research

Some academic research is available on the linguistics associated with speaking in tongues. The Linguist List (http://linguist.emich.edu) discusses various research activities, including the following results:

- Glossolalia consistently had a simple, primitive structure to it and consisted of significant repetition of individual sounds.

- A person's environment had a major impact on the words spoken. The sounds of tongues-speaking within a given church were similar and were quite different than what was observed in another church.

- The native language of the speaker was also a good indicator of the sounds that would be made when tongues-speaking. Sounds that sounded foreign would be used while speech typical of the native language would not be used. However, "exotic" sounds, those kinds of utterances unknown within the native language at all, were usually not used. English-speaking Americans, for example, didn't "produce clicks in their glossolalia." (A *click* is a popping sound produced by some African languages, such as Xhosa and Zulu.)

Noncharismatics may look at these findings and suggest that they imply that tongues is self-induced. They may contend that if glossolalia were truly an angelic language, it wouldn't be so dependent on one's environment. In contrast, charismatics might counter by saying that an angelic language need not be identical across the board but instead could allow for different dialects, just like human languages do.

Primitive versus complex

Another issue that surfaces concerning glossolalia as a heavenly language is the question of why angelic speech would be far more primitive and base than any known human language. After all, because God is infinitely more sophisticated than humans, it seems logical that any heavenly tongue would be linguistically far more complex and structured than even the most eloquent human language. Such a language could better express the kind of adoration to God that a human would be incapable of doing in normal speech.

In order to express any higher truth, you need a sophisticated means to describe it. Calculus and physics give you a truer picture of the scientific laws of the world than does simple arithmetic. But these advanced disciplines require you to use complex symbols, expressions, and algorithms to express their higher truths compared to arithmetic's rudimentary plus and equal signs.

Tongues critics say this is further evidence that all tongues-speaking referred to in the Bible is actually xenoglossia and that contemporary tongues-speaking is artificial. Proponents would counter that the linguistic complexity of glossolalia isn't what's important; what matters is that the speech brings glory to God.

Should tongues-speaking be a priority to a Christian?

One major problem of the Corinthian church that Paul deals with in his first letter to the members of the church is their preoccupation and overemphasis on tongues. They focused on this topic to the detriment of far more important issues, such as serving, discipling, and loving others. He makes his point very clearly in 1 Corinthians 14:19 when he says:

> *I would rather speak five words with my understanding, that I might instruct others also, than ten thousand words in another language.*

While Paul does say that he is glad that he speaks in tongues and wishes the same for others, he places the gift on the bottom of the totem pole of spiritual gifts, not at the top. Further, the New Testament history and teaching are consistent in indicating that not every Christian will speak in tongues.

Is tongues-speaking a sign of Christian maturity?

If you read the New Testament, you'll find no correlation between the maturity of a Christian and the ability to speak in tongues. Yes, Paul, Peter, and the other apostles were mature Christians and spoke in tongues, but not all people who spoke in tongues were long-time followers of Christ.

Ironically, tongues-speaking in the Bible is most often associated with new or immature believers. Think back to the accounts I discuss earlier in the chapter: Cornelius and the Gentiles were new converts, the Ephesus disciples had a newfound faith, and given all the weird stuff they were into, the Corinthians were obviously immature in their Christian faith.

Moreover, the vast majority of great, respected Christians throughout the centuries, be they Protestant, Catholic, or Orthodox, have not been charismatic.

Paging through the tongues instruction manual

If you have the gift of tongues, you need to know how to use this gift because its uncontrolled use is not allowed. Fortunately, the Bible is clear on this issue. In his letter to the Corinthian church, Paul provides the definitive instruction manual for tongues-speaking and sets out very clear guidelines to follow in 1 Corinthians 14:26–40:

> ✔ Everything that goes on in a worship service (including tongues-speaking) should strengthen the faith of the church as a whole. As a result, the church should always be put in front of specific desires of individuals.

✔ If tongues are to be spoken, limit the number of people to speak in tongues so that it doesn't dominate the service. Paul says that two or, at most, three should speak in tongues during a service.

✔ Tongues-speaking should be done one person at a time. Simultaneous speaking only causes confusion and disorder within the service.

✔ Tongues-speaking should be done only if someone is there to interpret the message. Otherwise, the speaker should keep quiet.

Keeping Your Tongue to Yourself

Many charismatics who talk about speaking in tongues often refer to it as their personal prayer language. In fact, many people speak in tongues privately but rarely or never do so in public. Those who practice private tongues-speaking say that, although they don't understand what they're saying, they sense the Spirit speaking through them, making sounds that bring glory to God. They feel strengthened by it and have a deep sense of God's presence as a result.

Although many people who practice private tongues as part of their prayer life find it strengthens them, Biblical support for this practice is actually pretty murky. In fact, nowhere in the Bible is private tongues-speaking discussed as an individual topic. Paul does mention the topic indirectly in 1 Corinthians 14 when he instructs the Corinthians on how public tongues should be conducted. Specifically, he says that if no one is present to interpret a tongue-speaker, then that person should keep quiet and "speak to himself and God." Paul doesn't prohibit private tongues-speaking, but you couldn't call his brief mention of it in this passage a resounding endorsement of the practice either.

Charismatics often point to Romans 8:23–26 as a text that approves the practice of personal tongues-speaking. This passage, which is discussed fully in Chapter 3, talks about the Holy Spirit's role as intercessor in your prayer life. However, charismatics argue that the words used by Paul in this verse indicate that tongues are part of this process: The Holy Spirit "himself makes intercession . . . with *groanings* which can't be uttered." Most Bible scholars disagree with this stance, saying the passage says nothing about tongues; that such an interpretation is reading into the text; and that this perspective doesn't hold up when you look at the full context of the passage.

The Bible is ambivalent at best on private tongues, but the decision as to whether you should practice it is a matter best left to you and God to discuss. However, if you choose to, make sure that it doesn't overwhelm or dominate your normal prayer life. If it does, it can become yet another pothole to prayer. The best prayer engages the mind *and* the spirit.

Balancing Perspective

Ouch! By now, I've been holding this hot potato in my hand long enough that the heat is starting to come through my oven mitt. But before I toss the potato again, I want to emphasize that, regardless of where you sit on the tongues-speaking debate, you should maintain a balanced perspective.

Tongues-speaking may receive a lot of attention in the Christian church today, but it is, frankly, a minor issue within the whole context of the Bible, referenced by a handful of verses within an ocean of thousands. The Bible is silent on whether Jesus ever spoke in tongues; the apostles did so only few times; and the Bible reports on only four instances of it.

Therefore, whether you're for or against tongues-speaking and whether you practice it or not, this issue should never distract the Christian church from what's really important. Fortunately, most charismatics and noncharismatics have been able to put this issue in its proper context. While they disagree on and debate this issue on the back burner, they've joined together to work to fulfill the true purposes of the Christian church.

All you need is love

In the middle of his discussion on tongues in 1 Corinthians 13, Paul gives sound advice to all Christians, whether they are prone to speak in tongues or not. He emphasizes in one of the most quoted passages in the Bible that the greatest gift God gives Christians is love:

If I speak with the languages of men and of angels, but don't have love, I have become sounding brass, or a clanging cymbal. If I have the gift of prophecy, and know all mysteries and all knowledge; and if I have all faith, so as to remove mountains, but don't have love, I am nothing. If I dole out all my goods to feed the poor, and if I give my body to be burned, but don't have love, it profits me nothing.

Love is patient and is kind; love doesn't envy. Love doesn't brag, is not proud, doesn't behave itself inappropriately, doesn't seek its own way, is not provoked, *takes no account of evil; doesn't rejoice in unrighteousness, but rejoices with the truth; bears all things, believes all things, hopes all things, endures all things. Love never fails. But where there are prophecies, they will be done away with. Where there are various languages, they will cease. Where there is knowledge, it will be done away with. For we know in part, and we prophesy in part; but when that which is complete has come, then that which is partial will be done away with. When I was a child, I spoke as a child, I felt as a child, I thought as a child. Now that I have become a man, I have put away childish things. For now we see in a mirror, dimly, but then face to face. Now I know in part, but then I will know fully, even as I was also fully known. But now faith, hope, and love remain — these three. The greatest of these is love.*

Part V
The Part of Tens

The 5th Wave   By Rich Tennant

"This is our family bible. It's truly a lamp to my feet, a light for my path and a balance unto our bookshelf."

In this part . . .

David Letterman, move over. *Christian Prayer For Dummies* has the definitive Top Ten lists on prayer. In this part, you get prayers for ten occasions when you really need them and ten prayers well worth teaching your children or grandchildren. I also include a list of ten prayer retreats and ten pilgrimage locations and top it off with the ten best prayer Web sites.

Chapter 22

Prayers for Ten Occasions When You Need It Most

. . . .

In This Chapter

▶ Asking for God's help when you're afraid, angry, or in despair

▶ Turning to prayer to help mend broken family relationships

▶ Praying for the sick and dying

▶ Surrendering to God

. . . .

A well-written prayer in a time of need is a godsend. It has a special ability to say what is in your heart, supplying you with the words you just can't quite articulate. This chapter supplies numerous prayers when you find yourself in different situations that cry out for prayer. Use these prayers as a starting point and then follow up by talking to God in your own words.

Fear

Whether you have lost your job, received bad news from the doctor, or are launching a new chapter in your life, the natural emotion you feel in your belly during such times is fear and trepidation. When you feel fear, go to the Lord in prayer, putting your concerns before him. Consider the following prayers to strengthen you in those fearful times.

Psalm 91

He who dwells in the secret place of the Most High
  Will rest in the shadow of the Almighty.
I will say of the Lord, "He is my refuge and my fortress;
  My God, in whom I trust."
For he will deliver you from the snare of the fowler,
  And from the deadly pestilence.

He will cover you with his feathers.
  Under his wings you will take refuge.
  His faithfulness is your shield and rampart.
You shall not be afraid of the terror by night,
  Nor of the arrow that flies by day;
  Nor of the pestilence that walks in darkness,
  Nor of the destruction that wastes at noonday.
A thousand may fall at your side,
  And ten thousand at your right hand;
  But it will not come near you.
You will only look with your eyes,
  And see the recompense of the wicked.
Because you have made Lord your refuge,
  And the Most High your dwelling place,
No evil shall happen to you,
  Neither shall any plague come near your dwelling.
For he will give his angels charge over you,
  To guard you in all your ways.
They will bear you up in their hands,
  So that you won't dash your foot against a stone.
You will tread on the lion and cobra.
  You will trample the young lion and the serpent underfoot.
Because he has set his love on me, therefore I will deliver him.
  I will set him on high, because he has known my name.
He will call on me, and I will answer him.
  I will be with him in trouble.
  I will deliver him, and honor him.
  I will satisfy him with long life,
  And show him my salvation.

The image depicted in this Psalm, "resting in the shadow of the Almighty," is one of the most comforting scenes imaginable, calling for God's protection in the midst of peril. This Psalm says that you may very well face dangerous situations, but the Lord is going to be with you during those times, so take refuge in him. (See Chapter 8 for more discussion on using the Psalms in your prayers.)

The Bookmark

Let nothing trouble you,
Let nothing scare you,
All is fleeting,
God alone is unchanging,
Patience

Everything obtains;
Who possesses God
Nothing wants,
God alone suffices.

St. Teresa of Avila, who lived in the 16th century, wrote this short prayer that expresses well the perspective you and I should have when panic and fear set in: God is constant throughout your triumphs and trials.

O Merciful Father

O merciful Father, who has taught me in your holy Word that you do not willingly trouble or grieve your children: Look with compassion on the sorrows of your servant. Remember me, O Lord, in mercy, nourish my soul with patience, comfort me with a sense of your goodness, shine your face upon me, and give me peace; through Jesus Christ our Lord. Amen.

Adapted from a prayer from *The Book of Common Prayer,* this prayer eloquently but succinctly asks God to nourish and comfort as you face troubles.

Anger

Anger can stem from both righteous and unrighteous sources, but whether your anger is justified or not, take your fury to God first before doing anything with it. Use the following prayers to get started.

For Our Enemies

Almighty God, have mercy on all that wish me evil will and would me harm, and their faults and mine together, by such easy, tender, merciful means as your infinite wisdom best can devise.

Heal and restore us that we may be together in Heaven together, where we may ever live and love together with you and your blessed saints, O glorious Trinity, for the bitter passion of our sweet Savior Christ. Amen.

Lord, give me patience in suffering and grace in everything to conform my will to yours, that I may truly say, "Thy will be done, on earth as it is in heaven." The things, good Lord, that I pray for, give me your grace to labor for.

Updated for today's English, this prayer by St. Thomas More reminds you to have an eternal perspective on your anger against an enemy. Instead of asking God to harm your enemy like some of the imprecatory Psalms do (see Chapter 8), this prayer supplies a most unexpected twist: asking God for mercy on them, so that you and your enemy can be saved together.

The Serenity Prayer

God, give us grace to accept with serenity
the things that cannot be changed,
courage to change the things
which should be changed,
and the wisdom to distinguish
the one from the other.

Living one day at a time,
Enjoying one moment at a time,
Accepting hardship as a pathway to peace,
Taking, as Jesus did,
This sinful world as it is,
Not as I would have it,
Trusting that You will make all things right,
If I surrender to Your will,
So that I may be reasonably happy in this life,
And supremely happy with You forever in the next.
Amen.

Author Reinhold Niebuhr wrote this prayer, expressing well the way you should look at life when anger threatens to disrupt your life. He also gives a refreshing viewpoint on how to look at life: asking for "reasonable happiness" in this life, with the certain knowledge that Christians will be "supremely happy" in heaven. The first part of this prayer is used by such groups as Alcoholics Anonymous.

Lord, Make Me an Instrument

Lord, make me an instrument of Thy peace
where there is hatred, let me sow love;
where there is injury, pardon;
where there is doubt, faith;
where there is despair, hope;
where there is darkness, light;
and where there is sadness, joy.
O Divine Master,

grant that I may not so much seek to be consoled as to console;
to be understood, as to understand;
to be loved, as to love;
for it is in giving that we receive,
it is in pardoning that we are pardoned,
and it is in dying that we are born to eternal life.
Amen.

This prayer was written by St. Francis of Assisi and has become one of the most beloved prayers of all time. Covering a wide range of areas, this prayer aligns you and me with God on all the major battles you may face: hatred, injury, doubt, despair, and sadness. And its closing phrase emphasizes the necessity of surrendering yourself to God in each of these ways.

Despair and Suffering

Sometimes life can get so bad that all you can do is hold up your hands in surrender to the circumstances and forces prevailing against you. God doesn't want you to give up, but he does want you to surrender everything to him. If you do, you'll rely not on your own druthers, but on the Lord to help you. So when you're at your wit's end, pray the following prayers as encouragement.

A Prayer of Hope

Lord Jesus, I pray this day for strength,
because there are times
when things get tough
and I feel like quitting.

Lord Jesus, I ask this day for the comforting
reassurance of Your love, because
there are times when people fail me,
and I am tempted to lose hope.

Lord Jesus, I seek this day for Your light
to guide my steps, because there
are times when life is confusing
and difficult, and I lose my way.

Help me, O Lord, to pick up the pieces,
wipe my tears, face the sun, and
start over again, for all is possible
when I place my faith and trust
in You, my Saving God. Amen.

Capuchin Franciscan Friars wrote this prayer as a way to stop focusing on the discouragement and circumstances in life, and instead ask God to help you focus on the hope that you can have in the Lord.

Lord, Give Me Patience in Tribulation

> *Lord, give me patience in tribulation.*
> *Let the memory of your Passion,*
> *and of those bitter pains you suffered for me,*
> *strengthen my patience,*
> *and support me*
> *in this tribulation and adversity.*

St. John Forrest wrote this short but effective prayer asking for help in times of strife. This prayer reminds you to forget about yourself and dwell on the price that Jesus Christ paid when he was crucified on the cross.

When in Trouble

> *O merciful Father, who has taught us in your holy Word that you don't willingly afflict or grieve the children of men: look with pity upon the sorrows of your servant.*
>
> *Remember me, O Lord, in mercy, nourish my soul with patience, comfort me with a sense of your goodness, lift up your countenance upon me, and give me peace; through Jesus Christ our Lord. Amen.*

Adapted from the original in *The Book of Common Prayer*, this prayer simply asks God for his mercy, comfort, and peace in times of affliction and grief.

Decision Making

Decision making can be one of the most heart-wrenching processes in your life: Should I move to Kansas or stay put? Should I take this job offer? Do I marry Jake even though he's old enough to be my father? Should I take the red or blue pill?

The scariest part of trying to make the right choice during a major decision is the finality of it: What if I make the wrong choice? I'll have to live with this for the rest of my life.

Use these prayers as a guide to your decision-making process, taking your choice to the Lord in prayer.

Prayers from The Book of Common Prayer

O God, by whom the meek are guided in judgment, and light rises up in darkness for the godly: Grant me, in all my doubts and uncertainties, the grace to ask what you would have me to do, that the Spirit of wisdom may save me from all false choices, and that in your light I may see light, and in your straight path may not stumble; through Jesus Christ our Lord. Amen.

*****

Direct me, O Lord, in all my doings with your most gracious favor, and further me with your continual help; that in all your works begun, continued, and ended in you, we may glorify your holy Name, and finally, by your mercy, obtain everlasting life; through Jesus Christ our Lord. Amen.

During times of decisions, the will of God may seem fuzzy to you. Go to the Lord in prayer, using these two prayers adapted from The Book of Common Prayer.

Prayer by John Henry Cardinal Newman

Give me, O Lord, that purity of conscience which alone can receive, which alone can improve your inspirations. My ears are dull, so that I cannot hear Thy voice. My eyes are dim, so that I cannot see Thy tokens. Thou alone can quicken my hearing, and purge my sight, and cleanse and renew my heart. Teach me, like Mary, to sit at your feet, and to hear your word. Give me that true wisdom which seeks your will by prayer and meditation, by direct intercourse with you, more than by reading and reasoning. Give me the discernment to know your voice from the voice of strangers, and to rest upon it and to seek it in the first place, as something external to myself; and answer me through my own mind, if I worship and rely on Thee as above and beyond it.

Written by John Henry Cardinal Newman, this prayer is an excellent one to pray in the midst of making a major decision in your life.

Wasted Time

Time is a precious gift from God. You and I never really *own* time, but it's easy to think of it that way. And, when you think your time is your own to use as you see fit, you can easily end up wasting days, weeks, months, years, and even decades.

Prayer to Redeem Lost Time

O my God! Source of all mercy! I acknowledge Your sovereign power. While recalling the wasted years that are past, I believe that You, Lord, can in an instant turn this loss to gain.

Miserable as I am, yet I firmly believe that You can do all things.

Please restore to me the time lost, giving me Your grace, both now and in the future, that I may appear before You in "wedding garments." Amen.

When you reach that moment of realization that the time you've been given is God's, not your own, and how you've wasted that time, pray this prayer from St. Teresa of Avila.

Guilt

Guilt over a wrong you have committed can weigh down the heart, causing you to sink ever lower into despair. You can try to put a bandage over the guilt and carry on as best you can, but that only prolongs the guilt feelings inside.

God offers a way out of this guilt with his forgiveness and grace. The heart of Christianity is that Jesus died on the cross for the sins of all humankind, so for anyone who accepts this forgiveness, God wipes away their wrongs and remembers their sins no more. Consider the following prayers that deal with God's grace even when you do bad things.

Psalm 51

Have mercy on me, God, according to your loving kindness.
  According to the multitude of your tender mercies, blot out my transgressions.
Wash me thoroughly from my iniquity.
  Cleanse me from my sin.
For I know my transgressions.
  My sin is constantly before me.
Against you, and you only, have I sinned,
  And done that which is evil in your sight;"
That you may be proved right when you speak,
  And justified when you judge.
Behold, I was brought forth in iniquity.
  In sin my mother conceived me.
Behold, you desire truth in the inward parts.
  You teach me wisdom in the inmost place.
Purify me with hyssop, and I will be clean.
  Wash me, and I will be whiter than snow.
Let me hear joy and gladness,
  That the bones which you have broken may rejoice.
Hide your face from my sins,
  And blot out all of my iniquities.
Create in me a clean heart, O God.
  Renew a right spirit within me.
Don't throw me from your presence,
  And don't take your holy Spirit from me.
Restore to me the joy of your salvation.
  Uphold me with a willing spirit.

Then I will teach transgressors your ways.
 Sinners shall be converted to you.
Deliver me from bloodguiltiness, O God, the God of my salvation.
 My tongue shall sing aloud of your righteousness.
Lord, open my lips.
 My mouth shall declare your praise.
For you don't delight in sacrifice, or else I would give it.
 You have no pleasure in burnt offering.
The sacrifices of God are a broken spirit.
 A broken and contrite heart, O God, you will not despise.
Do well in your good pleasure to Zion.
 Build the walls of Jerusalem.
Then you will delight in the sacrifices of righteousness,
 In burnt offerings and in whole burnt offerings.
 Then they will offer bulls on your altar.

This Psalm is attributed to King David after he had committed adultery with Bathsheba. After realizing his sin, David came to the Lord asking for God to show mercy and use God's cleansing power to blot out his sins. When you sin but are earnest in your desire to repent, God will always answer this prayer, showering you with his mercy and grace. (See Chapter 3 for more information on how sin impacts your prayer life.)

The Precious Blood

Blessed Lord Jesus,
Before your cross we kneel and see
the heinousness of our sin,
our iniquity that caused you to be 'made a curse,'
the evil that excites the severity of divine wrath.
Show us the enormity of our guilt by
the crown of thorns,
the pierced hands and feet,
the bruised body,
the dying cries.
Your blood is the blood of incarnate God,
its worth infinite, its value beyond all thought.
Infinite must be the evil and guilt that demands such a price.

Yet your compassions yearn over us,
your heart hastens to our rescue,
your love endured our curse,
your mercy bore our deserved stripes.
Let us walk humbly in the lowest depths of humility,
bathed in your blood,
tender of conscience,
triumphing gloriously as heirs of salvation.

This prayer was written by the Puritans, the group of English Protestants that sought reforms in the Church during the 17th century. After being persecuted in England and parts of Continental Europe, many came to America as early settlers in New England. This prayer focuses on the blood Jesus Christ shed on the cross for our sins. The source is www.worshipmap.com/prayers/puritans.html.

The Best Robe

O God of grace,
You have imputed my sin to my substitute,
and have imputed his righteousness to my soul,
clothing me with a bridegroom's robe,
decking me with jewels of holiness.
But in my Christian walk I am still in rags;
my best prayers are stained with sin;
my penitential tears are so much impurity;
my confessions of wrong are so many aggravations of sin;
my receiving the Spirit is tinctured with selfishness.

I need to repent of my repentance;
I need my tears to be washed;
I have no robe to bring to cover my sins,
no loom to weave my own righteousness;
I am always standing clothed in filthy garments,
and by grace am always receiving change of raiment,
for you always justify the ungodly;
I am always going into the far country,
and always returning home as a prodigal,
always saying, 'Father, forgive me,'
and you are always bringing forth the best robe.
Every morning let me wear it,
every evening return in it,
be married in it,
be wound to death in it,
stand before the great white throne in it,
enter heaven in it, shining as the sun.
Grant me never to lose sight of
the exceeding sinfulness of sin,
the exceeding glory of Christ,
the exceeding beauty of holiness,
the exceeding wonder of grace.

This Puritan prayer delves deep into the issues you face when you feel guilt and realize the extent of your sins. But each goes on to talk about the restorative hope you have when you submit to God.

Stressed Family Relationships

Stress in a family is natural. Each member has his own concerns and priorities, which may not always be in synch with the needs of the rest of the family. If left unchecked, this stress can cause separation. This prayer, adapted from *The Book of Common Prayer*, is focused on bringing unity to a family. It asks for God's presence in the home, his help in equipping each family member with Christian character traits, and his assistance in focusing each individual heart on others inside that family unit.

> *Almighty God, my heavenly Father, who creates unity in families: I ask for your continuing guiding and protecting hand over my home. Put far from us, every root of bitterness, selfish desire, and the pride of life. Fill us with faith, virtue, wisdom, self-control, patience, and integrity. Knit together in constant affection my spouse and I who, in holy marriage, have been made one flesh. Turn our hearts to the children, and the hearts of the children to us; and so light a spark of fervent charity among us all, that we may be joyfully bonded one to another; through Jesus Christ our Lord. Amen.*

In Need of Healing

God has been called "The Great Physician" and has demonstrated his healing touch countless times through the ages. Whether you or a loved one is sick, pray these prayers for healing and for your strength in the midst of illness.

Prayer of a Sick Person

> *Jesus Christ, my Lord and Savior, You became man and died on the cross for our salvation. You healed people of sickness and affliction through Your love and compassion. Visit me, Lord, and grant me strength to bear this sickness with which I am afflicted, with patience, submission to Your will and trust in Your loving care. I pray that You will bless the means used for my recovery and those who administer them. Grant that my sickness may be to my spiritual benefit and that I may live the rest of my life more faithfully according to Your will. For You are the source of life and healing and to You I give praise and glory, now and forever. Amen.*

This prayer from the Orthodox Church tradition emphasizes that just as Jesus Christ healed people during his ministry on earth, he can do the same in your situation.

Prayers for a Sick Person

Heavenly Father, physician of our souls and bodies, Who have sent Your only-begotten Son and our Lord Jesus Christ to heal every sickness and infirmity, visit and heal also Your servant (name) from all physical and spiritual ailments through the grace of Your Christ. Grant him (her) patience in this sickness, strength of body and spirit, and recovery of health. Lord, You have taught us through Your word to pray for each other that we may be healed. I pray, heal Your servant (name) and grant to him (her) the gift of complete health. For You are the source of healing and to You I give glory, Father, Son, and Holy Spirit. Amen.

O Lord our God, Who by a word alone did heal all diseases, Who did cure the kinswoman of Peter, You Who chastise with pity and heal according to Your goodness; Who are able to put aside every sickness and infirmity, do You Yourself, the same Lord, grant aid to Your servant (name) and cure him (her) of every sickness of which he (she) is grieved; and send down upon him (her) Your great mercy, and if it be Your will, give to him (her) health and a complete recovery; for You are the Physician of our souls and bodies, and to You do we send up Glory: to the Father, Son, and Holy Spirit, Both now and forever, and to the ages of ages. Amen

These prayers from the Orthodox Church tradition similarly emphasize the healing role of God the Father, affirming his power to heal and the glory given to him when he does it.

Approaching Death

It is easy and natural for people to put off life's big decisions for much of their lives, behaving like they're going to live forever. But when people are approaching death, they can no longer escape these decisions and questions. Christians have the certainty that this earthly life is not all there is, and that what comes next is far better than they can scarcely imagine. Therefore, in spite of the fear and dread of death, they can take comfort in the promises of the Lord.

Prayer for the Terminally Ill

Lord, Jesus Christ, Who suffered and died for our sins that we may live, if during our life we have sinned in word, deed, or thought, forgive us in Your goodness and love. All our hope we put in You; protect your servant (name) from all evil. We submit to Your will and into Your hands we commend our souls and bodies. For a Christian end to our lives, peaceful, without shame and suffering, and for a good account before the awesome judgment seat of Christ, we pray to you O Lord. Bless us, be merciful to us, and grant us life eternal. Amen.

This Orthodox Church prayer is especially for you or a loved one approaching death, as a preparation for a life of eternity with God.

Prayer by St. Thomas More

> *Lord God, give me the grace so to spend my life, that when the day of my death shall come, though I feel pain in my body, I may feel comfort in soul, and with faithful hope of thy mercy, in due love towards thee, and charity towards the world, I may, through thy grace, part hence into thy glory. Amen.*

This prayer is from *The Book of Catholic Prayer*.

Surrender

Chapter 16 explores the necessity of surrendering your own life and life's pursuits to God if you truly seek the Lord's will in your life. Surrendering is hard; it goes against our self-seeking nature, and you and I can fight it to the death. But God says that if you simply surrender, you'll find the freedom for which you are searching.

Prayer of Abandonment

> *Father,*
> *I abandon myself into your hands; do with me what you will.*
> *Whatever you may do, I thank you:*
> *I am ready for all, I accept all.*
> *Let only your will be done in me, and in all your creatures.*
> *I wish no more than this, O Lord.*
> *Into your hands I commend my soul;*
> *I offer it to you*
> *with all the love of my heart,*
> *for I love you, Lord,*
> *and so need to give myself,*
> *to surrender myself into your hands,*
> *without reserve,*
> *and with boundless confidence,*
> *for you are my Father.*

Written by Charles de Foucauld, this prayer of abandonment expresses what complete surrender to God entails: giving permission to God to do with you what he wills and doing so without reservation.

A Meditation on Detachment

Give me your grace, good Lord
to set the world at nought;
To set my mind fast upon you,
and not to hang upon the blast of men's mouths;
To be content to be solitary,
not to long for worldly company;
Little by little utterly to cast off the world,
and rid my mind of all its business;
Not to long to hear of any worldly things,
but that the hearing of worldly fantasies may be to me unpleasant;

Gladly to be thinking of God,
piteously to call for His help;
To lean unto the comfort of God,
busily to labor to love Him;
To know my own vileness and wretchedness,
to be humble and meeken myself under the mighty hand of God;
To grieve my sins passed,
for the purging of them patiently to suffer adversity;
Gladly to bear my purgatory here,
to be joyful of tribulations;
To walk the narrow way that leads to life,
to bear the cross with Christ;
To have the last thing in remembrance,
to have ever before my eye my death that is ever at hand;

To make death no stranger to me,
to foresee and consider the everlasting fire of hell;
To pray for pardon before the Judge come,
to have continually in mind the passion that Christ suffered for me;
For His benefits unceasingly to give Him thanks,
to buy the time again that I before have lost;
To abstain from vain conversations,
to avoid light foolish novelty and gladness;
Recreations not necessary to cut off,
of worldly substance, friends, liberty, life and all, to set the loss as nothing
for the winning of Christ;
To think my greatest enemies my best friends,
for the brethren of Joseph could never have done him so much good
with their love and favor as they did him with their malice and hatred.

These attitudes are more to be desired of every man
than all the treasure of all the princes and kings Christian and heathen,
were it gathered and laid together all upon one heap.

Written by St. Thomas More when he was a prisoner in the Tower of London in 1534, this prayer outlines a vast range of areas in which Christians need to surrender to God. (See Chapter 16 for more discussion on surrendering to God.)

TIP

Facing death courageously

While technically not a prayer per se, *Prospice* is a great poem written by Robert Browning. It provides an excellent window into the attitude and courage that Christians should have when they face death. In the poem, the speaker has lived a complete life fighting the good Christian fight and is now ready to encounter the "Arch Fear," meaning death.

> Fear death? — to feel the fog in my throat,
>
> The mist in my face,
>
> When the snows begin, and the blasts denote
>
> I am nearing the place,
>
> The power of the night, the press of the storm,
>
> The post of the foe:
>
> Where he stands, the Arch Fear in a visible form,
>
> Yet the strong man must go;
>
> For the journey is done and the summit attained
>
> And the barriers fall,
>
> Though a battle's to fight ere the guerdon be gained,
>
> The reward to it all.

> I was ever a fighter, so — one fight more,
>
> The best and the last!
>
> I would hate that death bandaged my eyes and forebore
>
> And bade me creep past.
>
> No let me taste the whole of it, fare like my peers,
>
> The heroes of old,
>
> Bear the brunt in a minute, pay glad life's arrears
>
> Of pain, darkness and cold.
>
> For sudden the worst turns the best to the brave,
>
> The black minute's at end,
>
> And the elements rage, the fiend-voices that rave,
>
> Shall dwindle, shall blend,
>
> Shall change, shall become first a peace out of pain,
>
> Then a light, then thy breast,
>
> O thou soul of my soul! I shall clasp thee again,
>
> And with God be the rest!

Chapter 23

Ten or So Prayers to Teach Children

In This Chapter

▶ Praying at bedtime and in the morning

▶ Saying prayers at meals and throughout the day

*W*hat image is more innocent and pure than a pajama-clad child kneeling beside his bed saying a heartfelt prayer? Indeed, watching your child or grandchild pray at bedtime is one of those Kodak moments you cherish all your life. Nearly all parents, even those without a personal faith, desire to teach their children prayers as a way to provide comfort and security to them during the early years of their lives. In this chapter, I provide a collection of ten or so prayers that you can teach the children around you.

What makes a children's prayer worth teaching your child? I think memorable children's prayers should have three qualities. A child's prayer should

✔ Be easy for the child to learn by heart. As a result, the prayer will typically rhyme and be simple to understand, not speaking in words over the child's head.

✔ Bolster a child's comfort and sense of security by reinforcing God's power, love, and dominion over earth and heaven.

✔ Be consistent with the teaching of the Bible. Not all children's prayers may be sound in what they teach, so Christian parents should carefully choose the best ones they know to be in line with the Bible.

Consider how you can use the prayer to serve as a way to instruct your child to discover more about God and the Christian faith. So when you teach them the prayer, don't just feed them words, but explain the prayer's underlying theology as well. Many prayers in this chapter have powerful truths that, if discovered, can help deepen your child's faith.

Although I heartily endorse a child's learning the prayers contained in this chapter, I also encourage you to not stop with these ready-made prayers.

Instead, use them as a starting point, after which you can teach your child how to pray on his own without a script. If you teach children how to pray on their own at an early age, they start to develop strong, meaningful prayer habits that can last them a lifetime. See Chapter 13 for more information on how to pray with your children.

Bedtime Prayers

After the daily grind, a bedtime prayer with your child or grandchild can be one of the most refreshing and tender moments you'll have all day. Consider the following bedtime prayers to teach your child.

The Lord Is My Shepherd

The Lord is my shepherd
I shall lack nothing.
He makes me lie down in green pastures.
He leads me beside still waters.
He restores my soul.
He guides me in the paths of righteousness for his name's sake.
Even though I walk through the valley of the shadow of death,
I will fear no evil, for you are with me.
Your rod and your staff, they comfort me.
You prepare a table before me in the presence of my enemies.
You anoint my head with oil.
My cup runs over.
Surely goodness and loving kindness shall follow me all the days of my life,
And I shall dwell in the house of the Lord forever.

If the Lord's Prayer is the most popular prayer of all time, the 23rd Psalm is surely a close second. The Psalm's promise of comfort, strength, and protection is expressed with the vivid imagery of a personal shepherd leading a scared and vulnerable sheep. This prayer works equally well for a child or adult.

Evening Offering

Dear God, we give you this day
All of our work, and all of our play
All that we do, and all that we say.
Amen.

This short and simple prayer expresses in a scant few words a concept that is at the core of Christianity: surrendering to God. This concept of surrender is such an important one to teach children because it helps them realize that faith is more than just asking God for stuff.

All Praise to You

> All praise to You, my God, this night,
> for all the blessings of the light.
> Keep me, O keep me, King of kings,
> beneath the shelter of Your wings.
>
> Forgive me, Lord, for this I pray,
> the wrong that I have done this day.
> May peace with God and neighbor be,
> before I sleep, restored to me.
>
> Lord, may I be at rest in You
> and sweetly sleep the whole night through.
> Refresh my strength, for Your own sake,
> that I may serve You when I wake.

All Praise to You provides a good comprehensive scope that touches on the important aspects of prayer: praising God and asking for protection, forgiveness, restoration, and the strength to serve God (see Chapter 6).

Now I Lay Me Down to Sleep

> Now I lay me down to sleep;
> I pray the Lord my soul to keep
> If I should die before I wake,
> I pray the Lord my soul to take.
> Keep me safely through the night
> And wake me up with morning light.
> Amen

Arguably the most ubiquitous children's prayer of all time, Now I Lay Me Down to Sleep was originally published in the 18th century in *The New England Primer,* a student's textbook, and has remained popular with families ever since.

The focus of the prayer is the Lord's control over the comfort and security of the child, regardless of what circumstances may arise. The child will see that she is in God's hands no matter what happens. The modern adult may view the line "if I should die before I wake" as a rather morbid phrase for a child to pray, so its use may be questioned. The phrase is undoubtedly included because death was something more children faced when the prayer was written in the 1700s, when the life expectancy of a child was far younger than it is today.

Before teaching your child the prayer, give careful thought to whether the phrase "if I should die" phrase may be disturbing to her. However, from my experience, unless children have experienced a personal tragedy, they often treat death very matter-of-factly and usually aren't scared to talk about death. A child who knows that a God is caring for her has that simple faith that Jesus commands everyone to have. Adults like you and me who try to grab control of their destiny have a much harder time talking about death than children do.

Morning Prayers

Mornings at my house can often be a flurry of activity as everyone does his or her own thing getting prepared for the day. However, just as I challenge myself and my children to begin the day with prayer, I also encourage you to instill in your child the practice of praying at the start of each day. Take a look at the following prayers for the morning to help in your efforts.

Morning Offering

Good morning, dear Jesus,
This day is for you.
We offer you all that
We think, say, and do.
Amen.

The morning counterpart to the Evening Offering prayer that I include in the "Bedtime Prayers" section, this prayer reinforces that concept of surrendering everything to God. Wonderful theology is packed into this simple prayer.

Child's Morning Prayer

My God, I offer to You this day all I think or
do or say, in union with all You have done
for me by Jesus Christ Your Son. Amen.

Dear Lord, I rise from bed to pray; then
soon go out to school or play. Let all I meet
along the way see You in me throughout the day.
Amen.

Another power-packed prayer, this child's prayer also focuses on surrendering your day to God so that you can be in his will. It also emphasizes the need to give God priority in the morning through prayer and to ask for God's help in being an ambassador of Christ throughout the day.

Dorothy's Morning Prayer

Dear God, I'm just a little child.
Take care of me today,
Guide my footsteps, calm my fears, and guard me while I pray.
Help me with my lessons and teach me to obey
Make me kind and honest, and let me be yours today.
God bless my mom and daddy, my brothers and sisters too
And may we all meet you in heaven when the trials of life are through.
Amen.

This prayer focuses on God's protection and help through the day and asks God to bless the child's family today and for eternity.

Mealtime Prayers

Mealtime prayers are rightly centered on God's provision and blessing of those burgers and fries on the table. Check out the following meal-focused prayers for children.

God Is Great

God is great, and God is good,
And we thank him for our food;
By his hand we all are fed;
Give us, Lord, our daily bread

An ever popular mealtime prayer, God Is Great is a simple prayer affirming God's divine greatness and goodness as well as his provision for meeting our daily needs.

Father in Heaven, We Ask of You

Father in Heaven
We ask of you
A blessing on each
plant and tree.

Bless each fruit
and bless each seed
and let them bear
the food we need.

Then bless the food
before we eat
Bless the bread
and bless the meat.

May all who share
these gifts today
Be blessed by you
we humbly pray.

Father in Heaven focuses on God's blessing for every aspect of the daily meal: fruits and vegetables, meat, and the people who are going to eat this food. This prayer shows how God plays an instrumental role in all you eat, from the planting stage through the harvest and food preparation.

We Thank You, Father, for This Food

We thank you, Father, for this food
And pray you'll bless it to our good;
Help us live your name to praise
In all we do through all our days.

This prayer thanks God for food and adds a plea to help give glory to him in all that you do.

To God, Who Gives Us Daily Bread

To God, who gives us daily bread
A thankful song we raise
and pray that He who sends us food
Will fill our hearts with praise.

Focused on God's role as provider, this prayer also asks God to help you praise him in all that you do.

Prayers for Any Time of Day

Don't teach your child to pray just at certain times in the day, such as morning, bedtime, and meals. Instead, teach them 24/7 prayer, as I talk about in Chapter 4. In this section, I list some prayers that are appropriate for a child to pray any time of the day.

Teach a Little Child to Pray

Lord, teach a little child to pray,
And oh, accept my prayer;
you can hear all the words I say,
For You are everywhere.
A little sparrow cannot fall,
Unnoticed, Lord, by You;
And though I am so young and small
You can take care of me. Amen.

Spoken from the perspective of a little child talking to a great God, this prayer affirms God's role as being in charge and caring for all creatures great and small. (See Chapter 3 for more on this topic.)

Trinity Prayer

Love of Jesus, Fill us.
Holy Spirit, Guide us.
Will of the Father be done.
Amen.

Given the fact that your eyes probably glaze over when you try to think about the Trinity, I don't think you'll want to dwell too much on the fullness of what it all means to an 8-year-old. However, don't let that make you shy away from this theology-filled prayer that I love. The Trinity Prayer shows that by asking Jesus to fill you with his love and asking the Holy Spirit to guide your path, then you'll be equipped to do God's will.

We Come to You in Prayer

Dear Lord, we come to you in prayer,
Knowing You are always there.
Joyfully, your songs we sing,
Praising You in everything.

Keep us safe by night and day,
As we travel on our way.
Teach us that it's when we share,
Others learn about your care.

Smile on us each time we give,
For that's how you would have us live.
Remind us friends should have our love,
For they are gifts from heaven above.

When we have special chores to do,
May we bring glory just to you.
This is your world that we love so,
We thank you, Lord, for things that grow.

With hearts as full as they can be,
We thank you for our family.
Amen

This prayer covers several topics, including worship, plea for protection, request for help to be a witness to others, the giving of glory to God through work, and thanks for the world, nature, and family.

Chapter 24

Ten Retreats and Ten Pilgrimages

· ·

In This Chapter

▶ Visiting ten prayer retreat centers
▶ Making ten prayer pilgrimages

· ·

At certain points in your life, sometimes the best way to get your prayer life refocused is to get away from your normal everyday life and visit a place where you can concentrate fully on God through prayer. Prayer retreat centers offer you a chance to do just that in serene, peaceful settings. Prayer pilgrimages, meanwhile, are visits to holy places around the world where you can enhance your walk with the Lord. (See Chapter 11 for more information on prayer retreats and pilgrimages.)

Literally hundreds, if not thousands, of choices are available to you for prayer getaways. In this chapter, I provide a sampling of ten prayer retreat centers and ten pilgrimages worth considering.

Ten Prayer Retreat Centers

Prayer retreat centers range from camps dedicated to individual prayer renewal to Christian retreat sites that host conferences on prayer. Ten prayer retreat centers are listed in the following sections.

College of Prayer

Sponsored by the Christian and Missionary Alliance denomination, the College of Prayer is a three-day seminar retreat offered four times a year. The retreat itself mixes training workshops with considerable quiet time for personal prayer. The College of Prayer is held at Beulah Beach Conference Grounds in Vermilion, Ohio. For more information, call 440-967-4861 or visit its Web site at www.beulahbeach.org/cop.html.

Ellel Ministries

If you really want to get away, consider Ellel Ministries, which offers prayer retreats at Kilravock Castle in the Highlands of Scotland. Retreats normally are scheduled for seven days, but you can adjust based on your scheduling needs. They're also unstructured to allow maximum time for personal prayer and reflection. Ellel also hosts regular prayer conferences at Kilravock Castle and other ministry locations. For more details, call 0-1524-751651 or visit its Web site at www.ellelministries.org.

Joseph House

Joseph House is described as a retreat center for "contemplative prayer in the classical Christian tradition." Located near Manchester, New Hampshire, the Joseph House was originally part of Ste. Marie Parish, serving as the residence for teachers who taught at the neighboring school. However, in 1986, it was transformed into a 21-room prayer retreat center. For more details, call 603-627-9493 or visit its Web site at www.specialink.com/JosephHouse/joseph.htm.

Christian Prayer Retreat House

Located in the Idaho Springs, Colorado, area, the Christian Prayer Retreat House offers a scenic location for single- or multiday personal prayer retreats. Accommodations are in a Swiss-style chalet. For more information, call 303-567-4601.

Prayer Valley

Prayer Valley is located in a serene setting on 185 acres of hills and valleys near La Crosse, Wisconsin, and offers periodic schools of prayer to teach ways to improve your prayer life. For more information, call 608-786-7729.

Mercy Center

Located in the San Francisco Bay Area of California, the Catholic-sponsored Mercy Center provides a quiet retreat center within this metropolitan region. Mercy Center can be used for private retreats, but it also has regularly scheduled prayer weekends and conferences. While here, you can spend your time alone or request guidance and mentoring. Accommodations include modest private bedrooms with shared bath facilities. Buffet style meals are served three times daily. For more information, visit its Web site at www.mercy-center.org.

Ashram of the Almighty

Ashram of the Almighty is located in the majestic Buena Vista, Colorado, region and intended as a place where individuals or couples may go for a relaxing, quiet prayer retreat. Spiritual mentoring and direction are available. Retreats include home-cooked meals on a wooden stove. For more information, call 719-395-6881.

Harvest Prayer Center

Harvest Prayer Center, sponsored by Harvest Ministries, is a 65-acre prayer retreat center located near Terre Haute, Indiana. The center focuses on providing a place of renewal for ministers, missionaries, church leaders, and their families. For more information, call 812-443-5703 or check out its Web site at www.harvestprayer.com/prayercenter.

Episcopal House of Prayer

The Episcopal House of Prayer is a five-acre prayer center provided by St. John's Abbey, a Roman Catholic Benedictine monastery in Collegeville, Minnesota. For more information, call 320-363-3293 or visit its Web site at www.csbsju.edu/sjuphysicalplant/episprayer.html.

The LaSalette Retreat Center

Part of the LaSalette Center for Christian Living, this Attleboro, Massachusetts-based retreat center features a variety of prayer retreats for people of all ages. According to its mission statement, the center was inspired by the tears Mary shed at LaSalette in France in 1846, prompting the founders to respond to the brokenness of the world today by providing a healing and peaceful environment. For more information, call 508-222-8530 or check out the Web site at www.ultranet.com/~lasalett.

TIP

Monastery, anyone?

Catholics interested in seeing monastic life up close and in person can spend a personal retreat at a Catholic monastery. While you're there, you can pray and work with the monks or nuns in the monastery and attend the worship services each day. For details and locations, visit www.vocationsplacement. org/MRetreats.

Prayer Pilgrimages

Although Christians from all backgrounds regularly visit prayer retreats, pilgrimages are primarily a focus of Catholics. So, with the exception of the Holy Land, nearly all the pilgrimage sites listed here are related to Catholic tradition.

Holy Land, Israel

Perhaps the prayer pilgrimage that is most meaningful to all Christians is the Holy Land, the land where Jesus walked. Millions of Christians make their way to Bethlehem, Nazareth, and Jerusalem each year. If you decide to go, consider making prayer a special focus while you're on the trip to enrich your prayer life during this once-in-a-lifetime experience.

Rome, Italy

Besides the Holy Land, Rome is perhaps the most popular center for Christian pilgrimages. Not only is the Vatican located here, but the city contains many historical sites associated with the early Christian church, such as the tomb of the Apostles.

Lourdes, France

Located in the Hautes-Pyrenees region of southern France, Lourdes is considered the favorite of all shrines for Catholics. Catholics believe that the Virgin Mary revealed herself to a poor shepherd girl in the 1850s a total of 18 times. Since that time, the town has attracted millions of Catholic visitors.

Fatima, Spain

Fatima in Spain is perhaps the best-known pilgrimage site on the Iberian Peninsula and among the more popular in the world. According to Catholics, Fatima served as the site of several appearances of the Virgin Mary in 1917, first to three young children and subsequently to thousands of people. Since that time, the town has attracted pilgrims from all over the world. The Catholic Church has recognized as miracles many cures of people who bathed in the springs.

Guadalupe, Mexico

Perhaps the most popular pilgrimage for Catholics in the Americas is the Basilica of our Lady of Guadalupe, located in Mexico City. Catholics believe that on this site in 1531 a poor Indian man had multiple visions of a beautiful lady whom he believed to be the Virgin Mary. After the bishop became convinced that his story was true, he built a church on the location. Millions of persons have visited this site over the centuries.

Auriesville, New York

The best-known pilgrimage in the United States, Auriesville is the location where Mohawk Indians murdered three Jesuit missionaries in the 17th century. The National Shrine of the North American Martyrs is the site commemorating where the first canonized martyrs in North America lost their lives: St. Rene Goupil, St. Isaac Jogues, and St. John Lalande. August 15 is the primary day of pilgrimage, but many people visit throughout the summer. See www.martyrshrine.org/info for more information.

Marytown, Illinois

Located in Libertyville, Illinois, Marytown is home of a group of Conventual Franciscans and the U.S. center of the MI (Militia of the Immaculata) movement founded by Saint Maximilian Kolbe. The facility includes liturgical and devotional events at a 24-hour chapel, a shrine in honor of St. Maximilian, and a retreat and conference center. See the Web site www.marytown.com/linktous.html for more information.

Basilica of the National Shrine of the Immaculate Conception, Washington, D.C.

Located in Washington, D.C., the Basilica of the National Shrine of the Immaculate Conception is the largest Catholic sanctuary in the Americas and is among the largest churches in the world. This pilgrimage site, built in honor of the Immaculate Conception, patroness of the United States, receives about a half million visitors annually. Visit its Web site at www.national-shrine.com.

Turin, Italy

Turin, Italy, is best known for the Shroud of Turin, which some people contend was the grave cloth of Jesus Christ. Many people travel on pilgrimages to view the shroud when it is periodically displayed. For more information on the shroud and display information, visit www.shroud.com.

Padua, Italy

Padua is the location where St. Anthony, called the "evangelical doctor" by Pope Pius XII, focused his preaching mission. As interest in St. Anthony has grown, so has the number of pilgrims to this shrine. Millions come to visit the Basilica di Sant'Antonio, which houses the relics of St. Anthony.

Chapter 25

Ten-Plus Recommended Web Sites

In This Chapter

▶ Finding sites to help you with daily prayer

▶ Linking to articles about prayer

▶ Praying for the president

*W*hen the Internet revolution began in the 1990s, everyone and his mother wanted to host a Web site about every conceivable topic, and those in the Christian community were no different. Churches, ministries, Christian-related companies, and dedicated individuals who simply loved talking about a given subject established a presence on the Web and hoped a lot of people would visit them.

So, well into the 21st century, the Web has evolved into a valuable resource and communication medium for prayer. Web sites not only serve as ways to find out more information on various prayer topics but can also host virtual "prayer meetings" for intercessory prayer requests and praises. (See Chapter 14 for more on prayer meetings.) Finally, the Web serves as a great vehicle for prayer ministries to get the word out on whom and what to pray for on any given day of the year.

The sites in this chapter, all of which are free, stand out in some way from the host of other prayer sites available on the Web. I heartily recommend that you take a close look at each of these.

Sacred Space

Web address: www.jesuit.ie/prayer

Why it's worth checking out: Well-written and well-designed interactive prayer devotional

Sacred Space is an interactive prayer site that guides you through a daily, ten-minute session of prayer. Every prayer is centered on a passage of Scripture and is in six stages. (You can read more about praying with Scriptures in Chapter 8.) As you step through these stages, you can click a Prayer Guide for more assistance and guidance. The site is hosted by the Irish Jesuits and is available in a dozen languages.

Prayer Central

Web address: www.prayercentral.org

Why it's worth checking out: Perhaps the best home base for all things related to prayer available on the Internet

Prayer Central serves as a solid online resource for equipping the praying Christian. On the site, you can browse articles about praying tips, read prayer quotes, find links to daily readings, and download aids to prayer, such as prayer cards (see Chapter 9) and church bulletin inserts.

Prayer Today Online

Web address: www.prayertoday.org

Why it's worth checking out: Solid, well-done Web site with helpful prayer resources

Prayer Today Online is another comprehensive prayer Web site that is focused on providing the tools and information to equip Christians in the discipline of prayer. It has a host of materials on how to improve your prayer life, prayer retreat ideas, a prayer calendar, and more.

The Book of Common Prayer

Web address: www.justus.anglican.org/resources/bcp

Why it's worth checking out: The granddaddy of prayer books for Anglicans and Episcopalians

Introduced originally over 500 years ago, *The Book of Common Prayer* (an actual book) is a collection of old and modern prayers and a guide to worship and daily devotions. The book is used by the Episcopal Church in the United States and the Anglican Church in England and worldwide. The first edition was written in 1549 and has been updated periodically ever since, the last revision coming in 1979. The latest edition provides prayers in updated modern English.

This Web site is devoted to making available the online versions of *The Book of Common Prayer* in most any format you want. It's available as a Web page (.html), Adobe Acrobat document (.pdf), or a Microsoft Word document (.doc). What's more, you can read any of the revisions of the *Book* dating from the 1600s to the present day. So, whether you are Episcopalian/Anglican or just want to use *The Book of Common Prayer* as a way to enhance your prayer and devotional time, this site is worth checking out.

Pray! Magazine Online

Web address: www.navpress.com/praymag.asp

Why it's worth checking out: Topical magazine articles on prayer

This Web site is the online companion to *Pray!*, a printed magazine published by Navpress that focuses on — you guessed it — prayer. Pray! Magazine Online serves as an excellent online prayer resource because it allows you to search for prayer-related articles in back issues.

Bible Gateway Audio Bible

Web address: www.biblegateway.com/bgaudio

Why it's worth checking out: An absolutely absorbing audio presentation of the Scriptures — for free!

Although this "listen-over-the-Web" Bible site is technically not a prayer site, you can certainly use this exceptional resource to enhance your prayer and devotional life. Most of the audio Bible versions I've heard before can lull you to sleep, but this version, read by actor Max McLean, is remarkably engaging and the finest version of the spoken Bible I've ever heard.

To listen to the audio Bible over the Web, you need a RealOne Player. If you don't have one installed already on your computer, you can download a free RealOne Player by going to www.real.com.

ePrayer.org

Web address: www.eprayer.org

Why it's worth checking out: Web home of the daily prayer and devotional e-mail newsletter written by fellow subscribers

ePrayer.org is a Web site that serves as a companion to the ePrayer.org Daily Devotional, an e-mail-based newsletter subscribed to by over 20,000 people. You can sign up for the newsletter and place and view prayer requests from other persons around the world.

International Day of Prayer for the Persecuted Church

Web address: www.persecutedchurch.org

Why it's worth checking out: To fully understand the attacks on Christians that still exist in many parts of the world

The International Day of Prayer for the Persecuted Church is a day dedicated to praying for Christians in certain parts of the world, such as the Sudan or China, where they're discriminated against, tortured, and even murdered because of their faith. Although the day itself comes only once each year, this Web site helps keep you informed all year long by providing specific prayer requests and telling you other ways in which you can get involved to help stop the persecution.

Presidential Prayer Team

Web address: www.presidentialprayerteam.org

Why it's worth checking out: United States citizens can discover how to offer prayer support to their country.

Christians living in the United States can participate in a new organization called the Presidential Prayer Team, which focuses on praying for the president, his cabinet members, and the nation as a whole. Although it has been around only for a short time, over 1 million members already belong to this prayer-focused organization. The Presidential Prayer Team makes a point in saying that it is nonpolitical and not associated in any way with any political party.

The Presidential Prayer Team Web site provides daily and weekly updated prayer requests, access to a variety of prayer resources, and an online form for joining the prayer team. Membership is free.

National Children's Prayer Network

Web address: www.childrensprayernet.org

Why it's worth checking out: Kid-focused prayer Web site that provides a prayer calendar and a regular listing of specific issues for children to pray for

Calling itself "America's Children's Prayer Movement," this Web site uniquely focuses on serving as a prayer resource for children living in the United States. The site features a well-done daily Quiet Time prayer calendar especially oriented for kids. It also provides a section updated periodically devoted to praying for specific nations around the world; the section provides background information on the country, its leaders, and some missionaries serving there.

America Praying On-Line

Web address: www.apol.org

Why it's worth checking out: Thriving online community to share prayer concerns and needs with others

Several Web sites allow you to view and submit prayer requests online, but America Praying On-Line seems to be one of the more active prayer request sites. If you'd like to get involved in a virtual community of Christians, this site is worth checking out.

Index

● *D* ●

combining with free prayer, 102–103
overview, 100–102
redemption, 27, 38, 39
reflection, 106–109
relationship, personal
benefits of prayer, 13
mending, 13
stress-relief prayer, 308
relationship with God
answered prayer, 235
fasting, 134–135
free prayer, 96
God's voice, 264
issues, 35–36
lost prayer, 252–253
surrender, 227
religion. *See specific religions*
remembering God's work, 123–124, 253
repentance
achieving X-factor, 22, 246
answered prayer, 246
definition, 43, 44
God's reaction, 43, 44
Psalm 51, 306
repetition, 209
repetitive prayer, 150, 153
respect, 80, 101
retreat, 154, 321–324
revival, 136
rhyming pattern, 111
ring finger, 99, 100
ritual
bad fast, 138
children, 182
meaningful, 153
Rome, Italy, pilgrimage, 324
Roosevelt, Theodore (U.S. president), 209
rope, prayer, 150, 151, 152
rosary, 150–151, 153

• S •

Sacred Space (Web site), 327–328
saint, 46. *See also specific saints*
Samuel (prophet), 116
Satan, 171, 172, 266

seeing sense, 98, 99
self-help technique, 28
self-interest, 221
selfishness
answered prayer, 237
lost prayer, 249
misconception about prayer, 34
origin, 219
senoglossia, 282
senses, 98–99
The Serenity Prayer (Niebuhr, Reinhold), 300
Sermon on the Mount, 114, 233
serving God, 165–166
share time, 181
Shroud of Turin (grave cloth of Jesus), 326
sibling rivalry, 180
sickness. *See* healing prayer
silent prayer, 194
simple obedience prayer, 118
sin
birth of Jesus, 40
effect on communication with God, 38–39
enemy of man, 114
forgiveness, 75
God's refusal to listen, 39
God's will, 219
guilt, 267, 305–307
healing prayer, 277
Jesus' death, 27, 38, 39
Jesus Prayer, 101
Lord's Prayer, 74
need for prayer, 27–28
original, 40
overlooked by God, 37
overview, 36
prayer time, 66
prayers, 305–307
presence in world, 37
recognizing, 84
singing, 146–147, 169
single-meal fast, 142
single-phrase prayer, 193–194
sleep, 57, 58–59
Small Group Ministries (Web site), 192
Small Group Network (Web site), 192
smelling sense, 98, 99

• T •

Notes

Notes

Notes

Notes

Notes

Notes

Notes

Notes

Notes